Fast Algorithms for 3D-Graphics

Georg Glaeser

Fast Algorithms for 3D-Graphics

With 94 Illustrations

With a diskette

Springer-Verlag

New York Berlin Heidelberg London Paris
Tokyo Hong Kong Barcelona Budapest

Georg Glaeser
Lehrkanzel für Geometrie
Hochschule für Angewandte Kunst
Oskar Kokoschka Platz 2
A-1010 Wien
Austria

Library of Congress Cataloging-in-Publication Data
Glaeser, Georg.
    Fast algorithms for 3D-graphics : with 94 figures / Georg Glaeser.
      p. cm.
    Includes bibliographical references and index.
    ISBN 0-387-94288-2
    1. Computer graphics. 2. Computer algorithms. 3. Three-
dimensional display systems. I. Title.
    T385.G575   1994
    006.6'7—dc20   94-8076

Printed on acid-free paper.

Production managed by Henry Krell; manufacturing supervised by Jacqui Ashri.
Photocomposed copy created from author's LaTeX files.
Printed and bound by Hamilton Printing Co., Rensselaer, NY.
Printed in the United States of America.

9 8 7 6 5 4 3 2 (Second corrected printing, 1995)

ISBN 0-387-94288-2 Springer-Verlag New York Berlin Heidelberg
ISBN 3-540-94288-2 Springer-Verlag Berlin Heidelberg New York

Preface

In this book, a variety of algorithms are described that may be of interest to everyone who writes software for 3D-graphics. It is a book that has been written for programmers at an intermediate level as well as for experienced software engineers who simply want to have some particular functions at their disposal, without having to think too much about details like special cases or optimization for speed.

The programming language we use is C, and that has many advantages, because it makes the code both portable and efficient. Nevertheless, it should be possible to adapt the ideas to other high-level programming languages.

The reader should have a reasonable knowledge of C, because sophisticated programs with economical storage household and fast sections cannot be written without the use of pointers. You will find that in the long run it is just as easy to work with pointer variables as with multiple arrays.

As the title of the book implies, we will not deal with algorithms that are very computation-intensive such as ray tracing or the radiosity method. Furthermore, objects will always be (closed or not closed) polyhedra, which consist of a certain number of polygons.

Ray tracing algorithms are necessary to get highly realistic pictures, and it is even possible to make ray-traced movies out of complicated scenes. If you want to do that, however, you will need the fastest computers available on the market and an enormous amount of disk space. In order to create hundreds of frames on less sophisticated computers, we need different algorithms. The loss of realism is more than offset by the increase in speed.

The method of the book is to introduce theoretical background and programming code at the same time. Type definitions, global variables and macros are described before their first applications. Because each chapter of the book builds upon the previous one, it is not advisable to skip any of them. If you are already familiar with a particular topic, at least skim over the relevant pages. All global variables, macros and function prototypes are listed in the index of the book.

In summary, it may be said that the intention of this book is to

- provide a mathematical background for 3D-graphics.

- gradually develop a complete graphics program that is able to render images of 3D-scenes comparatively quickly, including shadows and – to a limited degree – reflections. The images can be stored as PostScript files. The scene can be animated either interactively or by animation files. Series of scenes can be stored and replayed in real time. The program can be ported to any computer that is able to create palette colors by means of RGB-values and set pixels in those colors on the screen. The C compiler should provide a function to draw a line between two screen points and if possible a function to fill convex polygons.

- illustrate techniques of C programming with emphasis on portability and speed. Readers who are not so familiar with the programming language C may also find this book useful for a better understanding of pointer arithmetic.

- provide the reader with a source code of a graphics programming package. With the help of this source code, it is possible to adapt new code and to implement new information. (For example, one can easily introduce new spline types or new families of surfaces.)

Acknowledgments

A book like this can never be the achievement of one person only. It is not easy to start with anyone, because many people and institutions have helped to get the work done.

The idea of writing the book was born several years ago during the time I worked with Steve M. Slaby at Princeton University. Besides Steve, the man who came in with the most essential innovations and ideas from the very beginning was Silvio Levy from the Mathematics Department. It was he who strongly believed in the project.

At the same time, I received a lot of support from Dave Dobkin from the Computer Science Department and the individuals from the Interactive Computer Graphics Laboratory.

Back in Europe, Reinhard Thaller, Leonid Dimitrov and Emanuel Wenger from the Austrian Academy of Science helped me in many ways. During the same time, I worked together with two of my students, Thomas Grohser and Heinrich Pommer, both of whom brought in a lot of ideas to improve the code and the speed. Furthermore, I received advice from Hellmuth Stachel and Wolfgang Rath from the Institute of Geometry at the Technical University of Vienna and Otto Prem from the Handelsakademie St. Johann im Pongau, who also did the proofreading together with Silvio Levy.

Suggested Reading

The list of books on 3D-graphics is already very long and it is useless to recommend them all. The books listed below may be useful for a better understanding of this book:

- The C Programming Language: [DARN88], [KERN86].

- Theory of 3D-Graphics: [HEAR86], [HOSC89], [NEWM84], [PLAS86], [ROGE85], [ROGE90], [THAL87], [FOLE90], [VINC92].

Contents

A Basic Course in Spatial Analytic Geometry

In this chapter, we deal with the most common problems of analytic geometry and present possible solutions for them. We also include an introduction to pointer arithmetic for programmers with little experience, so that they may be able to understand more complex things later on.

If we do not start off with two-dimensional geometry, it is because we believe that, in reality, everyone is used to thinking in terms of spatial geometry and that speaking of objects in three-space does not necessarily make things more complicated. Furthermore, many principles of spatial geometry can also be applied to two-dimensional geometry without any major changes. As a matter of fact, most of the problems mentioned in 1.1–1.4 have an equivalent in two-space (such as intersecting lines and measuring angles between lines), which can be solved by simply ignoring the third coordinate. Nevertheless, some specific two-dimensional problems will be dealt with in other chapters.

1.1 Vectors

Let us consider a three-dimensional Cartesian coordinate system based on the three pairwise orthogonal axes x, y, z (Figure 1). Each point P in space has unique coordinates p_x, p_y, p_z, and we write $P(p_x, p_y, p_z)$. The vector $\vec{p} = \overrightarrow{OP}$ from the origin $O(0,0,0)$ to the point P is called the *position vector* of P, and we write

$$\vec{p} = (p_x, p_y, p_z) \quad \text{or} \quad \vec{p} = \begin{pmatrix} p_x \\ p_y \\ p_z \end{pmatrix}. \tag{1}$$

The vector $\vec{p}$ may also be interpreted as a linear combination of the three pairwise orthogonal unit vectors that determine the unit vectors:

$$\vec{p} = p_x \begin{pmatrix} 1 \\ 0 \\ 0 \end{pmatrix} + p_y \begin{pmatrix} 0 \\ 1 \\ 0 \end{pmatrix} + p_z \begin{pmatrix} 0 \\ 0 \\ 1 \end{pmatrix}. \tag{2}$$

Now let $Q(q_x, q_y, q_z)$, with position vector $\vec{q} = (q_x, q_y, q_z)$, be another point in space. The vector $\overrightarrow{PQ}$ is then given by

$$\overrightarrow{PQ} = \begin{pmatrix} q_x - p_x \\ q_y - p_y \\ q_z - p_z \end{pmatrix}, \quad \text{or more briefly,} \quad \overrightarrow{PQ} = \vec{q} - \vec{p}. \tag{3}$$

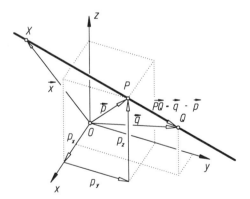

FIGURE 1. Cartesian coordinate system.

The vector $\overrightarrow{PQ}$ is called the *difference* between $\vec{p}$ and $\vec{q}$. An arbitrary point X with position vector $\vec{x}$ on the straight line PQ can then be given by the vector equation

$$\vec{x} = \vec{p} + \lambda \overrightarrow{PQ} \quad (\lambda \text{ real}), \tag{4}$$

which, in combination with Equation 3, leads to the general equation of a straight line:

$$\vec{x} = (1 - \lambda)\vec{p} + \lambda \vec{q} \quad (\lambda \text{ real}). \tag{5}$$

The points P and Q correspond to $\lambda = 0$ and $\lambda = 1$, whereas any point in between those two corresponds to the values $0 < \lambda < 1$.

Programming Techniques

Let us now take a short break from theory in order to write a simple C function that allows us to calculate a point on the straight line PQ, depending on the parameter λ.

First of all, however, we want to say a few words about a programming technique we will use for our graphics package.

The source code of a large program package should be split up into several modules `main.c`, `file1.c`, `file2.c`, `file3.c`, etc. The file `main.c` contains the *main()* function.

The files will share several global variables. In general, we will try to avoid global variables whenever possible. They make large programs hard to maintain and create the potential for conflicts between modules. On the other hand, such variables may speed up the code.

Global variables will be capitalized throughout this book. Thus, they can easily be distinguished from the local variables. We will put global variables into an include file named `Globals.h`. This file can then be included in the C code by writing

#**include** `"Globals.h"`

All type definitions that are going to be used should be put into an include file `Types.h`. The same is true for all the macros that will be developed ($\rightarrow$ `Macros.h`). Macro names will be capitalized, too, so that we can distinguish them from functions.

Finally, the function declarations ("function headers") should be written in the include file `Proto.h`. Throughout this book we will use the standard C language defined by Kernigham/Ritchie ("K&R standard") and not the more modern ANSI[1] Standard for the C language.

Now the definitions are at our disposal whenever we need them.

For more convenience, we put all the include files we need for our graphics package into a single include file `3d_std.h`, which may then look like this:

---

[1] "American National Standard Institute."

/* The include file *3d_std.h* */

#include `"stdio.h"`
#include `"math.h"`
#include `"Types.h"`
#include `"Macros.h"`
#include `"Globals.h"`
#include `"Proto.h"`
#include `"G_macros.h"`

(The system-dependent macros in **G_macros.h** will be developed in Chapter 4.)
At the beginning of each module we can now write

#include `"3d_std.h"`

and we do not have to worry about types or macros any more.

For the global variables we use a little trick: we first define two macros

#ifdef *MAIN*   ($\rightarrow$ `Macros.h`)
**define** *Global*
**define** *Init*(*var, value*) *var* $=$ *value*
#else
**define** *Global extern*
**define** *Init*(*var, value*) *var*
#endif

The file **Globals.h** looks somewhat like this:

Global **short** *Var1*, *Var2*[6];
Global **float** *Init*(*Var3*, 1.0), *Var4*[3];
Global **char** *Init*(*Var5*, 's');
Global **FILE** *Init*(*∗F*, *stdout*);

$\vdots$

In the file **main.c**, and nowhere else, the first statement is

#define *MAIN*

In this file the preprocessor now removes the word *Global* so that all the variables
are declared in the usual manner. In any other module, the variables are declared
extern.

This technique, however, does not allow us to initialize arrays. Thus, we write

#ifdef *MAIN*
Global **float** *Var4*[3] $=$ { 0.5, 1.5, -1 };

$\vdots$

#else
Global **float** *Var4*[3];

$\vdots$

#endif

into `Globals.h` when we want to conveniently initialize arrays.

The described technique is also very useful for the definition and initialization of pointers to functions: We define the macro

#ifdef *MAIN*   ($\rightarrow$ `Macros.h`)
 #   define *Init_fptr(ptr, function) (∗ptr)() = function*
#else
 #   define *Init_fptr(ptr, function) (∗ptr)()*
#endif

and write all the pointers to functions *at the end* of the File `Proto.h`. A typical example is:

Global Init_fptr(draw_polygon, fill_poly);   ($\rightarrow$ `Proto.h`)

$$\text{———} \quad \bullet \quad \text{———}$$

After this introduction we can finally write our first C function. We introduce a new type of variable called **Vector**, which is meant to be an array of three real numbers. These numbers may be the space coordinates of either a point or a vector in our sense. C distinguishes between double precision (**double**) and single precision (**float**). Since single precision should be sufficient for most cases, we choose **float** so as not to waste any space.

typedef float Vector $[3]$;   ($\rightarrow$ `Types.h`)

---

void *point_on_line(result, p, q, lambda)*   ($\rightarrow$ `Proto.h`)
    Vector *result*; /∗ The point to be calculated. ∗/
    Vector *p, q*; /∗ The vertices. ∗/
    float *lambda*; /∗ The parameter. ∗/
{   /∗ begin *point_on_line()* ∗/
    register [2] **float** *one_minus_lambda* = 1 − *lambda*;
    register short *i*;

    for ($i = 0;\ i < 3;\ i{+}{+}$)
        result[*i*] = *one_minus_lambda* ∗ *p*[*i*] + *lambda* ∗ *q*[*i*];
}   /∗ end *point_on_line()* ∗/

---

[2]**register** variables speed up the code. They are just a suggestion, however, and whether the program really profits from them depends on the compiler that is used.

This would not be C if the same thing could not be written in quite a different manner with the use of macros.

The use of macros helps to save time, considering that every call of a function takes time to copy variables into the stack.

Another advantage is that with a macro the type of the variables is of no consequence, which means that if you prefer to use **long** or **double** instead of **float**, it will work as well. Thus, the C macro

#define *Point_on_line*(*result, p, q, lambda*)\   ($\rightarrow$ `Macros.h`)
   (*result*[0] = *p*[0] + *lambda* * (*q*[0] − *p*[0]), \
    result[1] = *p*[1] + *lambda* * (*q*[1] − *p*[1]), \
    result[2] = *p*[2] + *lambda* * (*q*[2] − *p*[2]))

has exactly the same effect as the previous function, with the only difference being that, in most cases, it will work a little bit faster because the preprocessor replaces every call of the macro by the corresponding code, without jumping into a function. It will also be faster because the counting variable i does not exist any longer. In addition to that, we use Equation 4 instead of Equation 5 because in every line there is only one multiplication instead of two - a subtraction can be done a bit faster! When we compared the calculation times, the results were that the function *point_on_line*() runs 30% to 60% more slowly than the macro *Point_on_line*(), depending on the computers and compilers that were used (see Appendix A.4).

You may think that this obsession with speed is a little bit exaggerated, but you always have to keep in mind that the programming of 3D-graphics has to be extremely efficient in order to keep calculation times within limits. If we take every opportunity to save a little bit of time, the program as a whole will work much faster, which means that, in the end, we will be able to generate an animated picture 20 times a second instead of just 12 times a second.

Macros can be quite tricky, though, which means that for the purposes of pointer arithmetic it is advisable to write (*result*) instead of *result*, (*p*) instead of *p* and (*q*) instead of *q* in the macro! The reason for this will be explained at the end of Section 1.4. Furthermore, it is always a good idea to protect the whole macro with parentheses (we will soon have an example of this).

More About Vectors

But now back to theory. A very important lemma is that two non-vanishing vectors $\vec{a} = (a_x, a_y, a_z)$ and $\vec{n} = (n_x, n_y, n_z)$ are perpendicular if and only if their so-called *dot product* vanishes:

$$\vec{n}\,\vec{a} = \begin{pmatrix} n_x \\ n_y \\ n_z \end{pmatrix} \begin{pmatrix} a_x \\ a_y \\ a_z \end{pmatrix} = n_x\,a_x + n_y\,a_y + n_z\,a_z = 0. \tag{6}$$

If $\vec{n}$ is to be normal to another vector $\vec{b}$ as well, its components have to fulfill the additional condition $n_x\,b_x + n_y\,b_y + n_z\,b_z = 0$. The so-called *cross product*

$$\vec{n} = \vec{a} \times \vec{b} = \begin{pmatrix} a_x \\ a_y \\ a_z \end{pmatrix} \times \begin{pmatrix} b_x \\ b_y \\ b_z \end{pmatrix} = \begin{pmatrix} a_y\,b_z - a_z\,b_y \\ a_z\,b_x - a_x\,b_z \\ a_x\,b_y - a_y\,b_x \end{pmatrix} \tag{7}$$

is a vector that fulfills both conditions, and therefore, it is orthogonal to $\vec{a}$ and $\vec{b}$.

Macros[3] for the dot product and the cross product might look like this (for better reading we define X, Y, Z first):

#define $X\,0$ ($\rightarrow$ `Macros.h`)
#define $Y\,1$
#define $Z\,2$

#define $Dot\_product(a,\ b)\backslash$ ($\rightarrow$ `Macros.h`)
    $((a)[X] * (b)[X] + (a)[Y] * (b)[Y] + (a)[Z] * (b)[Z])$

#define $Cross\_product(n,\ a,\ b)\backslash$ ($\rightarrow$ `Macros.h`)
    $((n)[X] = (a)[Y] * (b)[Z] - (a)[Z] * (b)[Y], \backslash$
    $(n)[Y] = (a)[Z] * (b)[X] - (a)[X] * (b)[Z], \backslash$
    $(n)[Z] = (a)[X] * (b)[Y] - (a)[Y] * (b)[X])$

Again, the **Vector** variables should be written in parentheses for reasons of pointer arithmetic. Make sure that the whole expression is written in parentheses, too. Otherwise the expression $1 - \vec{a}\,\vec{b}$ will not be evaluated correctly by the expression $1 - Dot\_product(a, b)$.

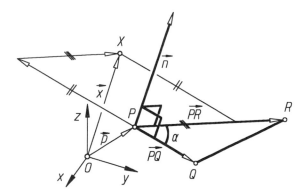

FIGURE 2. A plane is determined by three points.

---

[3]The reason why we use so many macros is explained in Appendix B.2.

In general, three points P, Q, R determine a plane (Figure 2). Any other point X on the plane can be expressed as a position vector $\vec{x}$, which is a linear combination of the vectors $\vec{p}$, $\overrightarrow{PQ}$ and $\overrightarrow{PR}$:

$$\vec{x} = \vec{p} + \lambda_1 \overrightarrow{PQ} + \lambda_2 \overrightarrow{PR} \quad (\lambda_1, \lambda_2 \text{ real}). \tag{8}$$

In order to eliminate the parameters λ_1 and λ_2 we simply multiply the vector equation by the normal vector $\vec{n} = \overrightarrow{PQ} \times \overrightarrow{PR}$, so that by Equation 6 we get the *parameter free (or implicit) equation of a plane*:

$$\vec{n}\,\vec{x} = \vec{n}\,\vec{p} = c = \text{constant}. \tag{9}$$

The constant c still depends on the length of the normal vector, which in turn depends on the points P, Q and R. For every point T (position vector $\vec{t}$) in space that is not on the plane PQR, we have $\vec{n}\,\vec{t} \neq c$. Two space points T_1 and T_2 lie on different sides of the plane if

$$\text{sign}(\vec{n}\,\vec{t_1} - c) \neq \text{sign}(\vec{n}\,\vec{t_2} - c). \tag{10}$$

The following function calculates the normal vector and the constant of a plane that is given by three points:

#define *Subt_vec*$(AB, a, b)\backslash$ ($\rightarrow$ **Macros.h**)
  $((AB)[X] = (b)[X] - (a)[X], \backslash$
  $(AB)[Y] = (b)[Y] - (a)[Y], \backslash$
  $(AB)[Z] = (b)[Z] - (a)[Z])$

typedef struct {
  Vector normal;
  float cnst;
} **Plane**;   ($\rightarrow$ **Types.h**)

---

void *plane_constants*(pqr, p, q, r) ($\rightarrow$ **Proto.h**)

  Plane $*pqr$; /* Pointer to the **struct Plane**.[4] */
  Vector p, q, r;[5] /* Three points on the plane. */

---

[4]One should always pass the *address* of a structure ("pass by reference") and not the structure itself ("pass by value"). A pass by value passes an entire *copy* of the structure. A pass by value guarantees that the function does *not* change the structure being passed!
[5]A **Vector** is by definition an array, i.e., an address. This is different from PASCAL: if you pass an array in PASCAL, the program makes a copy of the entire array unless you use the keyword **var**!

```
{   /* begin plane_constants() */
    Vector pq, pr; /* Difference vectors P⃗Q and P⃗R. */
    register Vector *n = (Vector *) pqr->normal;
        /* To speed up the macros. */
    Subt_vec(pq, p, q); Subt_vec(pr, p, r);
    Cross_product(*n, pq, pr);
    pqr->cnst = Dot_product(*n, p);
}   /* end plane_constants() */
```

1.2 How to Measure Lengths and Angles

If we want to measure the *distance between two points* P and Q, we simply have to measure the *length of the vector* $\vec{d} = \overrightarrow{PQ} = \vec{q} - \vec{p}$:

$$|\vec{d}| = \left| \begin{pmatrix} d_x \\ d_y \\ d_z \end{pmatrix} \right| = \sqrt{d_x^2 + d_y^2 + d_z^2} = \sqrt{\vec{d}\,\vec{d}}. \tag{11}$$

Now we can *normalize* every non-zero vector $\vec{d}$, which means that we scale the vector so that its length is one:

$$\vec{d}_0 = \frac{1}{|\vec{d}|}\,\vec{d} = \begin{pmatrix} d_x/|\vec{d}| \\ d_y/|\vec{d}| \\ d_z/|\vec{d}| \end{pmatrix}. \tag{12}$$

A C subroutine for the normalization of vectors might look like this:

#define *EPS* $1e - 7$ $\qquad\qquad$ ($\rightarrow$ `Macros.h`)
    /* This very small number is quite useful! */
#define *Length*(a) *sqrt(Dot_product(a, a))* $\qquad$ ($\rightarrow$ `Macros.h`)

```
void normalize_vec(v)                                    (→ Proto.h)
    Vector v; /* Pointer ≡ Address ⇒ Contents of v will be changed! */
{   /* begin normalize_vec() */
    register float len;

    len = Length(v);
    if (len < EPS ) {
        printf("Cannot normalize vector\n");
        return ;
    }
    v[X] /= len; v[Y] /= len; v[Z] /= len;
}   /* end normalize_vec() */
```

This time it turns out to be more efficient to use a function instead of a macro, because now we can use one register variable several times. You will have noticed that within the function we do not need to write (v) instead of v. For the compiler, the variable v is in fact a pointer to a **float**. The components of the vector are changed when the program leaves the subroutine (this would not have been the case if the variable had not been a pointer!).

With the help of normalized vectors, we can measure distances on given lines. For example, if we want to get a point R on the line PQ at a distance d from P, this point can easily be expressed by the equation

$$\vec{r} = \vec{p} + d \, \overrightarrow{(PQ)}_0, \tag{13}$$

where $\overrightarrow{(PQ)}_0$ is obtained by normalizing $\overrightarrow{PQ}$. Normalized vectors are also the key to the measuring of angles in space. If we want to measure the angle α of the two edges PQ and PR in Figure 2, we simply have to normalize the vectors $\vec{d} = \overrightarrow{PQ}$ and $\vec{e} = \overrightarrow{PR}$ and calculate their dot product to get the cosine of the angle α:

$$\cos \, \alpha = \vec{d}_0 \, \vec{e}_0. \tag{14}$$

Additionally, we have

$$\sin \, \alpha = \left| \vec{d}_0 \times \vec{e}_0 \right|, \tag{15}$$

though in most cases, we will prefer Formula 14 for reasons of speed. Every graphics programmer should avoid trigonometric functions, like sines, if possible. Unless you have an efficient mathematics coprocessor, such functions use up much more time than arithmetic operations. Fortunately, it is frequently possible to avoid those functions. An example is Lambert's cosine law, which says that the brightness of a polygon (a face of the object we intend to create) mainly depends on the cosine of the angle of incidence of the light rays. Thus we will do the following:

Before any drawings are begun, we determine and normalize the normal vectors of all faces. The cosine of the angle of incidence of a facet equals the dot product of the normalized normal vector and the normalized light ray.[6] The angle itself, however, does not have to be calculated because of Lambert's law. In this manner, we are able to avoid the function $arccos()$ for each facet of our scene.

---

[6]In fact, this is only true when the light rays are parallel. Otherwise the angle of incidence will be different for each point of the face. An "average angle of incidence" might be the angle of incidence of the light ray through the barycenter of the polygon. This point can be precalculated before any drawings are begun.

In order to determine the *angle between a plane and a straight line*, we measure the angle between the line and the normal of the plane and subtract the result from $\pi/2$. The *angle between two planes* equals the angle between the normal vectors of the planes.

1.3 Intersections of Lines and Planes

Let a straight line AB be given by its parametric equation $\vec{x} = \vec{a} + \lambda \overrightarrow{AB}$ and a plane be given by the implicit equation $\vec{n}\,\vec{x} = c$. (We have already developed subroutines to get the values of $\vec{n}$ and c). Now the intersection point S has to fulfill both conditions, and we have $\vec{n}\,(\vec{a} + \lambda \overrightarrow{AB}) = c$. Therefore, the parameter value for S is

$$\lambda = \frac{c - \vec{n}\,\vec{a}}{\vec{n}\,\overrightarrow{AB}}. \tag{16}$$

Let us look at the source code of a corresponding C function:

#define *INFINITE* 1*e*20   ($\rightarrow$ `Macros.h`)

#define *Linear_comb*(r, p, pq, l)\   ($\rightarrow$ `Macros.h`)
   ((r)[X] = (p)[X] $+ l * $($pq$)[$X$], /* Similar to *Point_on_line*(). */\
   (r)[Y] = (p)[Y] $+ l * $($pq$)[$Y$], \
   (r)[Z] = (p)[Z] $+ l * $($pq$)[$Z$])
typedef char Bool;   ($\rightarrow$ `Types.h`)
   /* Possible values *TRUE* and *FALSE*.[7] */
#ifdef *TRUE*
**undef** *TRUE*
#endif
#ifdef *FALSE*
**undef** *FALSE*
#endif
#define *TRUE* (**Bool**) 1   ($\rightarrow$ `Macros.h`)
#define *FALSE* (**Bool**) 0

#define *Is_zero*(x) ($fabs(x) < EPS$)   ($\rightarrow$ `Macros.h`)

---

[7]In C no type **Bool** is defined. The smallest fast-accessible type of a variable is **char**, which can still be assigned to the values -128 to $+127$. There will be no warning if you assign an arbitrary number to a **Bool** variable. Nevertheless, we will only assign *TRUE* and *FALSE*. These two values have to be (re)defined.

```
void sect_line_and_plane(s, lambda, parallel, a, ab, p)              (→ Proto.h)

    Vector s; /* Intersection point. */
    register float *lambda; /* Parameter to intersection point. */
    Bool *parallel;
    Vector a, ab; /* Point on line, direction of line. */
    Plane *p;

{   /* begin sect_line_and_plane() */
    register Vector *n = (Vector *) p->normal;
        /* To speed up the macro. */
    float n_ab;

    n_ab = Dot_product(*n, ab);
    if (Is_zero(n_ab)) {
        /* Either the line coincides with the plane or it is parallel to the plane.
        */
        *parallel = TRUE;
        if (Is_zero(Dot_product(*n, a) − p->cnst)) *lambda = 0;
        else *lambda = INFINITE;
    } else {
        *parallel = FALSE;
        *lambda = (p->cnst − Dot_product(*n, a)) / n_ab;
    } /* end if (Is_zero()) */
    Linear_comb(s, a, ab, *lambda);
} /* end sect_line_and_plane() */
```

For less experienced C programmers: if we want to have the variables *lambda* and *parallel* at our disposal outside the function, we have to pass them as pointer variables, because C "calls by value" (in PASCAL you would have to write the keyword **var** before the variable in the argument list). A pointer variable *ptr* to a **float**, for example, is declared by **float** *ptr*. The pointer *ptr* itself is then the *address* of the variable *ptr*. The pointer can only be changed within a function, whereas a change of its contents *ptr* will also be effective outside of it!

When calculating *lambda*, we had to make sure that there was no division by zero. It will occur when the direction of the line is parallel to the plane. In this case, λ is ∞ or it is not defined, if the point on the line coincides with the plane. If we now let $\lambda = INFINITE$ or $\lambda = 0$, the "intersection point" will be somewhere far out on the line or it will be the initial point itself, which is fine. Computer scientists prefer unconventional solutions like this one, rather than having to distinguish between several different cases. The flag *parallel* is set additionally in order to let us know when a special case has occurred.

Next we need to know how to intersect *two straight lines within a plane*. The two lines may have the parametric equations

$$\vec{x}_1 = \vec{a} + \lambda\,\vec{d}, \quad \vec{x}_2 = \vec{b} + \mu\,\vec{e} \quad \text{with} \quad \vec{e} = (e_x, e_y, e_z). \tag{17}$$

Now we intersect the lines by symbolically writing $\vec{x}_1 = \vec{x}_2$. When $\vec{e}$ is parallel to the z-axis ($e_x = 0$ and $e_y = 0$) (and when $\vec{d}$ is not parallel to the z-axis), we have

$$\lambda = \begin{cases} \frac{b_x - a_x}{d_x} & \text{if } d_x \neq 0; \\ \frac{b_y - a_y}{d_y} & \text{otherwise.} \end{cases} \tag{18}$$

When $\vec{e}$ is not parallel to the z-axis we multiply the vector equation $\vec{x}_1 = \vec{x}_2$ by the vector $\vec{n}_e = (-e_y, e_x, 0)$, which is normal to $\vec{e}$, according to Equation 6, and we get

$$\vec{a}\,\vec{n}_e + \lambda\,\vec{d}\,\vec{n}_e = \vec{b}\,\vec{n}_e, \tag{19}$$

so that the parameter λ can be evaluated directly:

$$\lambda = \frac{(\vec{b} - \vec{a})\,\vec{n}_e}{\vec{d}\,\vec{n}_e}. \tag{20}$$

When the lines are parallel or identical, we have $|\vec{d}\,\vec{n}_e| < EPS$. In this case, we let $\lambda = \infty$, if the nominator is not zero, or $\lambda = 0$, if the nominator is zero.

Here is a C function to accomplish the task:

First some two-dimensional equivalents to previous definitions:

typedef float Vector2 $[2]$; $(\rightarrow$ `Types.h`$)$
    /* A two-dimensional vector. */

#define *Subt_vec2(ab, a, b)*\ $(\rightarrow$ `Macros.h`$)$
    $((ab)[X] = (b)[X] - (a)[X], \ (ab)[Y] = (b)[Y] - (a)[Y])$

#define *Dot_product2(a, b)*\ $(\rightarrow$ `Macros.h`$)$
    $((a)[X] * (b)[X] + (a)[Y] * (b)[Y])$

#define *Linear_comb2(r, p, pq, l)*\ $(\rightarrow$ `Macros.h`$)$
    $((r)[X] = (p)[X] + l * (pq)[X], \backslash$
    $(r)[Y] = (p)[Y] + l * (pq)[Y])$

#define *Parallel_z(v)*\ $(\rightarrow$ `Macros.h`$)$
    $(Is\_zero((v)[X]) \ \&\& \ Is\_zero((v)[Y]))$

#define *Normal_vec2(n, v)*\ $(\rightarrow$ `Macros.h`$)$
    $((n)[X] = -(v)[Y], \ (n)[Y] = (v)[X])$

void *intersect_lines*(*s, lambda, parallel, a, d, b, e, dim*)   ($\rightarrow$ **Proto.h**)
   float *s*[ ];
   /* Intersection point. The reason why we use an array of **float**s instead of
      the types **Vector** or **Vector2** is because this function works without
      any changes when the vectors *a, b, d, e* in the argument list are two-
      dimensional! (Both **Vector** and **Vector2** are interpreted as pointers to
      a **float**.) The only difference between a 2D-version and a 3D-version is
      in the calculation of the intersection point. */
   float **lambda*;
   /* Parameter λ of the intersection point of the lines
      $\vec{x} = \vec{a} + \lambda\,\vec{d} = \vec{b} + \mu\,\vec{e}$. */
   Bool **parallel*;
   float *a*[ ], *d*[ ], *b*[ ], *e*[ ];
   short *dim*; /* 2D or 3D. */
{   /* begin *intersect_lines*() */
   Vector2 *ne, ab*;
   float *d_ne, ab_ne*;

   if (*dim* == 3 && *Parallel_z*(*e*)) {
       if ((**parallel = Parallel_z*(*d*))) {
           if (*a*[*X*] == *b*[*X*] && *a*[*Y*] == *b*[*Y*]) **lambda* = 0;
           else **lambda* = *INFINITE*; /* Lines are parallel. */
       } **else if** (!*Is_zero*(*d*[*X*])) **lambda* = (*b*[*X*] − *a*[*X*])/*d*[*X*];
       else if (!*Is_zero*(*d*[*Y*])) **lambda* = (*b*[*Y*] − *a*[*Y*])/*d*[*Y*];
   } **else** { /* $\vec{e}$ is not parallel to the *z*-axis. */
       /* Because of *ne*[*Z*] = 0, it is enough to make some
          of the following calculations only two-dimensionally. */
       Normal_vec2(*ne, e*);
       d_ne = *Dot_product2*(*d, ne*);
       Subt_vec2(*ab, a, b*);
       ab_ne = *Dot_product2*(*ab, ne*);
       if ((**parallel = Is_zero*(*d_ne*))) {
           if (*Is_zero*(*ab_ne*)) **lambda* = 0;
           else **lambda* = *INFINITE*;
       } **else** { /* This is the general case at last. */
           *lambda = *ab_ne*/*d_ne*;
       } /* end **if** (*Is_zero*(*d_ne*)) */
   } /* end **if** ($\vec{e}$ parallel *z*)) */
   if (*dim* == 2)
       Linear_comb2(*s, a, d, *lambda*);
   else
       Linear_comb(*s, a, d, *lambda*);
}   /* end *intersect_lines*() */

For some hidden line determinations (Section 7.2) we need another function *intersect_segments*() that is related to the function *intersect_lines*(). It calculates both the parameters t_1 and t_2 from the equation $\vec{p}_1 + t_1(\vec{p}_2 - \vec{p}_1) = \vec{q}_1 + t_2(\vec{q}_2 - \vec{q}_1)$ (and nothing else). When the segments are parallel (or identical) the function returns *FALSE*, else it returns *TRUE*.

```
Bool intersect_segments(t1, t2, p1, q1, p2, q2)              (→ Proto.h)
    float  * t1, *t2;
    float p1[ ], q1[ ]; /* The first segment. */
    float p2[ ], q2[ ]; /* The second segment. */
{   /* begin intersect_segments() */
    Vector2 dir1, dir2, p1p2;
    Vector2 n1, n2;
    double  det;

    Subt_vec2(dir1, p1, q1); Subt_vec2(dir2, p2, q2);
    Normal_vec2(n1, dir1); Normal_vec2(n2, dir2);
    det  =  Dot_product2(dir1, n2);
    if  (fabs(det) < EPS) return  FALSE;
    Subt_vec2(p1p2, p1, p2);
    * t1  =  Dot_product2(p1p2, n2) / det;
    * t2  =  Dot_product2(p1p2, n1) / det;
    return  TRUE;
}   /* end intersect_segments() */
```

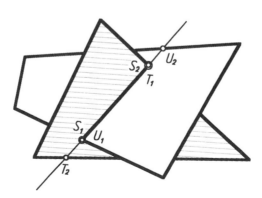

FIGURE 3. The line of intersection of two convex polygons.

The *intersection of two planes* can be achieved by the intersection of two lines of the first plane with the second plane. Since we do not usually deal with infinite planes, but rather with polygons that span the plane, we want to solve an additional problem: given two convex polygons (usually triangles or quadrilaterals) that intersect each other as in Figure 3, we look for the end points S_1 and S_2 of the intersection, which is a straight line.

Provided that such a line of intersection exists, we will always be able to find exactly two edges on the first polygon that intersect the plane of the second one. The two intersection points may be called T_1, T_2. The line joining them is represented by the parametric equation

$$\vec{x} = \vec{t_1} + \lambda\,(\vec{t_2} - \vec{t_1}) \quad (\lambda \text{ real}). \tag{21}$$

The point T_1 corresponds to the parameter value $\lambda = 0$, the point T_2 corresponds to the value $\lambda = 1$. Now we determine the edges of the second polygon, the vertices of which lie on different sides of the plane that is determined by the first polygon, and we intersect them with the edge $T_1 T_2$. These intersection points may be called U_1 and U_2, and they belong to two parameter values λ_1 and λ_2. We finally modify these values

$$\lambda_i = \begin{cases} 0, & \text{if } \lambda_i \leq 0 \ (\Rightarrow S_i = T_1); \\ \lambda_i, & \text{if } 0 < \lambda_i < 1 \ (\Rightarrow S_i = U_i); \\ 1, & \text{if } \lambda_i \geq 1 \ (\Rightarrow S_i = T_2); \end{cases} \quad (i = 1, 2) \tag{22}$$

and have the parameter values of the end points S_1, S_2 of the actual line of intersection.

Here is the corresponding C code:

```
#define Swap(a, b) (temp = a, a = b, b = temp)                    (→ Macros.h)
#define Sign(x) ((x < 0) ? (−1) : (1))                            (→ Macros.h)
#define Which_side(point, plane)\                                 (→ Macros.h)
    Sign(Dot_product((plane).normal, point) − (plane).cnst)
```

```
Bool sect_polys(section, n1, poly1, n2, poly2)                    (→ Proto.h)
    Vector section[2]; /* Intersection points. */
    short n1, n2; /* Number of vertices of the (convex!) polygons. */
    Vector poly1[ ], poly2[ ];[8] /* Vertices of the polygons. */
```

---

[8]This gives us the chance to explain the different writings we can use when we pass an **array** x as a function argument. The compiler will convert your writing into the **pointer** $*x$ in any case. Thus, it does not make any difference whether you really pass a pointer or the start address of an array. For better reading, however, it is preferable to write $x[\ ]$ or, when the size of the array is constant, $x[size]$. The compiler uses the size information only for bounds-checking (provided that it supports that feature).

```
{   /* begin sect_polys() */
    register short  i, j;
    Plane plane1, plane2;
    Vector t[2]; /* T₁, T₂ */
```

Vector $t1t2$; /* $\overrightarrow{T_1T_2}$ */
float $lambda[2]$; /* Parameters to section points. */

Vector $p1p2$; /* Difference vector. */

short $side1$, $side2$; /* Which side of the plane? */

short $found = 0$;
Bool $parallel$;

/* First calculate the intersection points T_1, T_2 of
   the first polygon with the plane of the second polygon. */
$plane\_constants(\&plane2$ [9], $poly2[0]$, $poly2[1]$, $poly2[2])$;
$side2 = Which\_side(poly1[0]$, $plane2)$;
for $(i = 0, j = 1; i < n1; i++, j++)$ {
    if $(j == n1) j = 0$;
    $side1 = side2$;
    $side2 = Which\_side(poly1[j]$, $plane2)$;
    if $(side1 != side2)$ {
        $Subt\_vec(p1p2$, $poly1[i]$, $poly1[j])$;
        $sect\_line\_and\_plane(t[found]$, $\&lambda[found]$, $\&parallel$,
                                   $poly1[i]$, $p1p2$, $\&plane2)$;
        if $(lambda[found]{>}{=}0$ && $lambda[found]{<}{=}1)$
            if $(++found == 2)$
                break;
    } /* end **if** $(side1)$ */
} /* end **for** (i) */
if $(found < 2)$
    return $FALSE$; /* No line of intersection. */

/* Now we intersect the line T_1T_2 with the edges of the second polygon. */
$plane\_constants(\&plane1$, $poly1[0]$, $poly1[1]$, $poly1[2])$;
$found = 0$;
$Subt\_vec(t1t2$, $t[0]$, $t[1])$;

$side2 = Which\_side(poly2[0]$, $plane1)$;
for $(i = 0, j = 1; i < n2; i++, j++)$ {
    if $(j == n2) j = 0$;
    $side1 = side2$;
    $side2 = Which\_side(poly2[j]$, $plane1)$;
    if $(side1{!}{=}side2)$ {
        $Subt\_vec(p1p2$, $poly2[i]$, $poly2[j])$;
        $intersect\_lines(section$, $\&lambda[found]$, $\&parallel$,
                                $t[0]$, $t1t2$, $poly2[i]$, $p1p2$, $3)$;

        /* Modify parameter. */

---

[9]For less experienced C programmers: we have to pass the argument *plane2*
as a pointer to a **Plane**. This is done by passing its *address* (= *&plane2*).

```
    if (lambda[found]  <  0)
        lambda[found] = 0;
    else if (lambda[found]  >  1)
        lambda[found] = 1;
    if (++found  == 2) {
        if (lambda[0]  >  lambda[1]) { /* Sort parameters. */

            float temp;¹⁰ /* Necessary in the Swap macro. */

            Swap(lambda[0],  lambda[1]);
        } /* end if (lambda) */
        break;
    } /* end if (found) */
} /* end if (side1) */
} /* end for (i) */
if (lambda[1] − lambda[0]  <  EPS) /* Line too short. */
    return FALSE;
/* Determine the actual intersection points. */

Linear_comb(section[0],  t[0],  t1t2,  lambda[0]);
Linear_comb(section[1],  t[0],  t1t2,  lambda[1]);
return TRUE;
} /* end sect_polys() */
```

1.4 Translations

By adding a translation vector $\vec{t}$ to the position vector of a space point we get the position vector of the translated point. Usually, translations are applied to hundreds or even thousands of points. Therefore, we want to have a subroutine that is able to accomplish the task as quickly as possible. With the help of pointer variables we can keep the coordinates of related points together in one storage block, which we will call a "pool." Let us have a look at the procedure in question:

#define *Add_vec(result, a, b)*\ $(\rightarrow$ `Macros.h`$)$
    $((result)[X] = (a)[X] + (b)[X], \backslash$
    $(result)[Y] = (a)[Y] + (b)[Y], \backslash$
    $(result)[Z] = (a)[Z] + (b)[Z])$

---

[10]C is very flexible in the declaration of variables. Sometimes programs become more readable when variables that are needed only in smaller loops etc., are declared locally. Such variables, however, cannot be used as **register** variables.

---

void *translate_pool*(*n*, *pool*, *trans*)   ($\rightarrow$ `Proto.h`)

    short *n*; /* Number of points to be translated. */
    Vector **pool*; /* Coordinate pool of arbitrary size. */
    Vector *trans*; /* Translation vector. */
{ /* begin *translate_pool*() */
    register Vector **vec* = *pool*, **hi_vec* = *vec* + *n*;

    for (; *vec* < *hi_vec*; *vec*++)
       Add_vec(**vec*, **vec*, *trans*);
} /* end *translate_pool*() */

The pointer *vec* is a pointer to a **Vector**, thus $hi\_vec = vec + n$ is a pointer to a new **Vector** **hi_vec*. In between *vec* and *hi_vec* there is space for *n* vectors. Because of the scaling nature of pointers in C [DARN88] they can be evaluated by means of

$$*vec = *(vec + 0),\ *(vec + 1),\ *(vec + 2),\ \text{etc.}$$

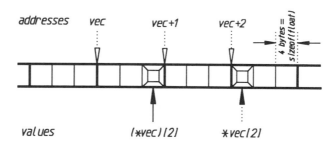

FIGURE 4. The difference between the evaluations of $(*vec)[2]$ and $*vec[2]$, where *vec* is a pointer to a **Vector**.

Once again, we have an example of a macro where it is important to write the arguments in parentheses. In C $(*vec)[2]$ is not the same as $*vec[2]$. The compiler will interpret the first expression as $(*vec)[2] = **vec + 2$, i.e., as the *z*-value of the **Vector** **vec*, which is correct. The second expression will be interpreted as $*vec[2] = **(vec + 2)$, which is the *x*-value of the vector $*(vec + 2)$![11] For better understanding see Figure 4. Pointer arithmetic may seem to be tricky, but after some time you will discover that it is one of the greatest things in C and that it speeds up the programs amazingly. If you look at the previous function again, you will see that almost all the calculations are done with **register** variables.

---

[11]**vec* is a **Vector**, i.e., a pointer to a **float**, ***vec* is a **float**!

Additions with such variables are probably among the fastest things a computer can do. There are no function calls, because *Add_vec* is a macro. If your computer is able to work with more than two register variables and if you have huge pools to transform, it may be worth declaring another variable

> **register Vector** *∗t* = (**Vector** ∗) *trans*;

Now write

> **for** (; *vec* < *hi_vec*; *vec*++)
>   *Add_vec*(∗*vec*, ∗*vec*, ∗*t*);

1.5 Matrices

Before we talk about rotations in space we will say a few words about matrix calculus, which is a very convenient way of abbreviating long and confusing calculations. In this context we will only speak of square 3×3-matrices. Such a matrix is an array of nine numbers (called elements) in three rows and three columns. The elements in a row may be interpreted as a vector ("row vector").

Let **A** and **B** be two 3×3 matrices:

$$\mathbf{A} = (a_{ik}) = \begin{pmatrix} a_{00} & a_{01} & a_{02} \\ a_{10} & a_{11} & a_{12} \\ a_{20} & a_{21} & a_{22} \end{pmatrix}, \quad \mathbf{B} = (b_{ik}) = \begin{pmatrix} b_{00} & b_{01} & b_{02} \\ b_{10} & b_{11} & b_{12} \\ b_{20} & b_{21} & b_{22} \end{pmatrix}. \quad (23)$$

The *product* of the matrices is defined as

$$\mathbf{A\,B} = \mathbf{C} = (c_{ik}) \quad \text{with} \quad c_{ik} = a_{i0}\,b_{0k} + a_{i1}\,b_{1k} + a_{i2}\,b_{2k}\,. \quad (24)$$

Note that $\mathbf{A\,B} \neq \mathbf{B\,A}$. The product of a vector $\vec{v} = (v_x, v_y, v_z)$ and a matrix **A** is defined as a new vector $\vec{r}$:

$$\vec{r} = \vec{v}\,\mathbf{A} = \begin{pmatrix} v_x\,a_{00} + v_y\,a_{10} + v_z\,a_{20} \\ v_x\,a_{01} + v_y\,a_{11} + v_z\,a_{21} \\ v_x\,a_{02} + v_y\,a_{12} + v_z\,a_{22} \end{pmatrix}. \quad (25)$$

Note the order of the operands in the multiplication. In many (especially in European) books, column vectors are used instead of row vectors and the order is turned around ($\mathbf{A}\,\vec{v}$ instead of $\vec{v}\,\mathbf{A}$). In this case the matrix **A** has to be "transposed" into a matrix $\mathbf{A}^T$ (Equation 26), i.e., its elements are reflected on the so-called *main diagonal*.

Every rotation in space by an arbitrary angle about an axis running through the origin can be described by a so-called *orthogonal* matrix or *rotation* matrix. The row vectors of such matrices are all normalized and pairwise orthogonal. The product of two rotation matrices is also a rotation matrix.

Because of the special properties of a rotation matrix we get its *inverse matrix* simply by transposing it:

$$\mathbf{A}^{-1} = \mathbf{A}^T = \begin{pmatrix} a_{00} & a_{10} & a_{20} \\ a_{01} & a_{11} & a_{21} \\ a_{02} & a_{12} & a_{22} \end{pmatrix}. \tag{26}$$

If $\mathbf{A}$ is a rotation matrix that describes the rotation of space by an angle φ about an axis a, its inverse matrix causes a rotation about the same axis a, but by the opposite angle $-\varphi$.

Let us now have a look at the corresponding C code. First we define a new type:

typedef float Rot_matrix[3][3];   ($\rightarrow$ `Types.h`)

A subroutine for a matrix multiplication might look like this:

void *matrix_mult(c, a, b)*   (*for the time being!*)
      Rot_matrix *c, a, b*;[12]

```
{   /* begin matrix_mult() */
    register short i, j;
    for (i = 0; i < 3; i++)
        for (j = 0; j < 3; j++)
            c[i][j] = a[i][0] * b[0][j] + a[i][1] * b[1][j] + a[i][2] * b[2][j];
}   /* end matrix_mult() */
```

The multiplication of a vector by a matrix is done by means of the function

void *vec_mult_matrix(result, v, a)*   (*for the time being!*)
      Vector *result*;
      Vector *v*;
      Rot_matrix *a*;

```
{   /* begin vec_mult_matrix() */
    register short i;
    for (i = 0; i < 3; i++)
        result[i] = v[X] * a[0][i] + v[Y] * a[1][i] + v[Z] * a[2][i];
}   /* end vec_mult_matrix() */
```

Now we will try to speed up this function, for which purpose we use pointers to **Vector** variables:

#define *Vec_mult_matrix(r, v, m)*\   ($\rightarrow$ `Macros.h`)
    $(r)[X] = (v)[X] * (m)[0][0] + (v)[Y] * (m)[1][0] + (v)[Z] * (m)[2][0], \backslash$
    $(r)[Y] = (v)[X] * (m)[0][1] + (v)[Y] * (m)[1][1] + (v)[Z] * (m)[2][1], \backslash$
    $(r)[Z] = (v)[X] * (m)[0][2] + (v)[Y] * (m)[1][2] + (v)[Z] * (m)[2][2]$

/* Faster version. */

---

[12]The type **Rot_matrix** is by definition a pointer. Therefore, the changes of the argument c will be valid outside the function.

```
void vec_mult_matrix(result, v, a)                        (→ Proto.h)
   Vector result;
   Vector v;
   Rot_matrix a;
{  /* begin vec_mult_matrix() */
   register Vector *res = (Vector *) result, *vec = (Vector *) v;

   Vec_mult_matrix(*res, *vec, a);
}  /* end vec_mult_matrix() */
```

In a similar way, we accelerate matrix multiplication.

/* Faster version. */

```
void matrix_mult(c, a, b)                                 (→ Proto.h)
   Rot_matrix c, a, b;
{  /* begin matrix_mult() */
   register Vector
       *vec = (Vector *) a,
       *hi_vec = vec + 3,
       *res = (Vector *) c;
   for ( ; vec < hi_vec; vec++, res++)
       Vec_mult_matrix(*res, *vec, b);
}  /* end matrix_mult() */
```

1.6 Rotations

A rotation of a point P *about the z-axis* by the angle ζ is done by the multiplication of its position vector $\vec{p}$ by the rotation matrix

$$
\mathbf{Z}(\zeta) = \begin{pmatrix} \cos\,\zeta & \sin\,\zeta & 0 \\ -\sin\,\zeta & \cos\,\zeta & 0 \\ 0 & 0 & 1 \end{pmatrix}. \tag{27}
$$

By convention, a rotation angle is declared to be positive if it appears as a positive angle when we "look into" the oriented axis.

When we rotate the unit point $E_x(1,0,0)$ on the x-axis about the *positive oriented z*-axis by $\pi/2$, it will coincide with the unit point $E_y(0,1,0)$ on the y-axis.

In order to rotate P *about the oriented x-axis* by the angle ξ, we multiply its position vector by the matrix

$$\mathbf{X}(\xi) = \begin{pmatrix} 1 & 0 & 0 \\ 0 & \cos \xi & \sin \xi \\ 0 & -\sin \xi & \cos \xi \end{pmatrix}. \tag{28}$$

This time the unit point E_y on the y-axis will coincide with the unit point $E_z(0, 0, 1)$ on the z-axis if we rotate it by $\xi = \pi/2$.

Finally, the *rotation about the oriented y-axis* by the angle η is achieved by a multiplication of the position vector by

$$\mathbf{Y}(\eta) = \begin{pmatrix} \cos \eta & 0 & -\sin \eta \\ 0 & 1 & 0 \\ \sin \eta & 0 & \cos \eta \end{pmatrix}. \tag{29}$$

Note the signs of cos and sin in this case! As a result, E_z will coincide with E_x when we rotate it by $\eta = \pi/2$.

Now we want to rotate a point about an *arbitrary axis g through the origin* by the angle φ. This can be done by a multiplication by a single general rotation matrix $\mathbf{R}$, the elements of which may be determined by the following geometric considerations (Figure 5):

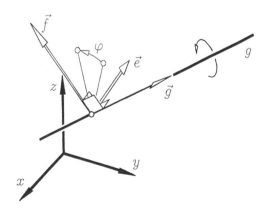

FIGURE 5. Rotation about a general axis.

Let the rotation axis g be the z-axis of a new Cartesian coordinate system Σ_g with the three pairwise orthogonal unit vectors $\vec{e}$, $\vec{f}$ and $\vec{g}$.

For the unit vector $\vec{g}$, we choose the normalized direction (g_x, g_y, g_z) of the axis g. Next we choose the horizontal normal vector $(-g_y, g_x, 0)$ of $\vec{g}$ and normalize it. Thus, we have found a second unit vector $\vec{e} = (e_x, e_y, e_z)$. (If $g_x = g_y = 0$, we let $\vec{e} = (1, 0, 0)$.) Finally, the unit vector $\vec{f} = (f_x, f_y, f_z)$ is the cross product of the two vectors: $\vec{f} = \vec{g} \times \vec{e}$.

Consider a rotation matrix $\mathbf{M}$ that describes the rotation of space so that the axes of Σ_g will coincide with the axes of the original system. By means of this matrix the rotation about g is transformed into a rotation about the z-axis, which we can already handle. The rotation back to the system Σ_g is described by the inverse matrix $\mathbf{M}^{-1}$. Thus, we have

$$\mathbf{R} = \mathbf{M} \ \mathbf{Z}(\varphi) \, \mathbf{M}^{-1}. \tag{30}$$

The inverse matrix $\mathbf{M}^{-1}$ can be determined easily. It is nothing but the rotation matrix

$$\mathbf{M}^{-1} = \begin{pmatrix} e_x & e_y & e_z \\ f_x & f_y & f_z \\ g_x & g_y & g_z \end{pmatrix}. \tag{31}$$

To prove this, we simply have to apply the rotation described by M^{-1} to the unit vectors of the original system. The rotated vectors are indeed $\vec{e}$, $\vec{f}$ and $\vec{g}$. Finally we come to the general case of a *rotation about an arbitrary axis*. If $\vec{a}$ is the position vector to a point A on the axis, we first translate the points that have to be rotated along the vector $-\vec{a} = \overrightarrow{AO}$; then we apply the rotation (Equation 30) to the translated points, and finally, we translate the points back by means of the vector $\vec{a}$.

2
Projections

From the physical point of view, one-eyed seeing is nothing but projecting three-dimensional objects onto a projection surface (projection plane) by means of a lens (the camera lens or the lens of the eyeball). The brain is then more or less capable of "reconstructing" the objects in space, i.e., of estimating the distance of the objects with the help of size comparisons or shadows. Misinterpretations are reduced by two-eyed seeing, because it enables the brain to intersect corresponding projection rays in space.

Geometrists distinguish between central projections (where the projection center is not at an infinite distance) and parallel projections. In reality, most projections are central projections ("perspectives"). For technical drawings we will mainly use "orthogonal projections" as a special case of parallel projections. Among these projections there are the "main views" (the top/bottom view, the front/back view, the right-hand side/left-hand side view) and axonometric views. Such projections permit us to compare or even measure lengths and to determine whether lines in space are parallel or not.

Since parallel projections can be interpreted as extreme cases of central projections, we will only talk about central projections in this book.

———— • ————

In this chapter we will learn how to deal with projections and how to submit the process of illumination to the rules of perspective. Furthermore, we will develop functions and macros that allow us to switch between different coordinate systems as quickly as possible. Finally, we will develop C functions for the clipping of lines and polygons.

2.1 Central Projections

A central projection is determined by the projection center C and the principal point T ("target point" or "look-at point"). The image plane π is defined as the normal plane to the "principal ray" CT through the principal point (Figure 1).

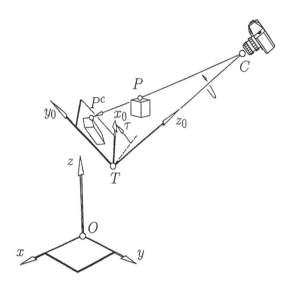

FIGURE 1. "World system" and "screen system."

The distance $d = |\overrightarrow{CT}|$ is called the *distance of the perspective*. This is the general case of a central projection. The camera itself may be rotated ("twisted") about the main projection ray by an angle τ. (The angle τ is measured with respect to the horizontal normal vector to the projection ray.)

In order to make the image plane π become the base plane xy, we now transform all the points that have to be projected so that
(1) the principal point T becomes the origin of the coordinate system,
(2) the projection center C becomes a point on the positive z-axis,
(3) the twist angle τ is eliminated.

Figure 2 illustrates what we have to do. In order to fulfill condition (1), we only have to apply a translation by the vector $\overrightarrow{TO}$ to all the points and to the projection center as well. To fulfill condition (2), first we rotate the translated world system about the z-axis until the translated projection center $C^t(c_x, c_y, c_z)$ lies on the yz-plane. According to Figure 2a, the rotation angle $-\gamma$ is given by

$$\gamma = \begin{cases} \frac{\pi}{2} + \arctan \frac{c_y}{c_x}, & \text{if } c_x \geq 0; \\ \frac{\pi}{2} + (\arctan \frac{c_y}{c_x} + \pi), & \text{otherwise.} \end{cases} \quad (-\pi < \gamma \leq \pi) \tag{1}$$

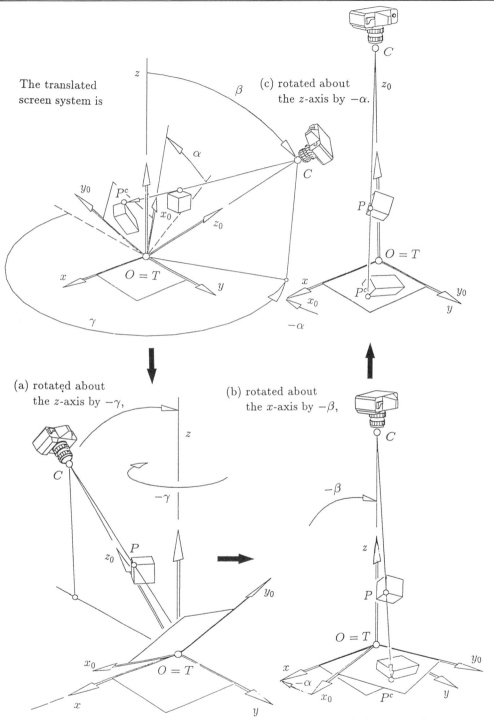

FIGURE 2. A transformation of the projection center and the image plane.

Now the image plane contains the x-axis. Thus, if secondly we rotate about the x-axis by the angle $-\beta$

$$\beta = \arccos \frac{c_z}{d} \quad (0 < \beta \leq \pi) \quad \text{with} \quad d = \sqrt{c_x{}^2 + c_y{}^2 + c_z{}^2}, \tag{2}$$

the image plane will become the xy-plane (Figure 2b). In order to eliminate the twist-angle (condition (3)), we finally rotate the transformed points about the transformed principal ray, which coincides with the z-axis, by the angle $-\alpha$ (Figure 2c)

$$\alpha = \tau \quad (-\pi < \alpha \leq \pi). \tag{3}$$

All three rotations can be performed in one step, which is described by the matrix

$$\mathbf{R} = \mathbf{Z}(-\gamma)\,\mathbf{X}(-\beta)\,\mathbf{Z}(-\alpha). \tag{4}$$

A point $P(p_x, p_y, p_z)$ with position vector $\vec{p}$ is rotated by means of $\mathbf{R}$ to a point $\overline{P}(\overline{p}_x, \overline{p}_y, \overline{p}_z)$ with position vector $\overrightarrow{\overline{p}}$:

$$\overrightarrow{\overline{p}} = \vec{p}\,\mathbf{R}. \tag{5}$$

We have not yet projected the rotated points $\overline{P}$ to the image plane (i.e., the xy-plane). The new projection center, which now lies on the z-axis, has the coordinates $\overline{C}(0, 0, d)$. If we intersect the projection ray

$$\vec{x} = \overrightarrow{\overline{c}} + \lambda\,(\overrightarrow{\overline{p}} - \overrightarrow{\overline{c}}), \tag{6}$$

with the plane $z = 0$, we get

$$\lambda = \frac{d}{d - \overline{p}_z}. \tag{7}$$

Thus, the image point P^c of $\overline{P}$ has the two-dimensional coordinates

$$p_x^c = \lambda\,\overline{p}_x, \quad p_y^c = \lambda\,\overline{p}_y. \tag{8}$$

The z-coordinate $\overline{p}_z$ of $\overline{P}$ is also the oriented distance $\overline{P\pi}$ of the original space point P from the image plane π.

The three angles α, β, γ can be interpreted as Euler angles [FOLE90]. First we translate our objects so that the target point becomes the origin of the coordinate system. If we then rotate our objects

(1) about the z-axis by the angle α,
(2) about the x-axis by the angle β,
(3) once again about the z-axis by the angle γ,

and if we finally project them from the point $C(0,0,d)$ on the xy-plane, we will get the same perspective of our scene. The rotation matrix that performs all three rotations in one step is given by

$$\mathbf{R}^{-1} = \mathbf{Z}(\alpha)\,\mathbf{X}(\beta)\,\mathbf{Z}(\gamma). \tag{9}$$

This means that each perspective can be given by the equivalent parametrizations[1]

$$(C,\ T,\tau) \Longleftrightarrow (d,\ \alpha,\ \beta,\ \gamma,\ T). \tag{10}$$

2.2 The Viewing Pyramid

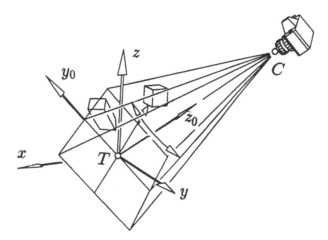

FIGURE 3. The "viewing pyramid."

The "neutral" or "vanishing" plane ν, which is parallel to the image plane and which coincides with the center of the projection, divides the space into two

---

[1]No parametrization by three numbers, however, can continuously parametrize the space of rotations. In the (C, T, τ)-parametrization, for example, the angle γ is ambiguous when the projection center is moved about during an animation and when $\overline{CT}$ points to the z-direction.

halfspaces. Of course it only makes sense to calculate the coordinates of images of those points that are in the halfspace that contains the image plane. Points in the other halfspace, however, may also play a part in the image of the scene. Imagine a polygon, some parts of which are in the visible halfspace and others in the "forbidden halfspace" (Figure 3). Nevertheless parts of the polygon have to be drawn. In this case, we have to calculate the intersection points with a "near clipping plane κ_n," which lies in between the image plane and the neutral plane ν. Their images replace the "forbidden points" of the polygon.

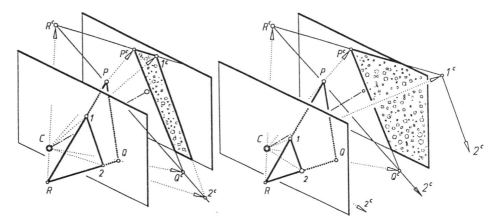

FIGURE 4. The neutral plane and the (near) clipping plane. The distance of the near clipping plane may have an influence on the appearance of the image polygons.

In some cases, it may also be useful to introduce a "far clipping plane κ_f" (Figure 4). Objects that lie behind this plane are not drawn at all. Such a plane should be used for animations of complex scenes, in which some objects are temporarily far away from the observer. The computer would spend precious calculation time on the display of the images of such objects, even though these images are hardly more than pixel size.

In general, we will not display objects that are outside the "viewing pyramid" or "viewing frustum," which is formed by the near and far clipping planes and by those four clipping planes that are spanned by one side of the rectangular field of view and by the projection center (Figure 3). In Section 2.5, we will develop routines for the clipping of lines and polygons.

An important question is which rectangle to choose for mapping on the screen. Figure 5 illustrates that it is a good idea to introduce a so-called "field-of-vision angle" $0° < \varphi < 90°$.

This is what we know of camera objectives with different focuses: a wide-angle lens has a greater field-of-vision angle than a telephoto lens. If you set up a camera at a fixed point and take pictures of a scene first with a telephoto lens and then with a wide-angle lens, the only difference between these pictures will be the scale factor. Thus, if you enlarge a detail of the picture taken with the wide-angle lens, it will be identical to the corresponding one taken with the telephoto lens.

Field-of-vision angles should not be too large ($\varphi < 60°$) because our images would not look natural any more (Figure 6a). Small field-of-vision angles ($\varphi < 10°$) create an impression similar to that of a telephoto lens (Figure 6c). For natural images, we can choose, for instance, $15° \leq \varphi \leq 40°$ (Figure 6b). For parallel projections, we will let the distance of the projection center be "large," but not infinite. Thus, we can still work with a "small," but non-vanishing field-of-vision angle.

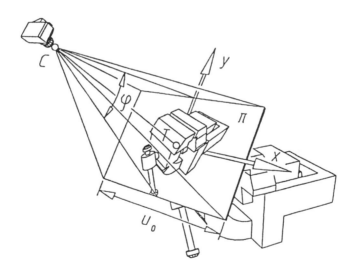

FIGURE 5. The field-of-vision angle.

Because many people are used to thinking in terms of focal distances f, we give a table of corresponding values,[2] valid for miniature cameras with a negative size of $24mm \times 36mm$ ([HECH74]).

φ	3.4°	6.7°	13.4°	26.5°	38°	46°	53°
$\overline{\varphi}$	6.2°	12°	24°	46°	63°	75°	84°
f	400mm	200mm	100mm	50mm	35mm	28mm	24mm

[2]The angle $\overline{\varphi}$ encloses the *diagonal* of the rectangular picture.

2.3 Coordinate Systems

According to the results of Section 2.1, we will work with three different coordinate systems:

1. The first system is the Cartesian *"world system,"* in which the coordinates of the vertices of our objects are given.

2. The second coordinate system is the non-Cartesian three-dimensional *"screen system."* In this system, the coordinates of a space point are the ordinary screen coordinates of the image of the point (Equation 8), plus, as a third dimension, the oriented distance $\bar{z}$ from the image plane π.

3. As a third type of coordinate system, we introduce the non-Cartesian *"light system,"* which is similar to the screen system. In such a system a space point can also be described by the two-dimensional coordinates of its shadow (=projection) on an arbitrary image plane plus the distance of the point from this image plane as a third coordinate.

When we talk about screen coordinates, we have to distinguish between the so-called screen coordinates on the image plane π (which are measured by orthogonal unit vectors) and the "pixel coordinates," which depend on the system that is used and which need not necessarily be normalized. Let us try to map the field $-\frac{u_0}{2} < x^c < \frac{u_0}{2}$, $-\frac{v_0}{2} < y^c < \frac{v_0}{2}$ into the rectangular field $0 < u < w$, $0 < v < h$, where w and h are the width and the height of our graphics window. The linear functions

$$u = \frac{w}{u_0} x^c + \frac{w}{2}, \quad v = \frac{h}{v_0} y^c + \frac{h}{2} \tag{11}$$

will fulfill this task. If we are lucky, a polygon on the image plane π will then appear undistorted on the screen. On many systems, however, the polygon will appear distorted and/or be turned upside down. This can be avoided by introducing a system-dependent variable ϱ:

$$u = \frac{w}{u_0} x^c + \frac{w}{2}, \quad v = \varrho \left(\frac{h}{v_0} y^c + \frac{h}{2} \right). \tag{12}$$

Even though the screen coordinates x, y are now system-dependent, it is fairly easy to transform these "physical device coordinates" into "normalized device coordinates" $0 \leq x_0, y_0 \leq 1$ by means of the linear functions

$$x_0 = \frac{u}{w}, \quad y_0 = \frac{v}{\varrho h}. \tag{13}$$

FIGURE 6. The influence of the field-of-vision angle.

We will need such normalized coordinates for plotter drawings or for the output on other devices.

According to the field-of-vision angle in Figure 5, the values of the variables u_0 and v_0 are:

$$u_0 = \frac{w}{h}\, d \tan \frac{\varphi}{2}, \ v_0 = \frac{1}{\varrho}\, d \tan \frac{\varphi}{2}. \tag{14}$$

The third dimension in the screen system (and in the light system) needs some more explanation. We will work with two transformations $\mathbf{T}_1 : \ P \to \overline{P}$ and $\mathbf{T}_2 : \ P \to P^*$ of space, both of which will have the property that the *normal projection* of the transformed scene on the projection plane π is identical with the *central projection* of the scene from the projection center (light center).

The first transformation

$$\mathbf{T}_1 : \ P(x,\, y,\, z) \to \overline{P}(\overline{x},\, \overline{y},\, \overline{z}) \tag{15}$$

is non-linear. It is defined by

$$\overline{x} = \lambda\, x, \ \overline{y} = \lambda\, y, \ \overline{z} = z = \overline{P\pi} \ \ \text{with } \lambda = \frac{d}{d - z}. \tag{16}$$

Similary to $\mathbf{T}_1$, the second transformation

$$\mathbf{T}_2 : \ P(x,\, y,\, z) \to P^*(x^*,\, y^*,\, z^*) \tag{17}$$

is defined by

$$x^* = \lambda\, x, \ y^* = \lambda\, y, \ z^* = k\,\lambda\, z \ \ \text{with } \lambda = \frac{d}{d - z} \ \ (k \text{ real}). \tag{18}$$

The transformation $P \to P^*$ is a linear one, i.e., the transformed edges are still straight lines. (Such a transformation is called a collineation. The center of the collineation is the principal point.) To prove this, it is enough to show that a plane in space is transformed into a plane. A straight line is then the intersection of two planes. When three points P, Q, R are coplanar, we have

$$D = \begin{vmatrix} p_x & p_y & p_z \\ q_x & q_y & q_z \\ r_x & r_y & r_z \end{vmatrix} = 0. \tag{19}$$

After the transformation $\mathbf{T}_2$, we have

$$D^* = \begin{vmatrix} p_x^* & p_y^* & p_z^* \\ q_x^* & q_y^* & q_z^* \\ r_x^* & r_y^* & r_z^* \end{vmatrix} = \begin{vmatrix} \lambda_p p_x & \lambda_p p_y & k\,\lambda_p p_z \\ \lambda_q q_x & \lambda_q q_y & k\,\lambda_q q_z \\ \lambda_r r_x & \lambda_r r_y & k\,\lambda_r r_z \end{vmatrix} = k\,\lambda_p\,\lambda_q\,\lambda_r\,D = 0. \tag{20}$$

Therefore, the three points P^*, Q^*, R^* are coplanar as well.

For $k = 1/d$, we have

$$z^* = \frac{z}{d - z} \tag{21}$$

and the reverse transformation

$$z = \frac{d\,z^*}{1 + z^*}. \tag{22}$$

Regular points, i.e., points that are not in the forbidden halfspace, have z^*-values in the interval $-1 < z^* < \infty$. For two points P and Q of the same halfspace, we have

$$p_z^* < q_z^* \iff p_z < p_z. \tag{23}$$

Figure 7a illustrates the perspective projection of a roller. Figures 7b and 7c show two rather diverse spatial objects, the images of which are identical to the image in Figure 7a when we apply a *normal* projection to the picture plane π. In Figure 7b, the transformation $\mathbf{T}_1$ was applied. As we can see, the edges of the roller are not straight lines any more (they are slightly bent hyperbola arches, which indicates that the transformation is quadratic). In Figure 7d, the roller was transformed by transformation $\mathbf{T}_2$.

When do we use which transformation? For our purposes it is enough to store the value $z = \bar{p}_z\,(\mathbf{T}_1)$ in the screen system and in the light systems. For intersections (e.g., for three-dimensional clipping or priority tests), however, we have to switch to the corresponding linear transformation $\mathbf{T}_2$ by transforming the z-values of the vertices of a point by means of the Formula (21).

One of the advantages of the non-linear transformation $\mathbf{T}_1$ is that it works perfectly when the projection center is at an infinite distance, whereas the linear transformation would fail in such a case.

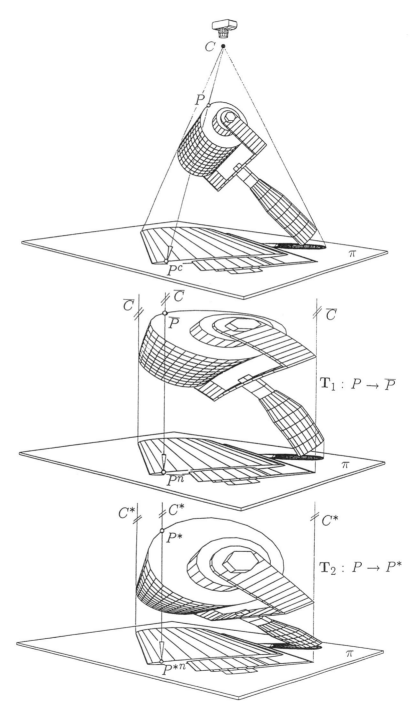

FIGURE 7. Different objects with identical images.

2.4 Back and Forth Between Coordinate Systems

In this section, we will develop functions and macros that permit us to switch between all the systems as quickly as possible. The speed factor is quite essential here, because for every new frame these calculations have to be done thousands of times.

Before we make any further calculations we translate our world system so that the principal point becomes the origin:

#define *MAX_LIGHTS* 5   ($\rightarrow$ `Macros.h`)
/* This limit is generous, because some algorithms in the program run in
        quadratic time with the number of lights, and the program would run
        more slowly if it were pushed to these limits. */
#define *MAX_SYST* $(1 + MAX\_LIGHTS)$ ($\rightarrow$ `Macros.h`)
/* Screen system plus light systems. */
#define *SCREEN_SYST* 0   ($\rightarrow$ `Macros.h`)

Vector *Proj_center*[*MAX_SYST*], *Target*;   ($\rightarrow$ `Globals.h`)
/* Projection centers (i.e., the eye point and the light sources) and target
        point are global variables. We may get their coordinates from an input
        file. */
Vector *∗Coord_pool*;   ($\rightarrow$ `Globals.h`)
/* The pool into which we write all the coordinates we want to have at our
        disposal. In Chapter 3.1, we will see how the pool is allocated. */
short *Total_vertices*; /* Number of all points. */   ($\rightarrow$ `Globals.h`)
short *No_of_lights*;   ($\rightarrow$ `Globals.h`)
/* This variable contains the exact number of lights. */
short *Total_systems*;   ($\rightarrow$ `Globals.h`)
/* The screen system plus all the light systems. Therefore, we let
        $Total\_systems = 1 + No\_of\_lights$;
        once we know the exact number of lights. */

#define *Turn_vec*(*t*, *v*) \   ($\rightarrow$ `Macros.h`)
        $((t)[X] = -(v)[X],\ (t)[Y] = -(v)[Y],\ (t)[Z] = -(v)[Z])$

---

void *translate_world_system*(*target*)   ($\rightarrow$ `Proto.h`)
        Vector *target*;

{   /* begin *translate_world_system*() */

        Vector *t*; /* The vector $-\overrightarrow{target}$ */
        short *syst*;

        Turn_vec(*t*, *target*);
        translate_pool(*Total_systems*, *Proj_center*, *t*);
        translate_pool(*Total_vertices*, *Coord_pool*, *t*);
}   /* end *translate_world_system*() */

In order to calculate the rotation matrices (Equation 4), we have to introduce a function that permits us to determine the "spherical coordinates" of a space point (radius, azimuth angle, and elevation angle):

---

void *spherical_coords*(*d, azimuth, elevation, point*)   (→ `Proto.h`)

    float *∗d*; /∗ Distance from the origin. ∗/
    double *∗azimuth, ∗elevation*;
    Vector *point*; /∗ Given point in 3-space. ∗/

{   /∗ begin *spherical_coords*() ∗/
  ∗d = Length(point);
  ∗azimuth = atan2(point[Y], point[X] + EPS);
     /∗ This is the extended *atan*()-function; *atan2*(*y, x*) returns $\arctan (y/x)$
      if $x > 0$, otherwise it returns $\arctan (y/x) + \pi$. ∗/
  ∗elevation = asin(($**double**$) point[Z]/(∗d + EPS));
     /∗ Do not forget to add EPS = 1e-7 to the dividends in *atan2*() and in
      asin() in order to avoid divisions by zero. The deviation from the cor-
      rect result is negligible. It is highly improbable that *point[X]* equals
      exactly $-EPS$ (which would cause a division by zero), whereas
      the case *point[X]* = 0 is quite common. For a point on the *z*-axis
      (*point[X]* = *point[Y]* = 0) we now have the value *∗azimuth* = 0. ∗/
}   /∗ end *spherical_coords*() ∗/

Now we need some additional global variables:

double *Dist[MAX_SYST], Azim[MAX_SYST], Elev[MAX_SYST],*
    Twist;   (→ `Globals.h`)
    /∗ Distance, azimuth angle, elevation of the projection centers in the different
      systems. The twist angle is only necessary for the screen system. ∗/

Rot_matrix *Rot[MAX_SYST], InvRot[MAX_SYST]*;   (→ `Globals.h`)
    /∗ Rotation matrices and their inverse matrices. ∗/

This enables us to determine the rotation matrices (Equation 4) for all the systems:

---

void *fill_rot_matrix*(*r, angle, axis*)   (→ `Proto.h`)
    Rot_matrix *r*;
    double *angle*;
    short *axis*;

{   /∗ begin *fill_rot_matrix*() ∗/
    register float *s, c*;   /∗ For reasons of speed.∗/

```
    s = sin(angle); c = cos(angle);
    switch(axis) {
        case X :
            r[0][0] =   1; r[0][1] =    0; r[0][2] =  0;
            r[1][0] =   0; r[1][1] =    c; r[1][2] =  s;
            r[2][0] =   0; r[2][1] =   -s; r[2][2] =  c;
            return;
        case Y :
            r[0][0] =   c; r[0][1] =    0; r[0][2] = -s;
            r[1][0] =   0; r[1][1] =    1; r[1][2] =  0;
            r[2][0] =   s; r[2][1] =    0; r[2][2] =  c;
            return;
        case Z :
            r[0][0] =   c; r[0][1] =    s; r[0][2] =  0;
            r[1][0] =  -s; r[1][1] =    c; r[1][2] =  0;
            r[2][0] =   0; r[2][1] =    0; r[2][2] =  1;
            return;
    }
}   /* end fill_rot_matrix() */
```

#define *PI* 3.1415926 $(\rightarrow$ `Macros.h`$)$

```
void calc_rot_matrix(syst)                                  (→ Proto.h)

    short syst;

{   /* begin calc_rot_matrix() */
    Rot_matrix z_alpha, x_beta, z_gamma, zx;
    double alpha, beta, gamma; /* The Euler angles α, β, γ. */

    spherical_coords(&Dist[syst],
                        &Azim[syst], &Elev[syst], Proj_center[syst]);
    alpha = Twist * (syst == SCREEN_SYST);
    beta = PI/2 − Elev[syst];
    gamma = PI/2 + Azim[syst];
    fill_rot_matrix(z_alpha, alpha, Z);
    fill_rot_matrix(x_beta, beta, X);
    fill_rot_matrix(z_gamma, gamma, Z);
    matrix_mult(zx, z_alpha, x_beta);
    matrix_mult(InvRot[syst], zx, z_gamma);
    inverse_rot_matrix(Rot[syst], InvRot[syst]);
}   /* end calc_rot_matrix() */
```

The inverse matrix is calculated by means of this simple function:

```
void inverse_rot_matrix(inv, mat)                          (→ Proto.h)
    Rot_matrix inv, mat;

{   /* begin inverse_rot_matrix() */
    register short i, j;

    for (i = 0; i < 3; i++)
        for (j = 0; j < 3; j++)
            inv[i][j] = mat[j][i];
}   /* end inverse_rot_matrix() */
```

float *Window_width, Window_height*;   (→ Globals.h)
  /* Dimensions of the drawing window in pixels. */
float *X_mid, Y_mid*;   (→ Globals.h)
  /* These are the coordinates of the center of the window on the screen:

$$X\_mid = Window\_width/2; \; Y\_mid = Window\_height/2;$$

  */
float *Pixel_ratio*;   (→ Globals.h)
  /* This is the system-dependent constant ϱ that corrects the distortion on
    the screen. (You can measure the distortion of a square.) If your coor-
    dinate system on the screen has its origin in the left *upper* corner, you
    will probably have $Pixel\_ratio \approx -1$.
  */
float *Scale_factor*;   (→ Globals.h)
  /* A stretch factor to fit the image of the scene into the drawing window. It
    is initialized by

$$Scale\_factor = Dist[0] * tan(Fovy/2);$$
    and may additionally be modified by an enlarge factor:
  */
float *Init(Enlarge, 1)*;   (→ Globals.h)
  /* To be able to zoom objects without changing the field-of-vision angle we
    let

$$Scale\_factor \mathrel{*}= Enlarge;$$
  */

Here is at last the code of the function:

```
void world_to_screen(screen, world)                          (→ Proto.h)
    Vector screen; /* result */
    Vector world; /* The point to be transformed. */
{   /* begin world_to_screen() */
    register float lambda;

    vec_mult_matrix(screen, world, Rot[SCREEN_SYST]);
    lambda = Scale_factor/(Dist[0] − screen[Z]);
    screen[X] = X_mid + lambda * screen[X];
    screen[Y] = Y_mid + lambda * Pixel_ratio * screen[Y];
}   /* end world_to_screen() */
```

If we use a macro instead, we can speed up the process (an application of this macro will be given in Section 3.1.)

```
#define Rotate_and_project(scr, wld)\              (→ Macros.h)
    (Vec_mult_matrix(*scr, *wld, *Rot),\
    lambda = Scale_factor/(Dist[0] − (*scr)[Z]),\
    (*scr)[X] = X_mid + lambda * (*scr)[X],\
    (*scr)[Y] = Y_mid + Pixel_ratio * lambda * (*scr)[Y])
```

———— • ————

The inverse function screen_to_world() is needed only a few times. Therefore, we are satisfied with the code

```
void screen_to_world(world, screen)                          (→ Proto.h)
    Vector world, screen;

{   /* begin screen_to_world() */
    register float lambda;
    Vector rotated;

    lambda = Scale_factor/(Dist[0] − screen[Z]);
        /* Undo projection */
    rotated[X] = (screen[X] − X_mid)/lambda;
    rotated[Y] = (screen[Y] − Y_mid)/(Pixel_ratio * lambda);
    rotated[Z] = screen[Z];
    vec_mult_matrix(world, rotated, InvRot[SCREEN_SYST]);
}   /* end screen_to_world() */
```

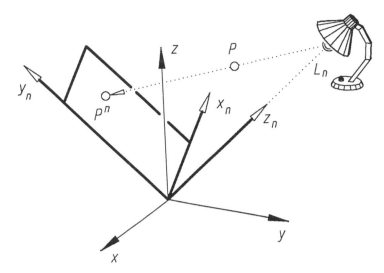

FIGURE 8. "World system" and "light system."

Let us now develop the equivalent functions (macros) for the light systems. This time the projection center is the n-th *light source* (given by *Proj_center*$[n]$). We can identify the origin (i.e., the former principal point) of the world system with a point on the "principal light ray." The plane that contains the origin and that is normal to the principal light ray is our image plane (Figure 8). The only difference from the usual perspective is that we do not have to deal with twist angles, because it does not make any difference whether or not we rotate the "light bulb" about its axis. Instead of the function *world_to_screen*(), we write an equivalent function *world_to_light*(), which uses a macro

#define *Rotate_and_illuminate*(*shad*, *wld*)\   ($\rightarrow$ `Macros.h`)
  (*Vec_mult_matrix*(**shad*, **wld*, *rot*), \
  lambda = *Dist*[n] / (*Dist*[n] − (**shad*)[Z]), \
  (**shad*)[X] **= lambda*, (**shad*)[Y] **= lambda*)

---

void *world_to_light*(*shadow*, *world*, *n*)   ($\rightarrow$ `Proto.h`)
  Vector *shadow*, *world*;
  short *n*; /* The *n*-th light system. */
{   /* begin *world_to_light*() */
  register float **rot* = (**float** ***) *Rot*[n];
  register Vector
    *shad = (**Vector** ***) *shadow*,
    *wld = (**Vector** ***) *world*;
  float *lambda*; /* Needed within the macro. */

  Rotate_and_illuminate(*shad*, *wld*);
}   /* end *world_to_light*() */

The inverse function *light_to_world*() is very similar to the function *screen_to_world*(). The only difference is that we do not have to care about scalings, distortions or translations to the center of the screen:

---
void *light_to_world*(*world, shadow, n*)   ($\rightarrow$ `Proto.h`)
   Vector *world, shadow*;
   short *n*; /* The *n*-th light system */
{ /* begin *light_to_world*() */
   register float *lambda*;
   Vector *rotated*;
   lambda = Dist[n]/(Dist[n] − shadow[Z]); /* Undo projection. */
   rotated[X] = shadow[X]/lambda;
   rotated[Y] = shadow[Y]/lambda;
   rotated[Z] = shadow[Z];
   vec_mult_matrix(world, rotated, InvRot[n]); /* Rotate back. */
} /* end *light_to_world*() */

Sometimes we want to make a direct switch from the screen system to one of the light systems and vice versa. For the time being, a detour over the world system will help us to do so.

2.5   Clipping Algorithms

When the scene contains "forbidden points" and we try to display the scene, we will realize that the image of the scene is wrong (unless your system supports hardware-clipping). But even if there are no forbidden points, we want to have clipping routines for lines and polygons at our disposal, for example, when we store drawings to replay them in real time afterwards (Chapter 10) or when we want to draw "rubber bands" (Section 4.6) and our compiler does not support such a feature.

The Two-Dimensional Clipping of a Line

Cohen and Sutherland [HEAR86] developed a very fast method of detecting whether and how a line in the drawing plane has to be clipped. They divide the drawing plane into nine regions (Figure 9). The region a point belongs to can be detected by means of fast bitwise operations. The algorithm works exclusively with integers.

If a point is inside the window, its region code is 0000. A point that is above and to the left of the window has a region code 0101, etc. When the region codes reg_1 and reg_2 of the end points of a line segment are identical, it follows that the line is either completely inside the window ($reg_1 = reg_2 = 0$) or completely outside the window. Otherwise the segment has to be clipped with the respective contour line of the window.

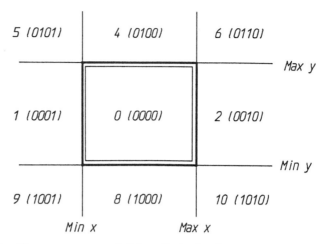

FIGURE 9. The nine regions of Cohen-Sutherland.

short *Min_x, Max_x, Min_y, Max_y;*   (→ Globals.h)
#define *LEFT*   0x01   (→ Macros.h)
#define *RIGHT* 0x02   (→ Macros.h)
#define *ABOVE* 0x04   (→ Macros.h)
#define *BELOW* 0x08   (→ Macros.h)
#define *Region(reg, x, y)* {\   (→ Macros.h)
   reg = 0; \
   if *(x > Max_x)*\
     reg |= RIGHT; \
   else if *(x < Min_x)*\
     reg |= LEFT; \
   if *(y > Max_y)*\
     reg |= ABOVE; \
   else if *(y < Min_y)*\
     reg |= BELOW; \
}

Bool *clip2d_line(exists, p0, q0, p, q)*   (→ Proto.h)
   Bool *∗ exists;* /∗ Is the line outside the clipping region? ∗/
   Vector *p0, q0;* /∗ The vertices of the clipped line. ∗/
   Vector *p, q;* /∗ The vertices of the line. ∗/
{   /∗ begin *clip2d_line()* ∗/
   register long $x1 = p[X], y1 = p[Y], x2 = q[X], y2 = q[Y];$
   char *reg1, reg2;*
   short *temp, outside = 0;*

```
    *exists = TRUE;
  Region(reg1, x1, y1);
  Region(reg2, x2, y2);
  if (reg1) ++outside;
  if (reg2) ++outside;
  if (!outside) return FALSE;
  while (reg1 | reg2) {
      if (reg1 & reg2) { /* Line outside window. */
          *exists = FALSE;
          return TRUE;
      }
      if (reg1 == 0) {
          Swap(reg1, reg2);
          Swap (x1, x2); Swap(y1, y2);
      }
      if (reg1 & RIGHT) {
          y1 += ((y2 - y1) * (Min_x - x1)) /(x2 - x1);
          x1 = Min_x;
      } else if (reg1 & LEFT) {
          y1 += ((y2 - y1) * (Max_x - x1)) /(x2 - x1);
          x1 = Max_x;
      } else if (reg1 & ABOVE) {
          x1 += ((x2 - x1) * (Max_y - y1)) /(y2 - y1);
          y1 = Max_y;
      } else if (reg1 & BELOW) {
          x1 += ((x2 - x1) * (Min_y - y1)) /(y2 - y1);
          y1 = Min_y;
      }
      Region(reg1, x1, y1);
  }
  p0[X] = x1; p0[Y] = y1; q0[X] = x2; q0[Y] = y2;
  return TRUE;
} /* end clip2d_line() */
```

The clipping region must be initialized. This is done by means of the function

float *Clip_vol*[6];   ($\rightarrow$ `Globals.h`)

```
void xy_region(xmin, xmax, ymin, ymax)              (→ Proto.h)
    float xmin, xmax, ymin, ymax;
{ /* begin xy_region() */
    Max_x = Clip_vol[0] = xmax;
    Min_x = Clip_vol[1] = xmin;
    Max_y = Clip_vol[2] = ymax;
    Min_y = Clip_vol[3] = ymin;
} /* end xy_region() */
```

When the graphics window is opened, we write

$xy\_region(0.0,\ Window\_width,\ 0.0,\ Window\_height);$

Now we introduce two pointers to a function

$Global\ Init\_fptr(clip\_line,\ clip2d\_line);$ ($\rightarrow$ `Proto.h`)

$Global\ Init\_fptr(draw\_line,\ quick\_line);$ ($\rightarrow$ `Proto.h`)
    /* The function $quick\_line()$ is explained in Section 4.2. */

A function $clip\_and\_plot\_line()$ looks like this:

```
void clip_and_plot_line(p, q)                            (→ Proto.h)
    Vector p, q;
{   /* begin clip_and_plot_line() */
    Vector p0, q0;
    Bool exists;
    if (!clip_line(&exists, p0, q0, p, q))
        draw_line(p, q);
    else if (exists)
        draw_line(p0, q0);
}   /* end clip_and_plot_line() */
```

When we have to do three-dimensional clipping or when we want to have other line styles (like XOR-lines) as well, we let $draw\_line$ point to the respective function. This makes the code more readable and also faster because a lot of conditional branchings can be avoided.

The Three-Dimensional Clipping of a Line

When the scene contains forbidden points, we let the pointer point to the function:

$clip\_line\ =\ clip3d\_line;$

In order to develop the code for the function $clip3d\_line()$, we extend the concept of the "regions" to three-space:

float $Min\_z,\ Max\_z;$ ($\rightarrow$ `Globals.h`)
    /* The z-values of the far and near clipping planes, given in the linear system
       (Transformation 21). */

#define MAX_POLY_SIZE 128   ($\rightarrow$ `Macros.h`)
char $Reg[MAX\_POLY\_SIZE];$ ($\rightarrow$ `Globals.h`)
    /* This space will also be used for the clipping of polygons. */

```
#define INFRONT 0x10                                              (→ Macros.h)
#define BEHIND   0x20                                             (→ Macros.h)
char  Clip_reg[6]  =
        { RIGHT,  LEFT,  ABOVE,  BELOW,  INFRONT,  BEHIND };
                                              /* Global in the current module. */

#define Region3d(reg,  x,  y,  z) {\                              (→ Macros.h)
    Region(reg,  x,  y); \
    if  (z > Max_z || z < −1)\
        reg | = INFRONT; \
    else  if  (z < Min_z)\
        reg | = BEHIND; \
}
```

For three-dimensional clipping it is important that the z-values of the points of the line are transformed by means of the linear transformation (21). The z-values of regular points will then be in the interval $-1 < z < \infty$.

Before we do any clipping, we initialize the clipping planes:

```
void z_region(far, near)                                          (→ Proto.h)
    float far, near;
{   /* begin z_region() */
    Max_z = Clip_vol[4]  = near;
    Min_z = Clip_vol[5]  = far;
}   /* end z_region() */
```

Good values for the initialization are

$$z\_region(-0.8, 4.0);$$

Then all the points behind the far clipping plane $\kappa_f : \bar{z} = -0.8\, d/(1-0.8) = -4\, d$ and all the points in front of the near clipping plane $\kappa_n : \bar{z} = 4\, d/(1+4) = 0.8\, d$ are outside the clipping volume (Formula (22)). The clipping with κ_n has to be done *before* the clipping with the drawing area: if one vertex of an edge is in the "forbidden halfspace," its image point may well be inside the drawing area. After clipping with κ_n, however, the vertex is replaced by a point, the image of which can be outside the drawing area.

The interpolation of the intersection point of the line with the clipping planes is done by means of the function

```
void intpol(r, a, b, i)                                    (→ Proto.h)
    register float * r; /* The interpolated result. */
    register float * a, *b; /* The two end points. */
    register short  i; /* Information about the order of x, y, z. */
{   /* begin intpol() */
    static char c[6][3] =
            { X, Y, Z,   X, Y, Z,   Y, Z, X,   Y, Z, X,   Z, X, Y,   Z, X, Y };
    char  c1, c2, c3;
    float t;

    c1 = c[i][X]; c2 = c[i][Y]; c3 = c[i][Z];
    t = (Clip_vol[i] − a[c1]) /(b[c1] − a[c1] + EPS);
    r[c1] = Clip_vol[i];
    r[c2] = a[c2] + t * (b[c2] − a[c2]);
    r[c3] = a[c3] + t * (b[c3] − a[c3]);
}   /* end intpol() */
```

Finally, the code for the three-dimensional clipping looks like this:

```
#define Point_region(reg, p) {\                            (→ Macros.h)
    x = (p)[X]; y = (p)[Y]; z = (p)[Z];\
    Region3d(reg, x, y, z);\
}
#define Copy_vec(r, v)\                                     (→ Macros.h)
    ((r)[X] = (v)[X], (r)[Y] = (v)[Y], (r)[Z] = (v)[Z])
#define Copy_vec2(r, v)\                                    (→ Macros.h)
    ((r)[X] = (v)[X], (r)[Y] = (v)[Y])
```

```
Bool clip3d_line(exists, p0, q0, p, q)                     (→ Proto.h)
    Bool * exists; /* Is the line outside the clipping volume? */
    Vector p0, q0; /* The vertices of the clipped line. */
    Vector p, q; /* The vertices of the line. */
{   /* begin clip3d_line() */
    register long  x, y;
    register short i;
    float z;

    Point_region(Reg[0], p);
    Point_region(Reg[1], q);
```

```
    if  (!(Reg[0] | Reg[1]))    /* No clipping. */
        return FALSE;
    * exists = FALSE;
    for (i = 5; i > = 0; i−−)
        if (Reg[0] & Reg[1] & Clip_reg[i])
            return TRUE;    /* Line is outside of box. */
    Copy_vec(p0, p); Copy_vec(q0, q);
    for (i = 0; i < 6; i++) {
        if (Reg[0] & Reg[1] & Clip_reg[i])
            return TRUE;    /* Line is outside of box. */
        if ((Reg[0] | Reg[1]) & Clip_reg[i]) {
            if (Reg[0] & Clip_reg[i])    /* First point is outside. */
                intpol(p0, q0, p0, i);
            else /* Second point is outside. */
                intpol(q0, p0, q0, i);
            if (i > 0) {
                Point_region(Reg[0], p0);
                Point_region(Reg[1], q0);
            }
        } /* end if (Reg[0]) */
    } /* end for (i) */
    return * exists = TRUE;
} /* end clip3d_line() */
```

The Two-Dimensional Clipping of a Polygon

Before we plot a two-dimensional polygon on the screen, we should clip it with the drawing window. This will save time when many of the polygons are outside the window. Clipping is also necessary when we store the polygons and replay them as fast as possible later on (Chapter 9).

Figure 10 shows how the "reentrant polygon clipping" developed by Hodgman and Sutherland [SUTH74/1] works. The polygon is clipped at each side of the window so that it will take a maximum of four steps to get a polygon that is clipped correctly. The algorithm is comparatively fast. For reasons of speed, we introduce two temporary polygons $Tmp1[\ ]$ and $Tmp2[\ ]$ where we store the provisional results. The code is written in such a manner as to make it work for both an array of **Vector2**s and **Vector**s. (We take advantage of the fact that both types are pointers to arrays of **float**s.)

```
float * Tmp1[MAX_POLY_SIZE], *Tmp2[MAX_POLY_SIZE];    (→ Globals.h)
short  Init(Dim, 2);                                   (→ Globals.h)
    /* When the polygon is an array of three-dimensional Vectors, Dim must
       equal 3! */
```

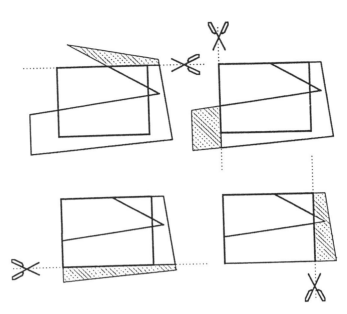

FIGURE 10. The Hodgman-Sutherland algorithm for the clipping of a polygon in four steps.

```
Bool clip2d_polygon(n0, poly0, n, poly)                        (→ Proto.h)
    short  *n0; /* Size of final polygon. */
    Vector poly0[ ]; /* Final polygon. */
    short  n; /* Number of vertices. */
    float  poly[ ]; /* Array of Vector2s or Vectors. */
{   /* begin clip2d_polygon() */
    static float additional[8 * sizeof(Vector)], *add;
        /* A maximum of eight intersection points plus a pointer. */
    register char  *reg = Reg;
    char  *hi_reg = reg + n, code;
    register short  x, y;
    register float  *p = poly, *q;
    short  edge, m, c1, c2;
    float **r;
    float **ppoly; /* Pointer to Tmp1 or Tmp2. */
    float **pp, **hi_pp; /* Pointers into ppoly[ ]. */
    float t;
    short  cut_off = 0;
```

```
cut_off = 0;
for ( ; reg < hi_reg; reg++, p += Dim) {
    x = p[X], y = p[Y];
    Region(*reg, x, y);
    if (*reg != 0)
        ++cut_off;
} /* end for (reg) */
*reg = Reg[0];

if (cut_off == 0)
    return FALSE;
else if (cut_off == n) { /* Pol. might be outside of window. */
    for (edge = 0; edge < 4; edge++) {
        code = Clip_reg[edge];
        for (reg = Reg; reg < hi_reg; reg++)
            if (!(*reg & code)) break;
        if (reg == hi_reg) { /* Polygon is outside of window. */
            *n0 = 0;
            return TRUE;
        } /* end if (reg) */
    } /* end for (edge) */
} /* end if (cut_off) */
p = poly; *n0 = n;
/* Assign pointers to the vertices of the polygon. */
hi_pp = (pp = ppoly = Tmp1) + n;
for ( ; pp < hi_pp; pp++, p += Dim)
    *pp = p;
c1 = X; c2 = Y;
add = additional;
for (edge = 0; edge < 4; edge++) {
    code = Clip_reg[edge];
    if (edge == 2)
        c1 = Y, c2 = X;
    for (hi_reg = (reg = Reg) + *n0; reg < hi_reg; reg++)
        if (*reg & code) break;
    if (reg < hi_reg) {
        m = Clip_vol[edge];
        hi_pp = (pp = ppoly) + *n0;
        *hi_pp = *pp;
        r = ppoly = (ppoly == Tmp1 ? Tmp2 : Tmp1);
        reg = Reg;
        while (pp < hi_pp) {
            p = *pp++; q = *pp;
            if (*reg++ & code) {
                if (!(*reg & code)) {
                    *r++ = add;
                    add[c1] = m;
```

```
                                t = (m − p[c1]) /(q[c1] − p[c1]);
                                add[c2] = p[c2] + (q[c2] − p[c2]) * t;
                                add += Dim;
                            } /* end if (*reg) */
                        } else {
                            *r++ = p;
                            if (*reg & code) {
                                *r++ = add;
                                add[c1] = m;
                                t = (m − q[c1]) /(p[c1] − q[c1]);
                                add[c2] = q[c2] + (p[c2] − q[c2]) * t;
                                if (Dim == 3)
                                    add[Z] = q[Z] + (p[Z] − q[Z]) * t;
                                add += Dim;
                            } /* end if (*reg) */
                        } /* end if (*reg) */
                    } /* end while (pp) */
                    pp = ppoly;
                    if (edge < 3) { /* Determine changed regions. */
                        for (reg = Reg; pp < r; reg++, pp++) {
                            p = *pp;
                            x = p[X]; y = p[Y];
                            Region(*reg, x, y);
                        } /* end for (reg) */
                        *reg = Reg[0];
                    } /* end if (edge) */
                    *n0 = r − ppoly;
                    if (*n0 < 3) {
                        *n0 = 0;
                        return TRUE;
                    } /* end if (*n0) */
                } /* end if (reg) */
            } /* end for (edge) */
            p = &poly0[0][0];
            hi_pp = (pp = ppoly) + *n0;
            if (Dim == 2)
                for ( ; pp < hi_pp; pp++, p += Dim)
                    Copy_vec2(p, *pp);
            else
                for ( ; pp < hi_pp; pp++, p += Dim)
                    Copy_vec(p, *pp);
            return TRUE;
        } /* end clip2d_polygon() */
```

Again we introduce a pointer to a function

Global Init_fptr(*clip_polygon, clip2d_polygon*);   (→ `Proto.h`)

A function *clip_and_draw_polygon*() looks like this:

Global Init_fptr(*draw_polygon, fill_poly*);   (→ `Proto.h`)
        /* The function *fill_poly*() is explained in Section 4.2. */

```
void clip_and_draw_polygon(n, poly)                    (→ Proto.h)
    short n;
    float poly[ ];
{   /* begin clip_and_draw_polygon() */
    static short n0;
    Vector poly0[MAX_POLY_SIZE];
        /* This is space reserved for the clipped polygon. */


    if (!clip_polygon(&n0, poly0, n, poly))
        draw_polygon(n, poly);
    else if (n0 >= 3)
        draw_polygon(n0, poly0);
}   /* end clip_and_draw_polygon() */
```

When we want to do three-dimensional clipping, to draw the outline of the polygon or to use other fill styles (e.g., smooth shading, see Section 4.6), we let *draw_polygon* point to the respective function. This makes the code more readable and faster because a lot of conditional branchings can be avoided.

The Three-Dimensional Clipping of a Polygon

For three-dimensional clipping, it is again important that the coordinates of the vertices of the polygon have been transformed by means of the *linear* transformation (21). Points in front of the observer then have z-values with $-1 < z < \infty$, whereas points in the forbidden halfspace have z-values < -1.

Of course, the routine *clip3d_polygon*() is similar to *clip_polygon*(). Only if 3d-clipping is really necessary, we let

        clip_polygon = *clip3d_polygon*;

For example, if we plot the faces of an object that is not to be clipped at all, it is a waste of time to do the 3d-clipping for each face.

```
Bool clip3d_polygon(n0, poly0, n, poly)                    (→ Proto.h)
    short  *n0; /* Size of final polygon. */
    Vector poly0[ ]; /* Final polygon. */
    short  n; /* Number of vertices. */
    float poly[ ]; /* Array of Vectors. */
{   /* begin clip3d_polygon() */
    static float additional[12 * sizeof(Vector)], *add;
        /* A maximum of 12 intersection points plus a pointer. */
    register char  *reg = Reg;
    char   *hi_reg = reg + n, code;
    register short x, y;
    float z;
    register float *p = poly, *q;
    short  i;
    float **r;
    float **ppoly; /* Points to Tmp1 or Tmp2. */
    float **pp, **hi_pp; /* Pointers into ppoly[ ]. */
    short  cut_off = 0;

    for ( ; reg < hi_reg; reg++, p += Dim) {
        Point_region(*reg, p);
        if (*reg != 0)
            ++cut_off;
    } /* end for (reg) */
    *reg = Reg[0];
    if (cut_off == 0)
        return FALSE;
    else if (cut_off == n) { /* Pol. might be outside of box. */
        for (i = 0; i < 6; i++) {
            code = Clip_reg[i];
            for (reg = Reg; reg < hi_reg; reg++)
                if (!(*reg & code)) break;
            if (reg == hi_reg) { /* Polygon is outside of box. */
                *n0 = 0;
                return TRUE;
            } /* end if (reg) */
        } /* end for (i) */
    } /* end if (cut_off) */
    p = poly; *n0 = n;
    /* Assign pointers to the vertices of the polygon. */
    hi_pp = (pp = ppoly = Tmp1) + n;
    for ( ; pp < hi_pp; pp++, p+= Dim)
        *pp = p;
    add = additional;
    for (i = 5; i >= 0; i--) {
        code = Clip_reg[i];
```

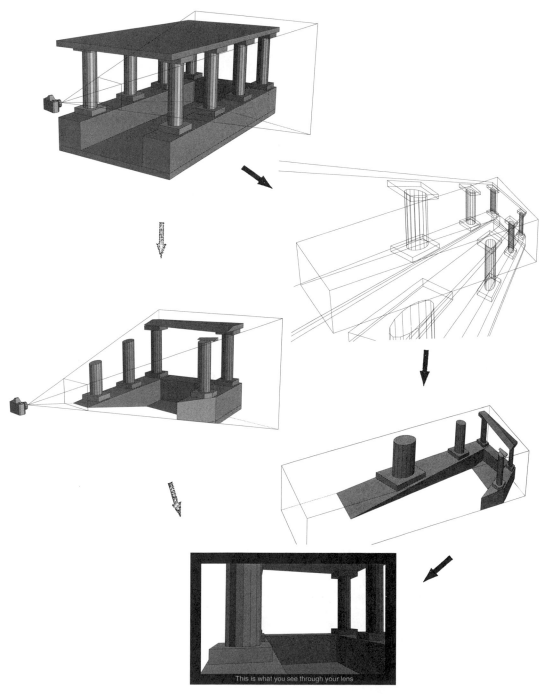

FIGURE 11. 3d-clipping can be done in world coordinates (left side) or it can be applied to the linearly transformed scene (right side). In the latter case the projection is parallel orthographic and the viewing frustum is a parallelepiped ("box").

```
    for  (hi_reg  =  (reg  =  Reg)  +  *n0; reg  <  hi_reg; reg++)
        if  (*reg & code) break;
    if  (reg  <  hi_reg) {
        hi_pp  =  (pp  =  ppoly)  +  *n0;
        * hi_pp  =  *pp;
        r =  ppoly  =  (ppoly  ==  Tmp1 ? Tmp2  :  Tmp1);
        reg  =  Reg;
        while  (pp  <  hi_pp) {
            p  =  *pp++;  q  =  *pp;
            if  (*reg++ & code) {
                if  (!(*reg & code)) {
                    * r++  =  add;
                    intpol(add, p, q, i);
                    add +=  Dim;
                }
            } else  {
                * r++  =  p;
                if  (*reg & code) {
                    * r++  =  add;
                    intpol(add, q, p, i);
                    add +=  Dim;
                } /* end if (*reg & code) */
            } /* end if (*reg) */
        } /* end while (pp) */
        pp  =  ppoly;
        if  (i  >  0) { /*  Determine changed regions. */
            for  (reg  =  Reg; pp  <  r; reg++, pp++) {
                p  =  *pp;
                Point_region(*reg, p);
            }
            * reg  =  Reg[0];
        } /* end if (i < 5) */
        * n0  =  r − ppoly;
        if  (*n0  <  3) {
            * n0  =  0;
            return  TRUE;
        } /* end if (*n0) */
    } /* end if (reg) */
} /* end for (i) */
/*  Now copy everything to poly0. */
p  =  *poly0;
hi_pp  =  (pp  =  ppoly)  +  *n0;
for  ( ; pp  <  hi_pp; pp++, p +=  Dim)
    Copy_vec(p, *pp);
return  TRUE;
} /* end clip3d_polygon() */
```

Figure 11 illustrates how 3d-clipping works: on the left side, the viewing frustum was used to clip the scene, and on the right side, the whole scene was transformed by means of the linear transformation $\mathbf{T}_2$).

3

How to Describe
Three-Dimensional Objects

One of the main problems of 3D-computer graphics is the description of geometrical objects. The most straightforward way is to give the computer a list of all the vertices, including a list that explains how to connect these vertices to faces or edges, respectively. Then the computer can apply a general hidden-line or hidden-surface algorithm.

Things get more complicated when the objects are not only defined geometrically, but also endowed with certain physical properties like transparency, reflecting surfaces, patterns, etc. In such a case, it turns out to be convenient to use a readable pseudo-code stored in data files, which may then be interpreted by an "object preprocessor" (i.e., a program that converts the pseudo-code into the above-mentioned lists).

The way in which the pseudo-code is produced is just a matter of taste. It may simply be done by a text editor (this is the way programmers are accustomed to producing it) or by another program, the "graphics object editor", which is more sophisticated (this is the way non-programmers want to do it). In principle, the way from the idea for a graphical scene to the solution of the problem is always:

idea $\xrightarrow{\text{object editor}}$ pseudo-code $\xrightarrow{\text{object preprocessor}}$ lists $\xrightarrow{\text{object processor}}$ image of the scene.

In this chapter, we will explain how an "object preprocessor" is written. However, we will *not* go into the creation of the corresponding data files by means of a sophisticated graphics object editor (i.e., a screen on which you can create and manipulate objects with a mouse).

Thus, it will be shown how data files like the following can be read and interpreted.

```
PYRAMID metallic gray convex hollow
   vertices
      2 0 0 , 1 2 0 , -1 2 0 , -2 0 0 , -1 -2 0 , 1 -2 0 ,
      2 0 4 , 1 2 1 , -1 2 1 , -2 0 4 , -1 -2 1 , 1 -2 1
   edges
      1 2 , 2 3 , 3 4 , 4 5 , 5 6 , 6 1 ,
      7 8 , 8 9 , 9 10 , 10 11 , 11 12 , 12 7 ,
      1 7 , 2 8 , 3 9 , 4 10 , 5 11 , 6 12 , 7 10
   faces
      1 2 3 4 5 6 ,
      1 2 8 7 , 2 3 9 8 , 3 4 10 9 , 4 5 11 10 ,
      5 6 12 11 , 6 1 7 12 , 10 11 12 7
```

The first thing we have to think of is how to organize memory. Arrays of pointers are extremely useful if we want to stay within certain storage limits (they also accelerate the program). In principle, we can say that we want to store every piece of information only once and that if we need this information elsewhere, we just store the address at which we can find it.

3.1 Data Pools

In Section 2.3, we learned how to get the screen coordinates and the light coordinates of a point. We will now see that it is possible to "fill coordinate pools" (i.e., memory allocation of the same type, in this case, arrays of **Vector**s) in quite an efficient manner. We will also see how we can apply the same principles to a variety of other arrays.

For the sake of convenience, we write two short functions that make the allocation and reallocation of memory safe and easy. The fact that C does not explicitly check many things, such as range errors and memory allocation failings, makes programs faster but also more sensitive to software errors. Therefore, memory allocation in particular should be checked every time!

FILE $Init(*Output, stdout)$; $(\rightarrow$ Globals.h$)$
> /* This is the file into which we write our messages. The file pointer can be
>   set to any other stream by
> $Output = fopen(" <$arbitrary file name$> ", "w")$;
> */

#define $Print(str)\backslash$ $(\rightarrow$ Macros.h$)$
   $fprintf(Output, str)$

Bool $Init(Window\_opened, FALSE)$; $(\rightarrow$ Globals.h$)$

```
void safe_exit(message)                                    (→ Proto.h)
   char *message;
{  /* begin safe_exit() */
   Print(message);
   if (Window_opened)
      G_close_graphics(); /* This will be explained in Section 4.2. */
   exit(0L);
}  /* end safe_exit() */
```

```
char * mem_alloc(n, size, name)                            (→ Proto.h)
   long n; /* Number of elements of the array. */
   short size; /* Size of each element in bytes. */
   char *name; /* Name of variable (array) we want to allocate. */
{  /* begin mem_alloc() */
   char *address;

   address = (char *) malloc(n * size);
        /* This is the (system-dependent) UNIX function
              char *malloc(long);
           for the allocation of memory. It returns NULL when the necessary
           memory is not available. If you use a different compiler, the function
           may have a slightly different name!
        */
   if (address != NULL) return address;
   else {
        Print("Cannot allocate ");
        safe_exit(name);
   }  /* end if */
}  /* end mem_alloc() */
```

```
char * mem_realloc(orig_address, n, size, name)            (→ Proto.h)
   char *orig_address; /* The original address of memory. */
   long n; /* Number of elements of the array. */
   short size; /* Size of each element in bytes. */
   char *name; /* Name of variable (array) we want to allocate. */
{  /* begin mem_realloc() */
   char *new_address;

   new_address = (char *) realloc(orig_address, n * size);
        /* System-dependent!!! See mem_alloc(). */
   if (new_address != NULL) return new_address;
   else {
        Print("Cannot reallocate ");
        safe_exit(name);
   }  /* end if */
}  /* end mem_realloc() */
```

In our object preprocessor, there are a few arrays, the size of which is unknown before allocation: *Coord_pool*, *Edge_pool*, *Face_pool*, *Object_pool*. Before any data are read, we allocate a reasonable amount of storage to the world coordinates of all points, edges, faces and objects:

#define *MAX_POINTS* 4000   ($\rightarrow$ `Macros.h`)

/* The number 4000 is just a suggestion. If you have enough RAM, take a higher number. Since a vector consists of three **floats** (**sizeof**(**float**) = 4 bytes), 4000 vectors need 48 Kbytes of RAM-memory. The pool is reallocated as soon as we know the precise number of points so that we do not waste any memory! */

#define *MAX_EDGES* 6000   ($\rightarrow$ `Macros.h`)

/* Takes 48 Kbytes, because for each edge we need two pointers to vectors of the size of 4 bytes each. */

#define *MAX_FACES* 2500   ($\rightarrow$ `Macros.h`)

/* The definition of the structure **Face** is given in Section 3.2. Because **sizeof**(**Face**) $\approx$ 40, 2500 faces need 100 Kbytes. */

#define *MAX_UBYTE* $(1L \ll (8 * \textbf{sizeof}(\textbf{Ubyte})))$ ($\rightarrow$ `Macros.h`)

/* This is $1 \ll 8 = 255$ or $1 \ll 16 = 65535$.[1]*/

typedef unsigned char Ubyte;   ($\rightarrow$ `Types.h`)

/* 0...*MAX_UBYTE*. */

/* The only reason why we introduce the type **Ubyte** is because it helps to save space (we will use more-dimensional arrays consisting of elements of this type). If you have a computer with enough RAM-memory, you can define **Ubyte** as a **short**. Then you will have no restrictions as to the number of objects (polyhedra) you want to display. */

#define *MAX_POL* $(MAX\_UBYTE - 1)$ ($\rightarrow$ `Macros.h`)

/* Maximum number of polyhedra. The definition of the structure **Polyhedron** is given in Section 3.2. */

Vector *Screen_pool*;   ($\rightarrow$ `Globals.h`)

/* The pool into which we write all the screen coordinates. */

Vector *Light_pool*[*MAX_SYST*];   ($\rightarrow$ `Globals.h`)

/* The pools into which we write all the coordinates in the different light systems. Since we may have several light sources, it is an array of pointers. */

---

[1]The C preprocessor will replace the constant by the *result* of the shift operation every time it appears in the code.

Vector $*Cur\_coord;$[2] $(\rightarrow$ `Globals.h`$)$

/* This is a pointer that indicates where we are in *Coord_pool* while we
read from the data file. It is initialized when we allocate the coordinate
pool. Whenever we store the world coordinates of a point of the scene
(including points like barycenters, etc.), we increase *Cur_coord* by one.
*/

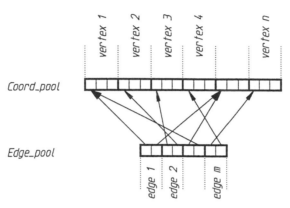

FIGURE 1. *Edge_pool* is an array of pointers into *Coord_pool*.

Vector $**Edge\_pool, **Cur\_edge;$ $(\rightarrow$ `Globals.h`$)$

/* Edge pool plus a pointer into the pool. *Cur_edge* is initialized when we
allocate the pool, and it is increased by two every time we store the
two vertices of an edge. Thus, the pointers to the vertices of all edges
are stored one after the other in an *Edge_pool*. The n-th edge has the
vertices $*Edge\_pool[2*n]$, $*Edge\_pool[2*n+1]$ (Figure 1). */

Face $*Face\_pool, *Cur\_face;$ $(\rightarrow$ `Globals.h`$)$

/* Face pool plus a pointer into the pool. *Cur_face* is initialized when we
allocate the pool, and it is increased by one every time we store a face.
*/

Polyhedron $*Object\_pool, *Cur\_object;$ $(\rightarrow$ `Globals.h`$)$

/* Object pool plus a pointer into the pool. *Cur_object* is initialized when
we allocate the pool, and it is increased by one every time we store an
object. */

[2]Pointers into pools will often begin with the prefix "*cur_*" (which stands for
"current" or, if you want, for "cursor"). This indicates that they will usually run
through loops. The upper limit of such a loop will frequently also be a pointer
of the same type, the name of which will usually have the prefix "*hi_*."

$Coord\_pool = Cur\_coord = (\textbf{Vector}\ *)^3$
     $mem\_alloc(MAX\_POINTS,\ \textbf{sizeof}(\textbf{Vector}),\ \texttt{"Coord\_pool"});$
$Edge\_pool = Cur\_edge = (\textbf{Vector}\ **)$
     $mem\_alloc(MAX\_EDGES,\ 2 * \textbf{sizeof}(\textbf{Vector}\ *),\texttt{"Edge\_pool"});$
$Face\_pool = Cur\_face = (\textbf{Face}\ *)$
     $mem\_alloc(MAX\_FACES,\ \textbf{sizeof}(\textbf{Face}),\ \texttt{"Face\_pool"});$

$Object\_pool = Cur\_object = (\textbf{Polyhedron}\ *)$
     $mem\_alloc(MAX\_POL,\ \textbf{sizeof}(\textbf{Polyhedron}),\ \texttt{"Object\_pool"});$

For more convenience, we can abbreviate the lines

$array = (type\ *)\ mem\_alloc(size,\ \textbf{sizeof}(type),\ string);$

$ptr\_array = (type\ **)\ mem\_alloc(size,\ \textbf{sizeof}(type\ *),\ string);$

by means of the macros:

#define $Alloc\_array(type,\ array,\ n,\ string)\backslash$ $(\rightarrow \texttt{Macros.h})$
     $array = (type\ *)\ mem\_alloc((\textbf{long})\ n,\ \textbf{sizeof}(type),\ string)$
#define $Alloc\_ptr\_array(type,\ ptr\_array,\ n,\ string)\backslash$ $(\rightarrow \texttt{Macros.h})$
     $ptr\_array = (type\ **)\ mem\_alloc((\textbf{long})\ n,\ \textbf{sizeof}(type\ *),\ string)$

The allocations of $Coord\_pool$ and $Edge\_pool$ can then be written like this:

$Alloc\_array(\textbf{Vector},\ Coord\_pool,\ MAX\_POINTS,\ \texttt{"Coord\_pool"});$
$Alloc\_ptr\_array(\textbf{Vector},\ Edge\_pool,\ 2 * MAX\_EDGES,\ \texttt{"Edge\_pool"});$

After having stored all the information, we make use of the scaling nature of pointers to calculate the actual sizes of the pools:

short $Total\_edges,\ Total\_faces,\ Total\_objects;$ $(\rightarrow \texttt{Globals.h})$
     /* $Total\_vertices$ was defined in Chapter 2. */
$Total\_vertices = Cur\_coord - Coord\_pool;$
$Total\_edges = Cur\_egde - Edge\_pool;$
$Total\_faces = Cur\_face - Face\_pool;$
$Total\_objects = Cur\_object - Object\_pool;$

Now we can reallocate the pools:

#define $Realloc\_array(type,\ array,\ n,\ string)\backslash$ $(\rightarrow \texttt{Macros.h})$
     $array = (type\ *)\ mem\_realloc(array,\ n,\ \textbf{sizeof}(type),\ string)$
#define $Realloc\_ptr\_array(type,\ p\_arr,\ n,\ string)\backslash$ $(\rightarrow \texttt{Macros.h})$
     $p\_arr = (type\ **)\ mem\_realloc(p\_arr,\ n,\ \textbf{sizeof}(type\ *),\ string)$

---

[3]If you do not cast the function $mem\_alloc()$, you will at least get a warning message from the compiler.

Realloc_array(**Vector**, *Coord_pool*, *Total_vertices*, `"coords"`);
Realloc_ptr_array(**Vector**, *Edge_pool*, *Total_edges*, `"edges"`);
etc.

Furthermore, we can allocate the exact amount of storage for the other coordinate pools:

Alloc_array(**Vector**, *Screen_pool*, *Total_systems* $*$ *Total_vertices*,

`"Screen and light pools"`);

for $(i = 0;\ i < no\_of\_lights;\ i{+}{+})$
   $Light\_pool[i] = Screen\_pool + i * Total\_vertices;$

> /$*$ We identify the zeroth light pool with the screen pool. This allows fast switches between the screen system and the light systems as we will see very soon. $*$/

The n-th point of the scene is given by $*(Coord\_pool + n)$ in the world system, by $*(Screen\_pool + n)$ in the screen system and by $*(Light\_pool[k] + n)$ in the k-th light system.

Provided that the n-th vector in the screen pool really contains the screen coordinates of the n-th vector of the coordinate pool, we can easily switch between the coordinate systems by means of macros:

#define *Screen_coords*(*world*)\ ($\rightarrow$ `Macros.h`)
   (*Screen_pool* + (*world* − *Coord_pool*))
#define *Light_coords*(*n*, *world*)\ ($\rightarrow$ `Macros.h`)
   (*Light_pool*[*n*] + (*world* − *Coord_pool*))

(The variable *world* must be a pointer to a **Vector**.) Here is an example of the usefulness of these macros: let p and q be pointers to the world coordinates of two vertices. Then we can draw a line that connects the images of these vertices simply by writing

plot_line($*Screen\_coords(p)$, $*Screen\_coords(q)$);

(The function *plot_line*() is explained in Section 4.6.)

Since we have identified the zeroth light system with the screen system, we can switch directly between these systems by means of the macro

#define *Switch_syst*(*old_syst*, *new_syst*, *v*)\ ($\rightarrow$ `Macros.h`)
   (*Light_pool*[*new_syst*] + (*v* − *Light_pool*[*old_syst*]))

In order to get the corresponding screen coordinates of a **Vector** v in the n-th light system, we now write

$v = Switch\_syst(n,\ SCREEN\_SYST,\ v);$

The following function shows how we can "fill the screen pool" very efficiently in the desired manner:

```
void fill_screen_pool()                                    (→ Proto.h)

{   /* begin fill_screen_pool() */
    register Vector
        *world = Coord_pool, /* Pointer into coordinate pool. */
        *screen = Screen_pool, /* Pointer into screen pool. */
        *hi_world = world + Total_vertices;
    register float lambda; /* Used within macro. */

    draw_line = quick_line;
        /* As long as no point is in the "forbidden halfspace,"
           we do not have to think about clipping. */
    for ( ; world < hi_world; world++, screen++) {
        Rotate_and_project(screen, world);
        if ((*screen)[Z] >= Dist[SCREEN_SYST])
            draw_line = clip3d_line;
    }
}   /* end fill_screen_pool() */
```

Note that the function does not call any other functions and that it works almost exclusively with register variables.

The *"n*-th *lightpool"* can be filled as quickly as the screen pool:

```
void fill_light_pool(n)                                    (→ Proto.h)
    short n; /* Index of light system. */

{   /* begin fill_light_pool() */
    register Vector
        *world = Coord_pool, /* Pointer into coordinate pool. */
        *shadow = (Vector *) Light_pool[n], /* Ptr into light pool. */
        *hi_world = world + Total_vertices;
    register float *rot = (float *) Rot[n], lambda; /* Used within macro. */

    for ( ; world < hi_world; world++)
        Rotate_and_illuminate(shadow, world);
}   /* end fill_light_pool() */
```

Another example of the scaling nature of pointers may be the following task: you want to get a list of the names of all the objects.

Polyhedron $* obj = Object\_pool$, $*hi\_obj = obj + Total\_objects$;
while $(obj < hi\_obj)$
    $fprintf(Output,$ "%s\n", obj++->$name$);

Several other pools like the "color pool," the "normal pool," the "mirror pool," the "contour pool" and so forth will be declared later on.

—————— • ——————

Sometimes we have to allocate *higher-dimensional arrays* dynamically. For example, let us assume that we want to allocate the two-dimensional array **short** $x[n][m]$. The array has $n\,m$ elements of the type **short**. The writing x[i][j] is turned into $*(x[i] + j)$ by the compiler. Thus, the computer needs information about the n pointers $x[i]$. Therefore, the allocation of the array has to be done in three steps:

```
/* First allocate the n pointers. */
x = (short **) mem_alloc(n, sizeof(short *), "x");
/* Now allocate space for the entire array. */
x[0] = (short *) mem_alloc(n, m * sizeof(short), "x[0]");
/* Finally, initialize the rest of the pointers. */
for (i = 1; i < n; i++)
    x[i] = x[i - 1] + m;
```

It is fairly complicated to rewrite these lines for every new allocation and there is always the danger of memory errors. This problem cannot be solved by a function, because we have to distinguish between different types of variables, if the pointers are to be cast correctly. In fact, this is exactly the case where a C macro comes in handy. (Note the use of commas and semicolons – we cannot use a comma before a loop.)

```
#define Alloc_2d_array(type, array, n, m)\
    array = (type **) mem_alloc((long) n, sizeof(type *), "pointers"),\
    array[0] = (type *) mem_alloc((long) n, m * sizeof(type), "2d-array");\
    for (i = 1; i < n; i++)\
        array[i] = array[i - 1] + m;
```

The macro can be very tricky if it is written like this. For example, if we write

```
for (j = 0; j < jmax; j++)
    Alloc_2d_array(...);
```

we will not get a syntax error, but only the first statement of the macro will be in the loop! Especially when we deal with memory functions, this is an error that cannot be traced easily and that will cause the program to crash. For this reason, we rewrite the macro by taking advantage of the fact that, in C, we can write whole sections of the code as macros, if we only write the code inside braces:

```
#define Alloc_2d_array(type, array, n, m) {\            (→ Macros.h)
    array = (type **) mem_alloc(n, sizeof(type *), "pointers");\
    array[0] = (type *) mem_alloc(n, m * sizeof(type), "2d-array");\
    for (i = 1; i < n; i++)\
        array[i] = array[i - 1] + m;\
}
```

To free the array, we introduce the macro

#define *Free_2d_array(array)*\   ($\rightarrow$ `Macros.h`)
    *(Free_array((***char** *) array[0]), Free_array((***char** *) array))*

To allocate and to free the array **short** $x[n][m]$, we write

*Alloc_2d_array(***short** , x, n, m);
Free_2d_array(x);

3.2   The 'Polyhedron' and 'Face' Structures

Before we start developing an "object preprocessor," let us think of what a
structure has to look like if it is to store all the necessary information about an
"object." As a matter of fact, in this book, an object will always be a (closed
or not closed) polyhedron that consists of a certain number of polygons. Thus,
we do not define every polygon as an object in its own right, as some compara-
ble algorithms do. Quite on the contrary, we will try to *keep together as many
polygons as possible* within units.

Let us first define a structure "Face" that contains all the necessary information
about the facets of the polyhedra:

typedef struct { /∗ **Face** ∗/
    short *no_of_vertices*; /∗ Number of vertices. ∗/
    Vector ∗∗*vertices*;
        /∗ An array of pointers to vectors. The n-th point is evaluated by
            ∗(*vertices*[n]) = ∗∗(*vertices* + n). ∗/
    Ubyte *color*; /∗ Index of corresponding color palette. ∗/
    Ubyte *physical_property*;
        /∗ The polyhedron can be metallic, shiny, transparent, etc. ∗/
    Vector *normal*; /∗ The normalized normal vector. ∗/
    float *cnst*; /∗ The constant of the plane of the polygon. ∗/
    float *incidence*;
        /∗ Average angle of incidence of the facet with the light rays. ∗/
    Ubyte *no_of_neighbor_faces*; **struct Face** ∗∗*neighbor_faces*;[4]
        /∗ Array of pointers to neighbor faces. The n-th neighbor face is
            ∗((**Face** ∗) *neighbor_faces*[n]) ∗/
    Vector ∗*barycenter*;
        /∗ "Center" of face (i.e., the arithmetic mean of the coordinates of the
            vertices). Useful for the calculation of the average depth of the facet
            or the average angle of incidence of the facet, etc. ∗/
} **Face**;   ($\rightarrow$ `Types.h`)

---

[4]We would prefer to simply write **Face** ∗∗*neighbor_faces*. However, this is not
possible, because the compiler does not yet know about the structure **Face**.

Here is an example of how a structure or record **Polyhedron** might look like:

typedef struct { /* **Polyhedron** */
    char *name*;
        /* Each object gets a name in the data file. When we write the data file,
        we call the objects by readable names. When the object preprocessor
        reads the file, it will thus be able to give readable information. */
    Ubyte *index*;
        /* In the program, the object is not called by a name but by an index.
        Because we keep many faces together, we limit the number of objects
        to $MAX\_UBYTE = 255$ (usually this is a very complicated scene with
        thousands of faces). The main reason for this is that we work with
        priority lists, where the priority of each object in comparison with
        all the other objects is stored. To work with more than 255 objects
        (see definition of **Ubyte**) should be left to really fast computers. */
    Ubyte *color_index*;
        /* Index of color palette.[5] The different shades of this special palette
        will be calculated during the program. Because of a minimum size
        for each color palette (necessary for smooth shading) and because of
        the limited number of colors that can be displayed simultaneousely on
        the screen, we will be able to create only a small number of palettes
        (e.g., 8 "parent palettes" plus 16 "subpalettes" in the case of 256
        displayable colors and a palette size of 32). */
    Ubyte *geom_property*;
        /* The polyhedron can be convex, hollow with convex outline, concave,
        etc. */
    Ubyte *physical_property*;
        /* The polyhedron can be reflecting, metallic, mat, transparent, etc. */
    short *type*;
        /* We distinguish between several kinds of polyhedra: polyhedra of re-
        volution, polyhedra of translation, general polyhedra, mathematical
        surfaces, etc. */
    short *no_of_vertices*;
        /* Number of vertices on the polyhedron. */
    Vector *vertices*;
        /* This is the pointer to the coordinate pool. From *vertices* to
        (*vertices* + *no_of_vertices*), the coordinates of all the points on
        the polyhedron are stored. The n-th point, for example, has the y-
        coordinate *vertices*[n][Y] or (*(*vertices* + n))[Y]. */
    Vector *hi_coord*;

---

[5]A "palette" in our sense is a chart of different shades of one and the same
color. Therefore, the constant $PALETTE\_SIZE$ means the number of the different
shades of *one single* color.

/* This pointer into *Coord_pool* is similar to the previous one. However, we will not let this variable point to the coordinates of the last vertex of the object, but a little bit further. After the coordinates of the vertices we store several other points of the object, the screen coordinates or light coordinates of which we want to calculate. */
short *no_of_edges*;
/* Number of edges. All the edges are stored in an "edge pool," which allows us to quickly draw wireframes or to remove hidden lines. */
Vector **edges*;
/* This is the pointer to where the edges of the object are stored. The "**" indicates that, in fact, it is an array of pointers. The storage works like this: the *n*-th edge has two end points, the pointers to which are stored at *edges*[2 * *n*] and *edges*[2 * *n* + 1]. Therefore, the points themselves are stored at *(*edges*[2 * *n*]) = **(*edges* + 2 * *n*) and *(*edges*[2 * *n* + 1]) = **(*edges* + 2 * *n* + 1). */
short *no_of_faces*;
/* The number of faces on the polyhedron. Complicated polyhedra like function graphs may have several thousands of them. */
Face **faces*;
/* This is the pointer to the beginning of the "face pool," where all the faces are stored. The *n*-th face of the polyhedron is stored at *faces*[n]. */
Vector **barycenter*;
/* The barycenter is a point, the coordinates of which are the arithmetic mean of the coordinates of all the vertices. In the case of convex polyhedra, this point is always inside the object. By means of the barycenter, we can orient the normals of the faces. Usually we can do a rough sorting of the priority list as well. In most cases, however, additional priority tests have to be applied. The memory for the point does not have to be allocated (the variable points into *Coord_pool*).
*/
} **Polyhedron**; /* end of **struct** */   (→ `Types.h`)

The structure looks rather complicated by now. In the following chapters, however, we will still add some more structure members.

3.3 General Convex Objects

A planar polygon is *convex* when it lies entirely on one side of each line that is determined by an edge. This occurs when no interior angle is greater than π. If an interior angle is greater than π, the polygon is *concave*. All the straight lines that cross the interior of a convex polygon cut two of its sides. Convex polygons are extremely important for many algorithms in computer geometry.

Our definition of convexity can be extended to 3-space: a polyhedron is convex when it lies entirely on one side of each plane that is determined by a face. The most common examples for such polyhedra are prisms and pyramids with convex base polygons. Special cases of these polyhedra, such as orthogonal parallelepipeds or regular prisms and pyramids, fulfill additional conditions and will be treated separately.

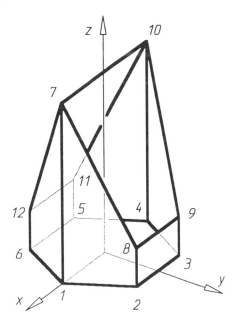

FIGURE 2. A simple object with convex outline.

If we want to describe a simple object like the one in Figure 2, we have to give the computer the following facts:

1. The object has 12 vertices, the coordinates of which are:

   $P_1(2,0,0)$, $P_2(1,2,0)$, $P_3(-1,2,0)$,
   $P_4(-2,0,0)$, $P_5(-1,-2,0)$, $P_6(1,-2,0)$,
   $P_7(2,0,4)$, $P_8(1,2,1)$, $P_9(-1,2,1)$,
   $P_{10}(-2,0,4)$, $P_{11}(-1,-2,1)$, $P_{12}(1,-2,1)$

2. We want to draw the following 19 edges of the polyhedron:

   P_1P_2, P_2P_3, P_3P_4, P_4P_5, P_5P_6, P_6P_1,
   P_7P_8, P_8P_9, P_9P_{10}, $P_{10}P_{11}$, $P_{11}P_{12}$, $P_{12}P_7$,
   P_1P_7, P_2P_8, P_3P_9, P_4P_{10}, P_5P_{11}, P_6P_{12},
   P_7P_{10}

In this case it is not absolutely necessary to give the computer the edge list. When each edge is defined as the side of a face, the computer can take them from the face list.

3. The polyhedron has 8 faces:

$$(P_1P_2P_3P_4P_5P_6), \ (P_1P_2P_8P_7), \ (P_2P_3P_9P_8), \ (P_3P_4P_{10}P_9),$$
$$(P_4P_5P_{11}P_{10}), \ (P_5P_6P_{12}P_{11}), \ (P_6P_1P_7P_{12}), \ (P_{10}P_{11}P_{12}P_7)$$

All this can be achieved by the data file in the introduction of this chapter. The first line of the data file contains some keywords that inform the object preprocessor about the kind of object we deal with, its color and its physical and geometrical properties.

Of course, it is tedious to count all the vertices, edges and faces. However, if we do not do that it will be more difficult to write a function that interprets the last three lines correctly.

Let us first write a function by means of which we can safely open a file:

```
FILE * safe_open(file_name, mode)                    (→ Proto.h)
    char *file_name, *mode;

{   /* begin safe_open() */
    FILE *fp;
    if ((fp = fopen(file_name, mode)) == NULL) {
        Print("Cannot open file ");
        safe_exit(file_name);
    }  /* end if (!fp) */
    return fp;
}   /* end safe_open() */
```

Now we introduce some new global variables:

```
FILE *Input;                                         (→ Globals.h)
    /* This is the file from which we read the data. It is initialized by
         Input = safe_open(" <arbitrary file name> ", "r"); */
char Comment[260];                                   (→ Globals.h)
    /* A string we read from the input file. */
#define Fread_vec(v)\                                (→ Macros.h)
    fscanf(Input, "%f%f%f", &((v)[X]), &((v)[Y]), &((v)[Z]))
#define Fread_str(string)\                           (→ Macros.h)
    fscanf(Input, "%s", string)
```

void *check_keyword*(*keywd*, *obj*)   ($\rightarrow$ `Proto.h`)
   char *∗keywd*;
      /* We check whether the word we read is this word. */
   Polyhedron *∗obj*; /* The object we read. */
{   /* begin *check_keyword*() */
   Fread_str(*Comment*);
   if (*strcmp*(*Comment*, *keywd*)) {
      fprintf(*Output*, `"Error while reading object %s:\n"`, *obj*→*name*);
      fprintf(*Output*, `"keyword '%s' \n"`, *keywd*);
      safe_exit(`"expected"`);
   }   /* end **if** (*strcmp*) */
}   /* end *check_keyword*() */

void *read_general_convex_polyhedron*(*obj*)   ($\rightarrow$ `Proto.h`)
   Polyhedron *∗obj*; /* The object we want to read now. */
{   /* begin *read_general_convex_polyhedron*() */
   register short *∗ indices*;
      /* This large array will be allocated and freed within the function. For
      the time being, it stores the indices of the vertices of all the faces of
      the polyhedron. */

   register short *∗ cur_index*, *∗hi_index*;
   Vector *∗∗world*;
   Face *∗ hi_face*;
   Bool *edgelist_is_given*;

   /* Now we read the vertices. When there is no comma after three coordinates, the vertex list is complete. */

   Fread_str(*Comment*);
   check_keyword(`"vertices"`, *obj*);
   obj→*vertices* = *Cur_coord*;
   /* Read coordinates of vertices until there is no commma left. */
   do {
      Fread_vec(*∗Cur_coord*); *Cur_coord*++;
         /* Do not write *Fread_vec*(*∗Cur_coord*++); (macro!) */
      Fread_str(*Comment*);
   } **while** (*Comment*[0] == ',');
   obj→*no_of_vertices* = *Cur_coord* − *obj*→*vertices*;
   /* Read edges. */

```
if (!strcmp(Comment, "edges")) {
    edgelist_is_given = TRUE;
    obj->edges = Cur_edge; obj->no_of_edges = 0;
    /* Read indices of vertices until there is no comma left. */
    do {
        obj->no_of_edges++;
        * Cur_edge++ = obj->vertices + read_pos_int() - 1;
        * Cur_edge++ = obj->vertices + read_pos_int() - 1;
        Fread_str(Comment);
    } while (Comment[0] == ',');
} else edgelist_is_given = FALSE;

/* Read faces. */

check_keyword("faces", obj);
Alloc_array(short, indices, 5000, "indices");
hi_index = (cur_index = indices) + 5000;
obj->no_of_faces = 0;
while (cur_index < hi_index) {
    Fread_str(Comment);
    * cur_index = atoi(Comment) - 1;
    if (*cur_index == -1) {
        obj->no_of_faces++;
        if (Comment[0] != ',' || feof(Input)) break;
    } /* end if (*cur_index) */
    cur_index++;
} /* end while (cur_index) */

/* Now copy everything to obj->faces. */

hi_face = (obj->faces = Cur_face) + obj->no_of_faces;

hi_index = indices;
for ( ; Cur_face < hi_face; Cur_face++) {
    cur_index = hi_index;
    /* Count vertices. */
    while (*hi_index >= 0) hi_index++;
    Cur_face->no_of_vertices = hi_index - cur_index;
    /* Allocate array of pointers to vertices. */
    world = Alloc_ptr_array(Vector,
            Cur_face->vertices, Cur_face->no_of_vertices, "v");
    for ( ; cur_index < hi_index; cur_index++, world++)
        * world = obj->vertices + (*cur_index - 1);
    hi_index++;    /* Forget index -1. */
} /* end for (Cur_face) */
Free_array(indices, "indices");
if (!edgelist_is_given)
    get_edges_from_facelist(obj);
} /* end read_general_convex_polyhedron() */
```

The subroutine calls a function *read_pos_int*(), which is quite useful for the detection of errors in the data file:

```
int read_pos_int()                                    (→ Proto.h)
{
    int n;
    fscanf(Input, "%d", &n);
    if (n >= 0  &&  n < 32000)
        return n;
    else {
        ftoa⁶((double ) n, Comment, 0, 1);
        Print("Positive integer expected instead of ");
        safe_exit(Comment);
    } /* end if (n) */
} /* end read_pos_int() */
```

When the edge list is not given, the computer looks for all the edges that any two faces have in common:

```
void get_edges_from_facelist(obj)                      (→ Proto.h)
    Polyhedron *obj;
{ /* begin get_edges_from_facelist() */
    Face *f1, *f2, *hi_f = obj->faces + obj->no_of_faces;
    Vector *p1, *p2;
    short i1, i2;   /* In this case only dummies. */

    obj->edges = Cur_edge; obj->no_of_edges = 0;
    for (f1 = obj->faces ; f1 < hi_f - 1; f1++)
        for (f2 = f1 + 1 ; f2 < hi_f; f2++)
            if (common_edge(&p1, &p2, &i1, &i2, f1, f2))
                *Cur_edge++ = p1, *Cur_edge++ = p2;
    obj->no_of_edges = (Cur_edge - obj->edges) / 2;
} /* end get_edges_from_facelist() */
```

The function *common_edge*() is useful for several purposes, e.g., for the detection of contour polygons:

---

⁶In TURBO C use the function *ltoa*() instead.

```
Bool common_edge(a, b, idx_a, idx_b, f1, f2)                    (→ Proto.h)
    Vector **a, **b;    /* Vertices of the edge. */
    short  * idx_a, *idx_b;   /* Indices of a, b in the f1-list. */
    Face * f1, *f2;   /* The two faces. */
{   /* begin common_edge() */
    register Vector **cur1, **cur2, **hi1, **hi2, **lo1, **lo2;

    hi1 = (lo1 = f1->vertices) + f1->no_of_vertices;
    hi2 = (lo2 = f2->vertices) + f2->no_of_vertices;

    * a = NULL;
    for (cur1 = lo1; cur1 < hi1; cur1++)
        for (cur2 = lo2; cur2 < hi2; cur2++)
            if (*cur1 == *cur2) {
                if (*a == NULL) {
                    * a = *cur1; *idx_a = cur1 − lo1; break;
                } else {
                    * b = *cur1; *idx_b = cur1 − lo1; return TRUE;
                } /* end if (*a) */
            } /* end if (*cur1) */
    return FALSE;
}   /* end common_edge() */
```

3.4 Surfaces of Revolution

Surfaces of revolution – or more accurately, polyhedra that approximate surfaces of revolution – are probably the best-known geometrical primitives. Figure 3 shows what we call a "surface of revolution" in this book. The polyhedron is determined by a "meridian polygon" and by the "order," i.e., by the number of the sides of the regular section polygons. By default, the "rotation angle" ϱ equals 2π. The process in which such polyhedra are generated is called "rotational sweeping" [THAL87].

When s is the "size" of the meridian polygon and r the order of the polyhedron, the polyhedron will normally have $r\,s$ vertices, $r(2s-1)$ edges and $r(s-1)+2$ faces (quadrilaterals). However, the number of vertices, edges and faces will decrease when a meridian point is on the rotation axis. (By default, the rotation axis is identical to the z-axis.) The meridian polygon should lie on a "meridian plane," which goes through the axis. (Otherwise, we would have to split the quadrilateral patches into triangles.)

In this section, we will see how the second line in the data file

```
CONE green revolution solid
    meridian 4 0 0 , 0 0 7 order 30
```

can be read and interpreted correctly. We will store a face list and an edge list for the respective convex polyhedron (Figure 3a). In addition to that, we will also work with data lines like

```
CYLINDER orange revolution hollow +bottom
    meridian 2.5 0 -5 , 2.5 0 5 order 40
```

which describe *hollow* surfaces of revolution – preferably with convex outlines (Figure 3b) – or

```
ROTSWEEP lightcyan revolution solid rot_angle 180
    meridian 2 0 -5 , 3 0 -2 , 3 0 3 , 0 0 5 order 20
```

which describe specific parts of such surfaces (Figure 3c).

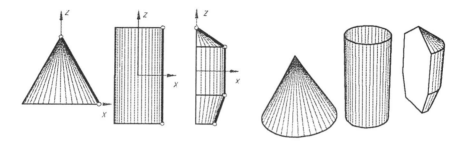

FIGURE 3. Approximations to a surface of revolution. The polyhedra can be a) solid, b) hollow, c) cut off.

For fast hidden-line (hidden-surface) removal (Chapters 5 and 7) and especially for the fast generation of shadows (Chapter 6), it is often a good idea to split the primitives into *convex* parts (Figure 4).

When we read the coordinates of a point on the meridian from the data file, a function

---

Bool *is_on_axis*(p)   ($\rightarrow$ Proto.h)
    Vector $*p$;

{ /* begin *is_on_axis*() */
    return $((*p)[X] == 0$ && $(*p)[Y] == 0)$? *TRUE* : *FALSE*;
} /* end *is_on_axis*() */

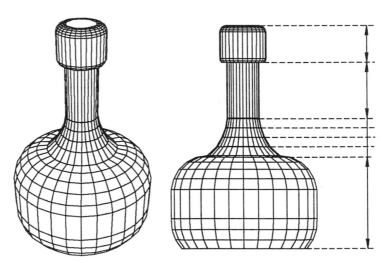

FIGURE 4. How to split a non-convex surface of revolution in order to speed up the rendering algorithms.

can decide whether this point is on the rotation axis ($\equiv z-$axis). Another function *corr_vertex*() helps to determine the pointer to a vertex of the polyhedron, when the order and the index of the corresponding point on the meridian are given:

```
Vector * corr_vertex(index, order)                           (→ Proto.h)
    short index, order;
{   /* begin corr_vertex() */
    register short i;
    register Vector *p = Cur_object->vertices;

    for (i = 1; i < index; i++)
        if (is_on_axis(p)) p++;
        else p += order;
    return p;
}   /* end corr_vertex() */
```

Now we store the vertex list of the polyhedron. First we read all the points on the meridian. When the polyhedron is not convex, the computer checks whether we want to add the top face or the bottom face. Then we calculate all the vertices and store them in *Coord_pool*. Finally, we store the edge list and the vertex list.

```
#define CONVEX 1                                          (→ Macros.h)
#define HOLLOW 2                                          (→ Macros.h)
#define Is_convex(obj)\                                   (→ Macros.h)
    ((obj->geom_property == CONVEX) ? TRUE : FALSE)
#define Store_coords(x, y, z)\                            (→ Macros.h)
    ((*Cur_coord)[X] = x, (*Cur_coord)[Y] = y, (*Cur_coord++)[Z] = z)
#define MAX_MERIDIAN 200                                  (local macro)
```

```
float read_float()                                       (→ Proto.h)
{   /* begin read_float() */
    float f;

    fscanf(Input, "%f", &f);
    return f;
}   /* end read_float() */
```

```
void must_be_keyword(keywd, obj)                         (→ Proto.h)
    char  *keywd;
    Polyhedron *obj;
{   /* begin must_be_keyword() */
    if (strcmp(keywd, Comment)) {
        fprintf(Output, "Reading obj %s:\n", obj->name);
        fprintf(Output, "keyword %s expected instead of %s\n",
                                                keywd, Comment);
        safe_exit(" ");
    }   /* end if (strcmp) */
}   /* end must_be_keyword() */
```

```
void read_convex_obj_of_rev(obj)                         (→ Proto.h)
    Polyhedron *obj;
{   /* begin read_convex_obj_of_rev() */
    short   order, meridian_size;
    short   i, j;
    float   sine, cosine, rot_angle = 2 * PI;
    double  angle;
    float   x, y, z, tmp;
    Vector  *meridian;
    Bool    bottom, top;

    /* Read meridian. */
    Fread_str(Comment);
    if (!strcmp(Comment, "rot_angle")) {
        rot_angle = PI /180 * read_float();
        Fread_str(Comment);
    }
    top = bottom = Is_convex(obj);
```

```
if (Comment[0] == '+') {
    if (!strcmp(Comment, "+top")) top = TRUE;
    else if (!strcmp(Comment, "+bottom")) bottom = TRUE;
    else safe_exit("\n+top or +bottom expected");
    Fread_str(Comment);
} /* end if (Comment[0]) */
must_be_keyword("meridian", obj);
Alloc_array(Vector, meridian, MAX_MERIDIAN, "meridian");
for (i = 0; i < MAX_MERIDIAN; i++) {
    Fread_vec(meridian[i]);
    Fread_str(Comment);
    if (Comment[0] != ',') break;
} /* end for (i) */
if (i == MAX_MERIDIAN)
    safe_exit("Meridian too large");
meridian_size = i + 1;
must_be_keyword("order", obj);
order = read_pos_int();
obj->vertices = Cur_coord;
if (rot_angle < 6.28) angle = rot_angle /(order - 1);
else angle = rot_angle /order;
sine = sin(angle); cosine = cos(angle);
for (i = 0; i < meridian_size; i++) {
    x = meridian[i][X]; y = meridian[i][Y]; z = meridian[i][Z];
    if (x == 0 && y == 0) { /* Point on the axis. */
        Store_coords(0, 0, z);
    } else {
        for (j = 0; j < order; j++) {
            Store_coords(x, y, z);
            tmp = cosine * x - sine * y;
            y = sine * x + cosine * y;
            x = tmp;
        } /* end for (j) */
    } /* end if (x) */
} /* end for (i) */
obj->no_of_vertices = Cur_coord - obj->vertices;
Fread_str(Comment);
trivial_edge_list(obj, meridian_size, order);
trivial_face_list(obj, meridian_size, order, bottom, top);
obj->no_of_edges = (Cur_edge - obj->edges) / 2;
Free_array(meridian, "meridian");
} /* end read_convex_obj_of_rev() */
```

The edge list of the polyhedron is "trivial," i.e., we can determine all the edges when we know the size of the meridian and the order.

```
void trivial_edge_list(obj, size, order)                          (→ Proto.h)
    Polyhedron * obj;
    short  size, order;
{   /* begin trivial_edge_list() */
    Vector * p, *q;
    short  i, j, index, other_index;
    obj→edges  =  Cur_edge;
    for  (index  =  1; index  <=  size; index++) {
        p  =  corr_vertex(index, order);
        for  (j  =  0; j  <  2; j++) {
            if  (j  ==  0) {
                if  (index  ==  size && is_on_axis(p)) return ;
                other_index  =  −index;
            } else  {
                other_index  =  index + 1;
                if  (index  ==  size) return ;
            }  /* end if (j == 0) */
            if  (other_index  >  0) {
                q  =  corr_vertex(other_index, order);
                for  (i =  0; i <  order; i++) {
                    if  (is_on_axis(p))  * Cur_edge++  =  p;
                    else   * Cur_edge++  =  p  +  i;
                    if  (is_on_axis(q))  * Cur_edge++  =  q;
                    else   * Cur_edge++  =  q  +  i;
                }  /* end for (i) */
            } else  {
                q  =  corr_vertex(−other_index, order);
                for  (i =  0; i <  order; i++) {
                    if  (is_on_axis(p))  * Cur_edge++  =  p;
                    else   * Cur_edge++  =  p + i;
                    if  (is_on_axis(q))  * Cur_edge++  =  q;
                    else  {
                        if  (i <  order − 1) * Cur_edge++  =  q  +  i + 1;
                        else   * Cur_edge++  =  q;
                    }  /* end if (is_on_axis) */
                }  /* end for (i) */
            }  /* end if (other_index) */
        }  /* end for (j) */
    }  /* end for (index) */
}   /* end trivial_edge_list() */
```

The same is true for the face list. In general, an approximation to a surface of revolution has $n = (size-1)*order$ faces with four vertices each plus the bottom face and the top face with *order* vertices. (When a point on the meridian lies on the rotation axis, the quadrilaterals degenerate into triangles.)

Therefore, the highest number of pointers to **Vector**s we need is $4*n + order*2$. These pointers can be allocated at one go, which saves both time[7] and memory.[8] The following two macros store the pointers to the vertices of a triangle and a quadrilateral, respectively, while making effective use of the allocated space:

#**define** *Set3*(*a*, *b*, *c*)\   ($\rightarrow$ `Macros.h`)
   (*Cur_face*–>*no_of_vertices* = 3, *Cur_face*++ –>*vertices* = *space*, \
   *space++ = *corner* + *a*, *space++ = *corner* + *b*, \
   *space++ = *corner* + *c*)

#**define** *Set4*(*a*, *b*, *c*, *d*)\   ($\rightarrow$ `Macros.h`)
   (*Cur_face*–>*no_of_vertices* = 4, *Cur_face*++ –>*vertices* = *space*, \
   *space++ = *corner* + *a*, *space++ = *corner* + *b*, \
   *space++ = *corner* + *c*, *space++ = *corner* + *d*)

Now we can write a subroutine that stores the trivial face list.

#**define** *NO_COLOR MAX_UBYTE*   ($\rightarrow$ `Macros.h`)

```
void trivial_face_list(obj, size, order, bottom, top)            (→ Proto.h)
    Polyhedron * obj;
    short size, order;
    Bool bottom, top;
{   /* begin trivial_face_list() */
    short n, j, index;
    Vector * corner;
    short v1, v2, v3, v4;
    static Vector **space;9

    n = (size − 1) * order + 2;
    obj−>no_of_faces = n;
    obj−>faces = Cur_face;
    v1 = 0; v2 = 1; v3 = 1 + order; v4 = order;
    Alloc_ptr_array(Vector, space, 4 *n + 2 * order, "TRI");
    /* Space for all the quadrilaterals (triangles) on the surface. */
```

---

[7]Memory organization can be a "bottleneck" even in fast programs.

[8]With many systems, the amount of bytes that are allocated by the function *malloc*() is always divisible by 8. If we allocate space for the three pointers of a triangle (which need 12 bytes), the system will provide 16 bytes and some memory will be wasted.

[9]The keyword **static** is essential for those local pointer variables that are used for a dynamic allocation of the memory that is needed outside the function. It prevents an error that is hard to find and that causes a program to do strange things or to crash later on.

```
for (index = 1; index < size; index++) {
    corner = corr_vertex(index, order);
    if (is_on_axis(corner)) {
        for (j = 1; j < order; j++)
            Set3(0, 1 + j, j);
        Set3(0, 1, order);
    } else {
        if (is_on_axis(corr_vertex(index + 1, order))) {
            for (j = 1; j < order; j++)
                Set3(j - 1, j, order);
            Set3(order - 1, 0, order);
        } else {
            for (j = 1; j < order; j++, corner++)
                Set4(v1, v2, v3, v4);
            Set4(v1, v2 - order, v3 - order, v4);
        } /* end if (is_on_axis(corr_vertex) */
    } /* end if (is_on_axis(corner)) */
} /* end for (index) */
if (!is_on_axis(corr_vertex(1, order))) {
    if (!bottom) Cur_face->color = NO_COLOR;
    set_f(Cur_face++, corr_vertex(1, order), order, -1, &space);
} else n--;
if (!is_on_axis(corr_vertex(size, order))) {
    if (!top) Cur_face->color = NO_COLOR;
    set_f(Cur_face++, corr_vertex(size, order), order, 1, &space);
} else n--;
obj->no_of_faces = n;
} /* end trivial_face_list() */
```

The top face and the bottom face are stored by means of the function

```
void set_f(f, corner, n, orientation, space)                    (→ Proto.h)
    Face * f;
    register Vector * corner;
    short n;
    short orientation;
        /* Seen from the outside of the polyhedron the face has to be oriented
           ccw. */
    Vector *** space;
        /* Pointer to **space. This is because we want to increase **space. */
{   /* begin set_f() */
    register Vector **v;
    register short i = 0, j = n - 1;
```

```
v = f->vertices = *space;
f->no_of_vertices = n;
if (orientation > 0)
    while (i < n) v[i] = corner + i++;
else
    while (i < n) v[i++] = corner + j--;
(*space) += n;
} /* end set_f() */
```

When we do not want the top face (bottom face) to be drawn, we indicate this by assigning the color *NO_COLOR* to the respective face. However, the face is stored and proceeded like any other face of the polyhedron, firstly, because it is possible to quickly determine the outline of the object by means of "frontfaces" and "backfaces" (Section 6.1), and secondly, because we can apply a fast hidden-line removal (Section 7.2).

3.5 Surfaces of Translation

All polyhedra that can be generated by "translational sweeping" [THAL87] will be called "surfaces of translation" in this book. They are defined by a planar base polygon and by a "translation vector." Figure 5 shows some examples of such polyhedra. A special case are the parallelepipeds, which also include the "boxes." A general polyhedron may be given by the data lines

```
TRANSLATIONAL_SWEEP yellow translation solid
    base_points 0 2 0 , 0 -1.4 0, 0 -2 0.6 ,
            0 -2 1.2 , 0 -1.4 1.6 , 0 2 1.6
    trans_vector -4.5 0 0
```

whereas a box may be given by the line

```
BOX gray box hollow 3 3 1 +bottom
```

("hollow" means that the top face and the bottom face are removed). A surface of translation is convex when the base polygon is convex. For reasons of speed, it is advisable to split non-convex polyhedra into convex polyhedra. (This can be done by a special subroutine.)

A polyhedron with b base points has $2b$ vertices and $3b$ edges. It has b faces with 4 vertices each and 2 faces with b vertices each. (Therefore, we have to allocate $6b$ pointers to the vertices.)

In combination with the functions and macros of the previous section, it is comparatively easy to store the lists:

```
#define MAX_BASE 200                          (local macro)
#define TRANSLATION   2                       (→ Macros.h)
#define BOX 3                                 (→ Macros.h)
```

FIGURE 5. Examples of "surfaces of translation": these scenes consist almost entirely of boxes and general polyhedra of translation.

```
void read_convex_obj_of_transl(obj)                              (→ Proto.h)
    Polyhedron * obj;
{   /* begin read_convex_obj_of_transl() */
    short i, size;
    Vector trans;
    float x, y;
    Vector *p, *q, *start, *corner, *hi_coord;
    static Vector **space; /* Space for all the pointers. */
    Bool top, bottom;
    /* Read base points until no comma is left. */
    obj->vertices = Cur_coord;
    if (obj->type == TRANSLATION) {
        Fread_str(Comment);
        must_be_keyword("base_points", obj);
        for (i = 0; i < MAX_BASE; i++) {
            Fread_vec(*Cur_coord); Cur_coord++;
            Fread_str(Comment);
            if (Comment[0] != ',') break;
        } /* end for (i) */
        if (i == MAX_BASE) safe_exit("too many base points");
        size = i + 1;
        must_be_keyword("trans_vector", obj);
        Fread_vec(trans);
    } else {        /* BOX */
        size = 4;
        trans[X] = trans[Y] = 0;
        x = read_float(); y = read_float(); trans[Z] = read_float();
        Store_coords(0, 0, 0); Store_coords(x, 0, 0);
        Store_coords(x, y, 0); Store_coords(0, y, 0);
    } /* end if (obj->type) */
    /* Translate base points. */
    hi_coord = Cur_coord;
    for (p = obj->vertices; p < hi_coord; Cur_coord++, p++)
        Add_vec(*Cur_coord, *p, trans);
    obj->no_of_vertices = Cur_coord - obj->vertices;
    top = bottom = Is_convex(obj);
    Fread_str(Comment);
    if (Comment[0] == '+') {
        if (!strcmp(Comment, "+top")) top = TRUE;
        else if (!strcmp(Comment, "+bottom")) bottom = TRUE;
        else safe_exit("\n+top or +bottom expected");
        Fread_str(Comment);
    } /* end if (Comment[0]) */
    /* Trivial edge list. */
    obj->edges = Cur_edge;
    start = obj->vertices;
```

```
for  (i  =  0; i <  size; i++) {
    p  =  start  +  i; q  =  p  +  1;
    if  (i == size − 1) q  =  start;
    *Cur_edge++  =  p; *Cur_edge++  =  q;
    q  =  p  +  size;
    *Cur_edge++  =  p; *Cur_edge++  =  q;
    p  =  q; q  =  p  +  1;
    if  (i == size − 1) q  =  start  +  size;
    *Cur_edge++  =  p; *Cur_edge++  =  q;
}  /* end for (i) */
obj−>no_of_edges  =  (Cur_edge − obj−>edges) /2;
/* Trivial face list. */
obj−>no_of_faces  =  size  +  2;
obj−>faces = Cur_face;
/* Allocate pointer pool. */
Alloc_ptr_array(Vector, space, 6 * size, "TRA");
p  =  obj−>vertices;
for  (i = 0, corner  =  p; i <  size  − 1; i++, corner++)
    Set4(0, 1, 1 + size, size);
corner  =  p;
Set4(0, size, 2 * size − 1, size − 1);
/* Bottom face and top face. */
if  (!bottom) Cur_face−>color  =  NO_COLOR;
set_f(Cur_face++, obj−>vertices, size, −1, &space);
if  (!top) Cur_face−>color  =  NO_COLOR;
set_f(Cur_face++, obj−>vertices  +  size, size, 1, &space);
}   /* end read_convex_obj_of_transl() */
```

3.6 The Intersection of Objects

In Section 3.3, we demonstrated how data files can be written that make it easy for the computer to create general object lists. In Section 3.4 and in Section 3.5, we learned how to interpret readable data for specific kinds of primitives. The computer then created general object lists like in Section 3.3. In this section, we will deal with the creation of general objects with complicated object lists by means of intersecting polyhedra.

When you look at Figure 6, you can imagine that it would be a waste of time to write down the lists of the illustrated objects. What we can do, however, is to make the computer itself write the data file of the intersection polygon of two given polyhedra.

Thus, we develop a function *intersect_objects()* with three parameters: the intersection polyhedron Θ and the polyhedra Θ_1 and Θ_2 that are to be intersected. The polyhedron Θ_2 should be convex. When Θ_1 is convex, Θ is convex as well.

A pseudo-code of the task might look like this:

1) Allocate enough space for a face list and a vertex list of Θ.
2) Determine the face list and the vertex list of Θ as follows:

> **for** all the faces f_1 of Θ_1
>> Copy f_1 to a temporary face f_0.
>> **for** all the faces f_2 of Θ_2
>>> Cut off f_0 by means of the plane of f_2.
>>> **break** the loop if f_0 has less than three vertices.
>>
>> **if** f_0 has at least three vertices
>>> Create a new face f of Θ.
>>> Copy the vertices of f_0 into the vertex list of Θ and store the corresponding pointers in the vertex list of f. For each vertex, make sure that it has not been stored before (or else most vertices will be stored two or three times).
>
> **if** Θ_1 and Θ_2 are convex
>> Swap Θ_1 and Θ_2 and repeat the process.
>
> **else**
>> **for** all the faces f_2 of Θ_2
>>> **for** all the faces f of Θ that have been found so far
>>>> Check if an edge of f is in the plane of f_2.
>>>> If there is such an edge, store it.
>>>
>>> **if** at least three edges are stored
>>>> Create a new face f of Θ.
>>>> Concatenate all the edges to a closed polygon and store the pointers to the vertices in the vertex list of f.

3) Allocate enough space for the edge list of Θ.
   Extract the trivial edge list from the face list.
4) Write a data file.
   Dump the lists of the object Θ in the format that is described in Section 3.2.

The corresponding C code looks like this:

Vector $* \, Add\_vertices,\ *Cur\_add$;
> /* A pool for the coordinates of temporary vertices
>   and a pointer to a vertex in this pool. */

#define $Alloc\_string(char\_ptr,\ n)\backslash$ ($\to$ `Macros.h`)
  $Alloc\_array(\textbf{char}\ ,\ char\_ptr,\ n+1,\ \texttt{"str"})$[10]
#define $Maximum(x,\ y)\ (\ (x) < (y)\ ?\ (x)\ :\ (y)\ )$ ($\to$ `Macros.h`)
#define $Minimum(x,\ y)\ (\ (x) > (y)\ ?\ (x)\ :\ (y)\ )$ ($\to$ `Macros.h`)

---

[10] A string str with $n = strlen(str)$ is stored as $str + \texttt{"\textbackslash 0"}$. Therefore, it needs $n+1$ instead of n characters. In most cases, the system function $malloc()$ allocates enough space anyway, because it takes the next number $n_0 \geq n$ that is divisible by 8, so that no error will occur, even if we forget about the additional byte. However, for $n = n_0$ ($n \bmod 8 = 0$), this may produce an error that is hard to find.

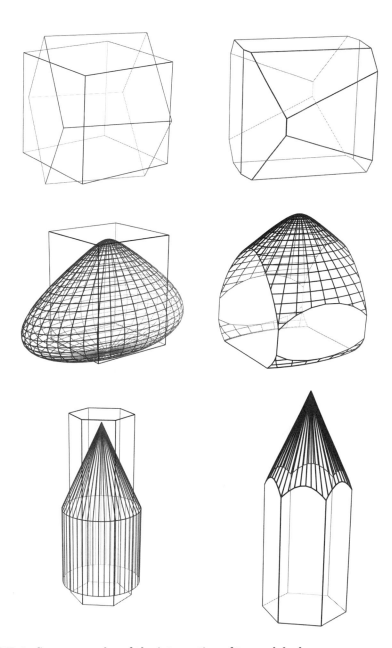

FIGURE 6. Some examples of the intersection of two polyhedra.

```
void normal_vector(n, points)                                  (→ Proto.h)
    Vector n, ** points;
{   /* begin normal_vector() */
    register  float len;
    register  Vector * a, *b, *c;
    Vector ab, ac;


    a = points[0]; b = points[1]; c = points[2];
    Subt_vec(ab, *a, *b); Subt_vec(ac, *a, *c);
    Cross_product(n, ab, ac);
    len = Length(n);
    if (len > 0) {
        n[X] / = len; n[Y] / = len; n[Z] / = len;
    } else
        Print("     warning: could not normalize Vector!");
}   /* end normal_vector() */
```

```
typedef struct  {
    Vector * v1, *v2; /* Pointers to the vertices of the edge. */
} Edge;                                                         (→ Types.h)
```

```
void intersect_objects(obj, obj1, obj2)                        (→ Proto.h)
    Polyhedron * obj, /* The intersection. */
             * obj1, /* Does not have to be convex. */
             * obj2; /* Should be convex. */
{   /* begin intersect_objects() */
    Face * f1, *hi_f1, *f2;   /* Faces of obj1 and obj2. */
    Face f0;   /* A temporary face. */
    Face * f, *hi_f; /* Faces of obj. */
    short  i, n, m;
    Plane * plane_pool, *plane, *hi_plane;
    static Vector **vtx_ptr_pool;
    Polyhedron * temp;


    Alloc_string(obj→name, strlen("INTERSECTION"));
    strcpy(obj→name, "INTERSECTION");
    obj→geom_property = obj1→geom_property;
    f = obj→faces = Cur_face;
    obj→vertices = obj→hi_coord = Cur_coord;
    obj→edges = Cur_edge;
```

```
/* Create section planes. */
if (Is_convex(obj1))
    n = Maximum(obj1->no_of_faces, obj2->no_of_faces);
else
    n = obj2->no_of_faces;
Alloc_array(Plane, plane_pool, n, "planepool");

Alloc_ptr_array(Vector, f0.vertices, MAX_POLY_SIZE, "f0");
Alloc_array(Vector, Add_vertices, 1000, "f0");
Alloc_ptr_array(Vector, vtx_ptr_pool, 2000, "space");
Cur_add = Add_vertices;

for (m = 0; m < 2; m++) {
    hi_plane = (plane = plane_pool) + obj2->no_of_faces;
    f2 = obj2->faces;
    for (; plane < hi_plane; plane++, f2++) {
        normal_vector(plane->normal, f2->vertices);
        plane->cnst = Dot_product(plane->normal, *f2->vertices[0]);
    } /* end for (plane) */

    /* Cut all the faces of obj1. */
    hi_f1 = (f1 = obj1->faces) + obj1->no_of_faces;
    for (; f1 < hi_f1; f1++) {
        /* Copy f1 to f0. */
        n = f0.no_of_vertices = f1->no_of_vertices;
        for (i = 0; i < n; i++)
            f0.vertices[i] = f1->vertices[i];
        /* Truncate f0. */
        for (plane = plane_pool; plane < hi_plane; plane++)   {
            cut_face_with_plane(&f0, plane);
            if (f0.no_of_vertices < 3) break;
        } /* end for (plane) */
        /* Copy f0 to a new face f of obj. */
        if (f0.no_of_vertices >= 3) {
            n = f->no_of_vertices = f0.no_of_vertices;
            f->vertices = vtx_ptr_pool; vtx_ptr_pool += n;
            for (i = 0; i < n; i++)
                f->vertices[i] = corr_ptr(f0.vertices[i], obj);
            f++;
        } /* end if (f0) */
    } /* end for (f1) */
```

```
    if (Is_convex(obj1)) Swap(obj1, obj2);
    else {
        Edge * edges;
        Face * prev_f;
        Alloc_array(Edge, edges, MAX_POLY_SIZE, "edges");
        hi_f = f;
        for (plane = plane_pool; plane < hi_plane; plane++) {
            prev_f = obj->faces; n = 0;
            for ( ; prev_f < hi_f; prev_f++)
                if (edge_in_plane(&edges[n], prev_f, plane)) n++;
            if (n >= 3) {
                f->vertices = vtx_ptr_pool; vtx_ptr_pool += n;
                if (concat_to_polygons(&i, &f->no_of_vertices,
                        &f->vertices, n, edges, FALSE)) {
                    if (f->vertices[0] == f->vertices[n])
                        f->no_of_vertices--;
                    f++;
                } /* end if (concat) */
            } /* end if (n) */
        } /* end for (plane) */
        break;
    } /* end if (Is_convex) */
} /* end for (m) */
obj->no_of_vertices = obj->hi_coord - obj->vertices;
obj->no_of_faces = f - obj->faces;
get_edges_from_facelist(obj);
Free_array(plane_pool, "PLP");
Free_array(f0.vertices, "f0v");
write_datafile(obj);
safe_exit("Your data file is ready.");
} /* end intersect_objects() */
```

The function *cut_face_with_plane*() has the code

```
void cut_face_with_plane(f, plane)                           (→ Proto.h)
    Face * f;
    Plane * plane;
{ /* begin cut_face_with_plane() */
    short n = f->no_of_vertices;
    Vector **v = f->vertices;
    short to_be_cut = 0;
    short i = 0, j, k = 0;
    Vector * tmp_ptr[MAX_POLY_SIZE];
    short side[MAX_POLY_SIZE];
```

```
for  (i = 0; i < n; i++, v++)
    if ((side[i] = Which_side(**v, *plane)) > 0) to_be_cut++;

if  (!to_be_cut)
    return ;
else  if  (to_be_cut == n) {
    f->no_of_vertices = 0;
    return ;
} else {
    Vector diff, *v1, *v2;
    float t;
    Bool parallel;

    k = 0;
    v = f->vertices;
    for  (i = 0, j = 1; i < n; i++, j++) {
        if  (j == n) j = 0;
        if  (side[i] > 0 && side[j] > 0) continue;
        v1 = v[i]; v2 = v[j];
        if  (side[i] < 0)
            tmp_ptr[k++] = v[i];
        if  (side[i] != side[j]) {
            Subt_vec(diff, *v1, *v2);
            sect_line_and_plane(*Cur_add, &t, &parallel, *v1, diff, plane);
            tmp_ptr[k] = ptr_to_vertex();
            if  (k == 0 || tmp_ptr[k] != tmp_ptr[k - 1]) k++;
        } /* end if (side[i]) */
    } /* end for (i) */
    f->no_of_vertices = k;
    v = f->vertices;
    for  (i = 0; i < k; i++)
        v[i] = tmp_ptr[i];
} /* end if (!to_be_cut) */
} /* end cut_face_with_plane() */
```

The function

```
Vector * ptr_to_vertex()                            (→ Proto.h)
{  /* begin ptr_to_vertex() */
    register  Vector *v = Add_vertices;

    for  ( ; v < Cur_add; v++)
        if  (close_together(v, Cur_add))
            return v;
    Cur_add++;
    return v;
} /* end ptr_to_vertex() */
```

checks whether the vertex has been stored before and returns the corresponding pointer to the vertex. It calls a function

```
Bool close_together(a, b)                                    (→ Proto.h)
    register Vector * a, *b;
{   /* begin close_together() */
    register short i;

    for (i = 0; i < 3; i++)
        if (fabs((*a)[i] − (*b)[i]) > 1e − 3) return FALSE;
    return TRUE;
}   /* end close_together() */
```

which determines whether two points have the same coordinates. (Because of the limited accuracy of floating point calculations, we have to admit a certain tolerance.)

The function $corr\_ptr()$ picks a vertex from the temporary coordinate pool and copies it to the vertex list of the object:

```
Vector * corr_ptr(v, obj)                                    (→ Proto.h)
    Vector * v;
    Polyhedron * obj;
{   /* begin corr_ptr() */
    register Vector * v0 = obj−>vertices, *hi_v0 = obj−>hi_coord;

    for ( ; v0 < hi_v0; v0++)
        if (close_together(v0, v)) return v0;
    /* Vertex has to be copied into obj−>vertices. */
    Copy_vec(*v0, *v);
    obj−>hi_coord++;
    return v0;
}   /* end corr_ptr() */
```

To find out whether a face has an edge on a plane, we use the function

```
Bool edge_in_plane(edge, face, plane)                        (→ Proto.h)
    Edge *edge;
    Face * face;
    Plane *plane;
```

```
{   /* begin edge_in_plane() */
    register  Vector  **v  =  face->vertices,
                     **hi_v  =  v +  face->no_of_vertices;
    register  Vector  *p, *n  =  (Vector *) plane->normal;
    register  float c =  plane->cnst;

    for  (++v; v <  hi_v; v++) {
        p =  *v;
        if  (fabs(Dot_product(*p, *n) − c)  < 1e − 4) break;
    }  /* end for (v) */
    if (v++  ==  hi_v) return  FALSE;
    edge->v1 =  p;
    edge->v2 =  p  =  (v <  hi_v) ? *v :  face->vertices[0];
    return  (fabs(Dot_product(*p, *n) − c)  < 1e − 4);
}   /* end edge_in_plane() */
```

The important **Bool** function *concat_to_polygons*() is listed in Section 6.1.

Finally, we give the listing of a function that writes the desired data file:

#define *P_vec(v)*\   (*local macro*)
    fprintf(df, "%8.3f␣%8.3f␣%8.3f", *(v)[X], (v)[Y], (v)[Z])*

```
void write_datafile(obj)                                      (→ Proto.h)
    Polyhedron * obj;
{   /* begin write_datafile() */
    FILE * df;
    short  i, j, n, idx;
    Vector * v, *hi_v;
    Face * f, *hi_f;
    Vector **e, **hi_e;

    df  =  safe_open("intersect.dat", "w"),
    fprintf(Output, "filename = intersect.dat\n");
    fprintf(df, "%s␣", obj->name);
    fprintf(df, "%s␣␣␣", "magenta");
    fprintf(df, "general␣");
    if  (Is_convex(obj)) fprintf(df, "solid\n");
    else  fprintf(df, "hollow\n");
    fprintf(df, "␣␣␣vertices");
    v =  obj->vertices; hi_v  =  obj->hi_coord;
    for  (i =  0; v <  hi_v; v++) {
        if  (i > 0) fprintf(df,"␣,␣");
        if  (i++ % 2  ==  0) fprintf(df, "\n ␣␣␣␣␣␣");
        P_vec(*v);
    }  /* end for (i) */
```

```
    fprintf(df, "\n ␣␣␣edges\n ␣␣");
    hi_e = (e = obj–>edges) + 2 * obj–>no_of_edges;
    for (i = 0; e < hi_e; ) {
        fprintf(df, " ␣␣");
        for (j = 0; j < 2; j++, e++) {
            idx = *e − obj–>vertices;
            fprintf(df, "%4d␣", idx);
        } /* end for (j) */
        if (e < hi_e − 1) fprintf(df, ",␣");
        if (++i % 5 == 0) fprintf(df, "\n ␣␣");
    } /* end for (i) */
    fprintf(df, "\n ␣␣␣faces\n");
    hi_f = (f = obj–>faces) + obj–>no_of_faces;
    for ( ; f < hi_f; f++) {
        short prev_idx, first_idx;

        if ((n = f–>no_of_vertices) < 3) continue;
        hi_e = (e = f–>vertices) + n − 1;
        fprintf(df, "␣␣␣␣␣␣");
        prev_idx = −1;
        for (i = 0; e <= hi_e; e++) {
            if (++i % 12 == 0) fprintf(df, "\n ␣␣␣␣␣␣");
            idx = *e − obj–>vertices;
            if (e == f–>vertices) first_idx = idx;
            if (idx != prev_idx && !(e == hi_e && idx == first_idx))
                fprintf(df, "%4d␣", idx);
            prev_idx = idx;
        } /* end for (i) */
        if (f + 1 < hi_f && (f + 1)–>no_of_vertices)
            fprintf(df, ",␣");
        fprintf(df, "\n");
    } /* end for (f < hi_f) */
    fclose(df);
} /* end write_datafile() */
```

The data file for the two cubes in Figure 6 looks like this:

```
CUBE1 yellow box solid 6 6 6
    translation -3 -3 -3
CUBE2 green box solid 6 6 6
    translation -3 -3 -3
    rotation x 40 rotation z 20
```

To create the pencil in Figure 6, we used the following file:

```
CONE gray revolution solid
    meridian 5 0 -10, 5 0 0, 0 0 11 order 45
PRISM yellow revolution solid
    meridian 4 0 -12, 4 0 12 order 6
```

4

Graphics Output

In this chapter, we will see how we can write graphics programs that are more or less independent of the hardware that is used. If we want to adapt these programs to different kinds of computers, we only have to change a few lines in one of the include files and in the system-dependent module.

We will create color palettes and use them for the shading of our facets. For the shade, we will take into account factors like the angle of incidence of the facet with the light rays and the distance from the light source.

Furthermore, we will learn how to write a program that allows us to manipulate a wireframe model of an arbitrary scene.

4.1 Graphics Hardware

Before we can make any drawings on the screen, we have to know the graphics commands. These commands are system-dependent. Graphics workstations provide a lot of functions, most of which are executed by graphics coprocessors. This helps to speed up the programs considerably. Less sophisticated computers are only supplied with very few graphics commands so that everything has to be done by the software.

We will try to write programs that use as few graphics-dependent functions and macros as possible and that still allow the program to take advantage of the graphics hardware. You will see that we do not need a lot of these commands. They should all be written into the include file **G_macros.h**. When it is necessary to write functions, the macros just call these system-dependent functions that are collected by the system-dependent module **g_functs.c**. The include file **G_macros.h** has to be included in the file **3d_std.h** (Section 1.1), whereas the object file **g_functs.o** has to be linked with the program.

In order to reproduce all the features presented in this book, you need a computer that

- is able to create palette colors by means of RGB values (the more, the better, with a minimum of 16 for the shading).

- is able to set pixels in these colors on the screen. The compiler should provide a function for the drawing of a line between two screen points and, if possible, a function for the filling of convex polygons.

- has an acceptable screen resolution (the absolute minimum is 320×200 like on a Standard-VGA-Card for PCs), if possible with two "pages" for "double buffering" (page flipping).

4.2 System-Dependent Macros and Functions

Throughout the book, we will only use our own macro names, even if we want to do something that depends on the hardware that is used. If you want to adapt the program to any specific graphics computer you only have to replace the macros listed in this chapter. In Appendix A.1 you will find the corresponding listings of the following macros (and functions) for a variety of different computers in connection with certain compilers. Some compilers might use the same names as we do, and in order to avoid that, we start every macro name with a "G_":

(**void**) *G_open_graphics* (**void**);   ($\rightarrow$ **G_macros.h**)
　　/* Open a graphics window/screen. For some computers this means that the whole screen switches over to graphics mode, on others (with multi-tasking or a separate graphics monitor), part of the screen is reserved for your drawings. When the window is opened, we let the global variable *Graph_on* be *TRUE*. This is important for safe exits from the program. */

(**void**) *G_close_graphics* (**void**);   ($\rightarrow$ **G_macros.h**)
　　/* Close the open screen. */

(**void**) *G_clear_screen* (**short** *col*);   ($\rightarrow$ **G_macros.h**)
　　/* Clear screen in color *col*. */

(**void**) *G_swap_screens* (**void**);   ($\rightarrow$ **G_macros.h**)
　　/* Turn over screen pages (if there is more than one page). This is also called "double buffering." The availability of a double-buffer mode is important for animation. In double-buffer mode, the framebuffer is split into a frontbuffer and a backbuffer. While the image is drawn into the backbuffer, the frontbuffer is displayed. The function *G_swap_screens*() will exchange the buffers. */

(**void**) *G_create_RGB_color* (**short** *n*, **short** *r*, **short** *g*, **short** b);

$\qquad\qquad\qquad\qquad\qquad\qquad\qquad\qquad\qquad\qquad$ ($\rightarrow$ `G_macros.h`)

/* Create a color given by RGB values (red, green, blue) and store it as the *n*-th color in a color lookup-table. Full RGB mode allows detailed, high-quality renderings of full color displays. However, only few graphics computers have that much video memory. The use of color maps is an economical way of using fewer bits per pixel, so that 2^n colors can be displayed at the same time (where *n* is the number of bit planes). */

short *Cur_color*; $\qquad\qquad\qquad\qquad\qquad\qquad\qquad\qquad$ ($\rightarrow$ `Globals.h`)

/* Current pixel color. This pixel color is set when we call the following macro *G_set_color*(). */

(**void**) *G_set_color* (**short** *n*); $\qquad\qquad\qquad\qquad\qquad\qquad$ ($\rightarrow$ `G_macros.h`)

/* Set the *n*-th color from the color lookup-table before a line is drawn or a polygon is filled. */

(**short**) *G_get_pixel_color* (**short** *x*, **short** *y*); $\qquad\qquad$ ($\rightarrow$ `G_macros.h`)

/* Return the index from the color lookup-table for the pixel position (x, y). This function is necessary only for the drawing of "rubber bands" (Section 4.6). */

(**void**) *G_set_pixel* (**short** *x*, **short** *y*); $\qquad\qquad\qquad\qquad$ ($\rightarrow$ `G_macros.h`)

/* Set pixel in current color. */

/* Commands for the drawing of a (poly)line: */

(**void**) *G_move_xy* (**short** *x*, **short** *y*); $\qquad\qquad\qquad\qquad$ ($\rightarrow$ `G_macros.h`)

/* Move to (x, y). */

(**void**) *G_draw_xy* (**short** *x*, **short** *y*); $\qquad\qquad\qquad\qquad$ ($\rightarrow$ `G_macros.h`)

/* Draw a line to (x, y). */

(**void**) *G_move* (**Vector** *v*); $\qquad\qquad\qquad\qquad\qquad\qquad$ ($\rightarrow$ `G_macros.h`)

/* Move to the first vertex of a (poly)line. */

(**void**) *G_draw* (**Vector** *v*); $\qquad\qquad\qquad\qquad\qquad\qquad$ ($\rightarrow$ `G_macros.h`)

/* Draw to the next vertex of a (poly)line. */

/* Commands for the filling of a (convex) polygon: */

(**void**) *G_move_area* (**Vector** *v*); $\qquad\qquad\qquad\qquad\qquad$ ($\rightarrow$ `G_macros.h`)

/* Buffer first vertex of a polygon. */

(**void**) *G_draw_area* (**Vector** *v*); $\qquad\qquad\qquad\qquad\qquad$ ($\rightarrow$ `G_macros.h`)

/* Buffer next vertex. */

(**void**) *G_close_area* (**void**); $\qquad\qquad\qquad\qquad\qquad\qquad$ ($\rightarrow$ `G_macros.h`)

/* Fill buffered (convex) polygon. */

/* For the manipulation of the scene by means of the keyboard: */

(**Ubyte**) *G_key_pressed* (**void**); $\qquad\qquad\qquad\qquad\qquad$ ($\rightarrow$ `G_macros.h`)

/* Returns 0 if no key is pressed, otherwise it returns the ASCII-code of the key that is pressed. */

/* Finally, a command for an acoustic signal: */

(**void**) *G_beep* (**void**); $\qquad\qquad\qquad\qquad\qquad\qquad\qquad$ ($\rightarrow$ `G_macros.h`)

With the help of these basic functions, we can write all of the other functions we need for the graphics output. A function for the connection of two points on the screen, for example, might look like this:

```
void quick_line(p, q)                                    (→ Proto.h)
    register float *p, *q;
{   /* begin quick_line() */
    G_move(p), G_draw(q);
}   /* end quick_line() */
```

A function for the filling of polygons might have the code

```
void fill_poly3(n, poly)                              (for the time being!)
    short n; /* Number of vertices. */
    register Vector *poly; /* Array of vectors. */
{
    register Vector *hi_poly = poly + n;

    G_move_area(*poly);
    for (poly++; poly < hi_poly; poly++)¹
        G_draw_area(*poly);
    G_close_area();
}
```

When the coordinates of the polygon are only two-dimensional, we have to use another function:

```
void fill_poly2(n, poly)                              (for the time being!)
    short n; /* Number of vertices. */
    register Vector2 *poly; /* Array of vectors. */
{
    register Vector2 *hi_poly = poly + n;

    ⋮ /* Same code as above.² */
}
```

Without any mentionable loss of speed, the functions $fill\_poly3()$ and $fill\_poly2()$ can be replaced by a single function $fill\_poly()$. This method was also used for the function $intersect\_lines()$ (Section 1.3). One advantage of such a compression of codes is that we do not have to change several parts of the code when we want to elaborate the function.

---

[1]Even though the variable *poly* is a pointer, any change of *poly* is undone outside the function $fill\_poly()$. We can only change *poly, i.e., the contents of the vector.

[2]For the macros $G\_move\_area()$ and $G\_draw\_area()$, it does not make any difference whether *poly* is a two-dimensional **Vector2** or a three-dimensional **Vector**, because both types are interpreted as pointers to a **float** and only the first two elements of the array are taken.

```
void fill_poly(n, poly, dim)                                      (→ Proto.h)
    short n;
    register float *poly;
    register short dim; /* Two or three. */
{   /* begin fill_poly() */
    register float *hi_poly = poly + dim * n;

    G_move_area(poly);³
    for (poly += dim; poly < hi_poly; poly += dim)
        G_draw_area(poly);
    G_close_area();
}   /* end fill_poly() */
```

4.3 How to Create Color Palettes and How to Use Them

Consider a green polyhedron. Its faces will appear in hues or shades of green –
the collection of these shades is called a green palette. Even though the human
eye can distinguish hundreds of different "greens," a comparatively small number
of different shades is sufficient for our purposes (the pictures in this book were
created with palettes of 32 different shades). Sophisticated shading models like
"ray tracing" [GLAS90] or "Phong shading" [BUIT75] may use larger palettes.

The problem is that we can only display a limited number of colors on the screen
at one and the same time. This is why we prefer several smaller palettes to one
or two huge palettes. To give you an example: many computers can display 256
different colors on the screen.[4] In this case, we will use 8 parent palettes with 32
shades each plus a variety of additional palettes created out of the prototypes
(once we have created a "green palette," we can extract a "light green" palette
and a "dark green" palette without wasting any further video memory).

Every color can be synthesized by means of a red component R, a green component G and a blue component B ($0 \leq R, G, B \leq 1$). These three components
form a **Vector**. Each color in a certain palette has a RGB value somewhere in
between a "lower" RGB vector and an "upper" RGB vector. (In [ROGE85] or
[PURG89] you can find some other possibilities of defining a color between two
RGB vectors. A system that is more intuitive, and thus, more user-oriented, is

---

[3]Now we must not write *poly* any more, because this would be a **float**,
whereas the macro expects a **Vector**, i.e., a pointer to a **float**.

[4]This requires at least 8-bit planes for single buffering and 16-bit planes for
double buffering (page flipping).

the HLS system (Hue, Lightness, Saturation).) If we have n shades in a palette ($lower\_rgb \rightarrow upper\_rgb$), the k-th shade can be interpolated linearly:

$$\overrightarrow{rgb(k)} = \overrightarrow{lower\_rgb} + k. \underbrace{\frac{\overrightarrow{upper\_rgb} - \overrightarrow{lower\_rgb}}{n}}_{\overrightarrow{delta\_rgb} \ (constant)} \tag{1}$$

This enables us to create any kind of palette by means of a function *make_spectrum*(). This function uses several macros that will turn out to be useful in the following chapters as well:

#define *Scale_vec*(*r, v, k*)\   ($\rightarrow$ Macros.h)
  $((r)[X] = k * (v)[X], \ (r)[Y] = k * (v)[Y], \ (r)[Z] = k * (v)[Z])$
#define *Round_vec*(*r, v*)\   ($\rightarrow$ Macros.h)
  $((r)[X] = (v)[X] + 0.5, \ (r)[Y] = (v)[Y] + 0.5, \ (r)[Z] = (v)[Z] + 0.5)$
        /* In C type conversion is automatic. When i is an **integer** variable and
          f is a **float** variable, the assignment $i = f + 0.5$; quietly converts i
          into the round value of f. */

/* First, we predefine the parent palettes we want to have at our disposal (the
  color names are of course only a suggestion): */
typedef struct { /* **Palette** */
    Ubyte *index*;
    Bool *in_use*;
    Vector *lower_rgb, upper_rgb*;
    char **name*;
} **Palette**;   ($\rightarrow$ Types.h)

#ifdef *MAIN*
Palette *Parent_palette*[8] = {   ($\rightarrow$ Globals.h)[5]
/* *index in_use*   *lower_rgb*   *upper_rgb*   *name* */
    0,   *FALSE*,   0.00, 0.00, 0.00,   1.00, 1.00, 1.00,   "gray",
    1,   *FALSE*,   0.00, 0.30, 0.00,   0.80, 1.00, 0.80,   "green",
    2,   *FALSE*,   0.50, 0.30, 0.00,   1.00, 1.00, 0.50,   "yellow",
    3,   *FALSE*,   0.00, 0.25, 0.45,   0.70, 0.70, 1.00,   "blue",
    4,   *FALSE*,   0.50, 0.00, 0.25,   1.00, 0.85, 0.80,   "pink",
    5,   *FALSE*,   0.00, 0.25, 0.25,   0.50, 1.00, 1.00,   "cyan",
    6,   *FALSE*,   0.10, 0.10, 0.10,   1.00, 0.20, 1.00,   "magenta",
    7,   *FALSE*,   0.50, 0.15, 0.00,   1.00, 0.60, 0.40,   "orange"
}; /* end *Parent_palette* */
#else
Palette *Parent_palette*[8];
#endif

---

[5]This requires at least 8-bit planes for single buffering and 16-bit planes for double buffering (page flipping).

void *make_spectrum(pal, start_idx, n)*   ($\rightarrow$ Proto.h)
    Palette *∗pal*; /∗ Pointer to palette. ∗/
    short *start_idx, n*;
        /∗ The palette will be stored in the color lookup-table between the indices *start_index* and *start_index + n*. ∗/
{   /∗ begin *make_spectrum()* ∗/
    short *color_idx, hi_color_idx*; /∗ Index of the current color. ∗/
    Vector
        lower_rgb, upper_rgb,
        cur_rgb, /∗ Current RGB in between these vectors. ∗/
        delta_rgb; /∗ "Increase of color." ∗/
    short *rgb[3], prev_rgb[3]*;
        /∗ Current triplet of round RGB values, previous triplet. ∗/
    color_idx = start_idx;
    /∗ The following constants *MAX_COLORS* and *RGB_RANGE* are defined in the system-dependent include file G_macros.h:
    MAX_COLORS is the number of colors that can be displayed simultaneously, *RGB_RANGE* is the number of values for the red, green and blue components of a color. Thus, the colors that are to be displayed can be chosen from of a palette of $(RGB\_RANGE)^3$ colors. ∗/
    /∗ Copy extreme color vectors from table and fit them into *RGB_RANGE*. ∗/
    Scale_vec(lower_rgb, pal→lower_rgb, RGB_RANGE);
    Scale_vec(upper_rgb, pal→upper_rgb, RGB_RANGE);
    /∗ Calculate *delta_rgb*. ∗/
    Subt_vec(delta_rgb, lower_rgb, upper_rgb);
    Scale_vec(delta_rgb, delta_rgb, 1.0/n);
    /∗ Initialize previous color with impossible RGB values. ∗/
      prev_rgb[0] = prev_rgb[1] = prev_rgb[2] = −1;
    Copy_vec(cur_rgb, lower_rgb); /∗ We start with *lower_rgb*. ∗/
    hi_color_idx = Minimum(MAX_COLORS, start_idx + n);
    for (; *color_idx < hi_color_idx*[6]; *color_idx++*) {
        Round_vec(rgb, cur_rgb);
        /∗ Take the nearest possible color. Since the RGB values are rounded off, it may happen that a palette has two identical colors. In order to avoid that, we compare the current color with the previous one. If they are identical, we increase one of the three components by one. ∗/

---

[6]Note that in C the loop
    for (*i*= 0; *i < complicated expression*; *i++*)
is slower than the loop
    for (*i*= 0; *i < i_max*; *i++*)
because its upper limit will be calculated every time.

```
        if (rgb[0] == prev_rgb[0] &&
            rgb[1] == prev_rgb[1] && rgb[2] == prev_rgb[2]) {
            if (rgb[0] < RGB_RANGE) ++rgb[0];
            else if (rgb[1] < RGB_RANGE) ++rgb[1];
            else if (rgb[2] < RGB_RANGE) ++rgb[2];
        } /* end if (rgb...) */
        G_create_RGB(color_idx, rgb[0], rgb[1], rgb[2]);
        Copy_vec(prev_rgb, rgb);
        Add_vec(cur_rgb, cur_rgb, delta_rgb);
    } /* end for (color_idx) */
} /* end make_spectrum() */
```

Now it is easy to create all the necessary palettes according to our predefined
standard colors. In order to have fast access to all the colors, we introduce an
array of pointers $*Map\_color[\ ]$:

#define $MAX\_PAL\backslash$
$\quad ((MAX\_COLORS - COLOR\_OFFSET)/PAL\_SIZE)$[7] $(\rightarrow$ `Macros.h`$)$

short $*Map\_color[3 * MAX\_PAL]$; $(\rightarrow$ `Globals.h`$)$
/* PAL_SIZE and $COLOR\_OFFSET$ are defined in `G_macros.h`. Default for
$COLOR\_OFFSET$ is zero. If your computer has enough bit planes, you
can skip the first color entries. These colors are usually predefined by the
system. Otherwise your "Desk Top" alters the colors. The reason why
we allocate space for $3 * MAX\_PAL$ palettes is that from each parent
palette we can extract two "subpalettes." However, they have only half
of the shade range. */

```
void create_palettes()                              (→ Proto.h)
{ /* begin create_palettes() */
    register short *pal, *dark, *bright;
    short  i, p0 = COLOR_OFFSET, idx;

    for (idx = 0; idx < MAX_PAL; idx++) {
        make_spectrum(Parent_palette + idx, p0, PAL_SIZE);
        /* Allocate space for three palettes. */
        Alloc_array(short , Map_color[idx], 3 * PAL_SIZE,"pal");
        pal = Map_color[idx];
        bright  = Map_color[idx + MAX_PAL] = pal + PAL_SIZE;
        dark  = Map_color[idx + 2 * MAX_PAL]  =  pal  + 2 * PAL_SIZE;
```

[7]The C preprocessor will replace the constant MAX_PAL by the *result* of the
division $(MAX\_COLORS-COLOR\_OFFSET)/PALSIZE$ every time it appears in
the code. The constants PAL_SIZE and $COLOR\_OFFSET$ are system-dependent
and have to be defined in `G_macros.h`.

```
for (i = 0; i < PAL_SIZE; i++)
    pal[i] = p0 + i;
p0 += PAL_SIZE;
```

/* We get two more palettes "for free," even though these secondary
   palettes only have half of the shade range of the "parent palette."
   Thus, they should only be used when you run out of parent palettes.
*/

```
for (i = 0; i < PAL_SIZE; i++) {
```
/* The dark subpalette consists of the shades in the lower half of
   the parent palette *pal*, and the light subpalette consists of the
   shades in the upper half (Figure 1). */
```
    dark[i] = pal[i/2];
    bright[i] = pal[(PAL_SIZE + i)/2];
    } /* end for (i...) */
    } /* end for (idx...) */
} /* end create_palettes() */
```

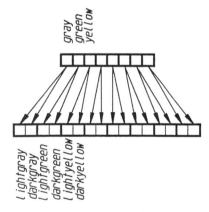

FIGURE 1. How to extract two "subpalettes" from a "parent palette."

Remember that we wrote the color of our object into the datafile itself (Section 3.3 and Section 3.6). Here is the listing of a function that interprets the name of the color palette and that returns the index of the corresponding palette:

Ubyte *color_index(color_name)*   ($\rightarrow$ Proto.h)
    char **color_name*;

{   /* begin *color_index()* */
    register Palette **pal, *hi_pal*;

    /* Is *color_name* the name of a parent palette? */

    hi_pal = Parent_palette + MAX_PAL;

```
        for (pal = Parent_palette; pal < hi_pal; pal++)
            if (!strcmp(pal->name, color_name))
                return pal->index;

        /* Is color_name the name of a subpalette? */

        if (!strncmp("light", color_name, 5)) {
            /* "lightgray", "lightgreen", "lightyellow" etc. */
            color_name += 5; /* What is the color name after "light"? */
            for (pal = Parent_palette; pal < hi_pal; pal++)
                if (!strcmp(pal->name, color_name)
                    return pal->index + MAX_PAL;
        } /* end if */
        if (!strncmp("dark", color_name, 4)) {
            /* "darkgray", "darkgreen", "darkyellow" etc. */
            color_name += 4; /* What is the color name after "dark"? */
            for (pal = Parent_palette; pal < hi_pal; pal++)
                if (!strcmp(pal->name, color_name)
                    return pal->index + 2 * MAX_PAL;
        } /* end if */
        fprintf(Output, "color %s not found (gray taken)\n", color_name);
        return Parent_palette->index;
    } /* end color_index() */
```

If we have

$$idx = color\_index(color\_name);$$

in our code, we let

$$Parent\_palette[idx \ \% \ MAX\_PAL].in\_use \ = \ TRUE;$$

so that the program knows whether the palette is really going to be used. This allows us to create larger palettes.

Finally, if we want to set a particular shade of a color palette, we write

$$G\_set\_color(Map\_color[palette][shade\_value]);$$

or we use the macro

#define $Set\_map\_color(pal, \ shade)\backslash$ ($\rightarrow$ `Macros.h`)
    $G\_set\_color(Map\_color[pal][shade]);$

and write

$$Set\_map\_color(palette, \ shade\_value);$$

As a special case, the color of the background can be defined by

#define $BACKGROUND \ Map\_color[0][0]$ ($\rightarrow$ `Macros.h`)

4.4 Wire Frames and Depth Cuing

In Chapter 3, we learned how to create vertex lists, edge lists and face lists of the objects we want to draw. In order to draw a wireframe, we simply have to draw all the edges of all the polyhedra we want to display:

```
void draw_wireframe()                                              (→ Proto.h)
{  /* begin draw_wireframe() */
   register Vector *v1, *v2; /* Pointers to Coord_pool. */
   register Vector **ptr, **hi_ptr; /* Pointer to Edge_pool. */
   Polyhedron *obj = Object_pool, *hi_obj = obj + Total_objects;

   fill_screen_pool();
   for ( ; obj < hi_obj; obj++) {
       hi_ptr = (ptr = obj->edges) + 2 * obj->no_of_edges;
       Set_map_color(obj->color_index, PAL_SIZE/2);
       while (ptr < hi_ptr) {
           v1 = Screen_coords(*ptr++);⁸
           v2 = Screen_coords(*ptr++);
           draw_line(*v1, *v2);
       } /* end while */
   } /* end for (obj) */
} /* end draw_wireframe() */
```

(After the screen pool is filled, the pointer *draw_line* points either to *quick_line*() or to *clip3d_line*() .)

Wireframes are a bit confusing, especially when we deal with unusual views. On the other hand, they enable us to quickly move and rotate a scene before we do the final rendering.

If we apply the so-called "depth cuing" [ROGE87] to the wireframe, the pictures look much more three-dimensional (Figure 2). The color of the image of a point (i.e., a "pixel") is not only determined by the color of the object the point belongs to, but it is also influenced by the distance from the projection center. To save calculation time, this distance may be replaced by the distance from the

---

⁸For less experienced C programmers: the operation ++ is done **after** *vertex* has been assigned, because ++ stands after *ptr*. Be careful with such abbreviations of the code when you use macros! A typical example of an error that is hard to be found is the line
    *Add_vec(a, a, *b++);*
(Where *a* and *∗b* are **Vector**s.) The value of *b* will increase by 3 instead of 1 at the end of the line, because the macro *Add_vec*() will replace this line by 3 lines.

projection plane (the latter being the third coordinate of the point in the screen system).

If we want to draw a line from the image of a point P to the image of a point Q, theoretically, we have to calculate the depths of several points between P and Q, which takes a lot of time. Therefore, we will only calculate the average depth of the points between P and Q (i.e., the arithmetic mean of the z-coordinates of P and Q in the screen system). The result still looks much better than an ordinary wireframe.

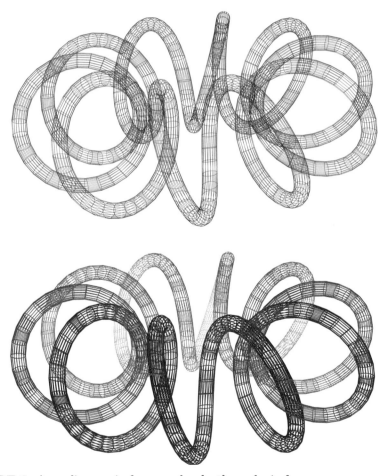

FIGURE 2. An ordinary wireframe and a depth-cued wireframe.

Some graphics workstations are provided with hardware depth cuing. In this case you should use the hardware according to the user's manual. Usually, it is enough to set a Boolean variable *depthcuing* (or similar) *TRUE*, to store the minimum and the maximum depths in some predefined variables and to indicate the color palette by its start index and its last index in the color lookup-table. This may be done by the macros

#**define** *HARDWARE_DEPTH_CUING*

(**void**) *G_depth_cuing* (*on_off*);	($\rightarrow$ G_macros.h)

   /* *TRUE* or *FALSE*. */

(**void**) *G_depths_for_depth_cuing* (*min_depth*, *max_depth*);	($\rightarrow$ G_macros.h)
(**void**) *G_colors_for_depth_cuing* (*min_color*, *max_color*);	($\rightarrow$ G_macros.h)

Before we draw the depth-cued wireframe, we allocate and fill a "color pool" with the shade values of all the points:

Ubyte *Init*(*Color_pool*, *NULL*);	($\rightarrow$ Globals.h)
float *Min_depth*, *Max_depth*, *Total_depth*;	($\rightarrow$ Globals.h)

   /* We need these values for the shading of the faces. */

#**define** *T2*(*w*, *z*, *syst*)\   ($\rightarrow$ Macros.h)
   $((w) = (z) /(Dist[syst] - (z)))$
   /* Apply the transformation $\mathbf{T}_2$: Formula (2.3.9). */
#**define** *UndoT2*(*z*, *w*, *syst*)\   ($\rightarrow$ Macros.h)
   $((z) = (w) * Dist[syst] /(1 + (w)))$
   /* Apply the inverse transformation $\mathbf{T}_2^{-1}$: Formula (2.3.10). */

---

void *fill_color_pool*()   ($\rightarrow$ Proto.h)

```
{   /* begin fill_color_pool() */
    register float min_z, max_z;
    register float *z = &Screen_pool[0][Z];
    float *hi_z = &Screen_pool[Total_vertices][Z];
    register  Ubyte *cur_color;
    register float lambda;
    float z1, z2, z0;

    /* First determine the extreme depths. */

    if (!Color_pool)
        Alloc_array(Ubyte, Color_pool, Total_vertices, "Color_pool");
    cur_color = Color_pool;
    min_z = max_z = *z;
    for (z += 3; z < hi_z; z += 3) {  9
        if (*z < min_z) min_z = *z;
        else if (*z > max_z) max_z = *z;
    }  /* end for */
    Max_depth = max_z + EPS;  Min_depth = min_z - EPS;
    /* The EPS helps to avoid a division by zero. */
```

---

[9]If *z* points to the *z*-coordinate of a vertex stored in coord_pool, *z*+3 points to the *z*-coordinate of the following vertex.

```
    UndoT2(z1, Min_z, SCREEN_SYST);
    UndoT2(z2, Max_z, SCREEN_SYST);
    if (Min_depth < Min_z || Max_depth > Max_z) {
        Min_depth = Maximum(z1, Min_depth);
        max_z = Max_depth = Minimum(z2, Max_depth);
    }
    Total_depth = Max_depth - Min_depth;
    min_z = Max_depth - 1.25 * Total_depth;
```

/* The shade of the vertex depends on the distance from the image plane
and on the width of the palette. (In our case, we do not use the lowest
20% of the shades, because then we would hardly be able to see the
vertices on the black screen.) */

```
#ifdef HARDWARE_DEPTH_CUING
    G_depthcuing(TRUE);
    G_depths_for_depthcuing(min_z, max_z);
#else
    lambda = PAL_SIZE/(max_z - min_z);
    if (draw_line == quick_line)
        for (z = &Screen_pool[0][Z]; z < hi_z; z += 3)
            *cur_color++ = (*z - min_z) * lambda;
    else
        for (z = &Screen_pool[0][Z]; z < hi_z; z += 3) {
            z0 = (*z - min_z) * lambda;
            *cur_color++ = (z0 < z1) ? z1 : ((z0 > z2) ? z2 : z0);
        }
#endif
}  /* end fill_color_pool() */
```

Now we can calculate the average depth of a line with the help of pointer arithmetic (compare the following code with the one in *draw_wireframe()* at the
beginning of this section):

```
void draw_depthcued_wireframe()                              (→ Proto.h)
{  /* begin draw_depthcued_wireframe() */
    register Vector *v1, *v2; /* Pointer into Coord_pool. */
    register Vector **ptr, **hi_ptr; /* Pointer into Edge_pool. */
    register short shade;
    Polyhedron *obj = Object_pool, *hi_obj = obj + Total_objects;
    short *cur_pal;

    calc_rot_matrix(SCREEN_SYST);
    fill_screen_pool();
    fill_color_pool();
```

```
    for ( ;  obj < hi_obj;  obj++) {
        hi_ptr = (ptr = obj–>edges) + 2 * obj–>no_of_edges;
        cur_pal = Map_color[obj–>color_index];
#ifdef HARDWARE_DEPTH_CUING
        G_colors_for_depth_cuing(cur_pal[0], cur_pal[PAL_SIZE − 1]);
#endif
        while (ptr < hi_ptr)) {
            v1 = Screen_coords(*ptr++);
            v2 = Screen_coords(*ptr++);
#ifdef HARDWARE_DEPTH_CUING
            /* Average shade value of line. */
            shade  = (Color_pool[v1 − Screen_pool] +
                            Color_pool[v2 − Screen_pool]  +  1) >> 1;¹⁰
            G_set_color(cur_pal[shade]);
#endif
            draw_line(*v1, *v2);
        }  /* end while (ptr < hi_ptr)) */
    }  /* end for (obj...) */
}   /* end draw_depthcued_wireframe() */
```

We have mentioned above that wireframes can be manipulated (rotated and translated, zoomed, etc.) quickly. Here is one way of manipulating a scene interactively by means of the keyboard.

#define *ESCAPE* (**Ubyte**) 27   (→ Macros.h)

Global Init_fptr(display_scene, draw_wireframe);   (→ Proto.h)
    /* When certain keys (e.g., the *s*-key for "shade" or the *h*-key for "hidden lines") are pressed, the pointer will point to other functions. */

```
void manipulate_scene()                                    (→ Proto.h)
{  /* begin manipulate_scene() */
    Ubyte key;
    static Vector delta = { 0.05,  0.05,  0.05 };
    static float lambda = 1.03;
    while ((key = G_key_pressed()) != ESCAPE) {
        if (!key) continue;
        switch (key) {
            /* Change azimuth angle, elevation angle, twist angle. */
```

---

[10]Usually, the shift operator works much faster than an ordinary division. If you shift an integer value to the right by 1, this is equivalent to dividing it by 2.

```
        case 'a': Azim[SCREEN_SYST] += delta[0]; break;
        case 'A': Azim[SCREEN_SYST] -= delta[0]; break;
        case 'e': Elev[SCREEN_SYST] += delta[1]; break;
        case 'E': Elev[SCREEN_SYST] -= delta[1]; break;
        case 't': Twist += delta[2]; break;
        case 'T': Twist -= delta[2]; break;

        /* Change distance and scale factor. */

        case 'd': Dist[SCREEN_SYST] *= lambda; break;
        case 'D': Dist[SCREEN_SYST] /= lambda; break;
        case 'x': Scale_factor *= lambda; break;
        case 'X': Scale_factor /= lambda; break;

                ⋮

        /* Change the draw mode. */
        case 'w':
            display_scene = draw_depthcued_wireframe;
            break;
        /*
        case 's': display_scene = shade_scene; break;
        case 'h': display_scene = remove_hidden_lines; break;
        etc.
        */
    } /* end switch key */
    G_clear_screen(BACKGROUND);
            /* Do this before any calculations. In this manner, the processor
               can keep on calculating, while the graphics hardware clears the
               screen, and no time is wasted. */
    display_scene();
    G_swap_screens(); /* Show contents of backscreen. */
  } /* end while (key != ESCAPE) */
} /* end manipulate_scene() */
```

4.5 Shading

Of course, wireframes are not very satisfactory. The next step towards realistic computer-generated images is to "shade" the facets of our objects. The brightness of a face (i.e., the shade in the corresponding color palette) depends on various factors. Sophisticated shading models are described in detail in [THAL87] and [HEAR86]. In Section 8.8, we will extend the formulas derived in this section.

For our purposes, we try to simplify the determination of the shade. First let us assume that we only have *one light source* (Figure 3). The shade value s can then be calculated in the following three steps:

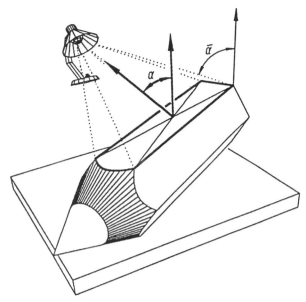

FIGURE 3. The shading of a face (one light source).

1. According to Lambert's cosine law (Section 1.2) the amount of light reaching the surface depends mainly on the angle of incidence α of the light rays. If the light rays are not parallel, their angles of incidence will be slightly different for each vertex of the face. In order to keep calculation time within limits, we simply take the "average angle of incidence" (i.e., the angle of incidence with the   barycenter of the face).[11] We have maximum brightness when the light rays hit the face perpendicularly ($\alpha = 0$) and minimum brightness when the light rays coincide with the plane of the face ($\alpha = \pi/2$). The shade value s can be calculated by

$$s = reduced\_palette \, [\cos(\alpha)]^{c}. \qquad (2)$$

The value of the variable *reduced_palette* depends on the amount of "background light." In the pictures in this book, 20% of the total palette size are reserved for background or "ambient" light. Therefore, *reduced_palette* comprises 80% of the palette size ($0.8 * PAL\_SIZE$), provided that the light rays really illuminate the face. "Dark faces" (i.e., faces where the light rays fall on the invisible side of the polygon) can be treated in a similar manner. There is always a certain amount of light that is reflected from surrounding objects and that will illuminate the face. As a rule of thumb, we can say

[11]If we deal with large polygons or with polyhedra that approximate smooth surfaces, we can also calculate a shade value for each vertex and interpolate the shades of the pixels between the vertices (see "Gouraud shading" in Section 4.6).

that this reflected light comes more or less "from the back." Therefore, the brightness of a dark face also depends on the angle of incidence of the light rays so that we can again use Formula 2 with a reduced shade value (for example: $s \to 0.3\,s$).

FIGURE 4. The influence of the constant c in Equation 4.2.

The exponent c has an influence on the appearance of the object (Figure 4). For "normal material" (neither mat nor shiny) we let $c = 1$. For metallic material we may set $c \geq 2$. [12] For mat materials like wood, we let $0.5 < c < 1$.

[12]The use of the constant c like in Equation 2 represents a very rough simplification of the law of reflection. It will not place highlighted spots exactly

Remember that $\cos(\alpha)$ is nothing but the dot product of the normalized normal vector of the facet and the normalized vector to the light source (Section 1.2). In any case, a first approximation of the shade value is

$$0 \le s \le reduced\_palette. \tag{3}$$

2. A second criterion for the brightness of the face is its (average) distance from the light source.

   To increase the speed of the program, we replace the distance from the light source by the distance from the base plane of the light system.

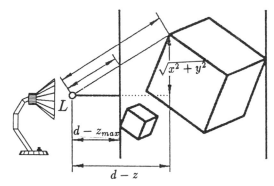

FIGURE 5. When the light source is close to the scene, we have to take into account the distance from the light source.

Let d_{light} be the z-value of the light source in the light system (i.e., the distance of the light source from the base plane, see Figure 5), let $(z_{light})_{max}$ be the maximum z-value of the scene in the light system and let z_{light} be the average z-value of the face in the light system. The shade value 2 can then be modified by

$$s \to s \underbrace{\left(\frac{d_{light} - (z_{light})_{max}}{d_{light} - z_{light}} \right)^2}_{\le 1}. \tag{4}$$

(The brightness of the face decreases with the *square* of the distance.)

When the light source is far away from the objects, the above-mentioned modification is negligible.

where they ought to be. For *smooth* reflecting surfaces, it is better to use a more sophisticated model, which will be described in Chapter 9 in connection with mathematical surfaces and spline curves.

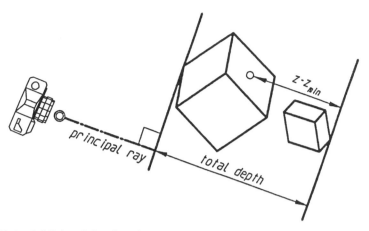

FIGURE 6. Additional depth cuing.

3. A third factor that has an influence on the brightness of the face is its
distance from the projection center. We can call this factor "additional depth
cuing."

To increase the speed of the program, we replace the distance from the
projection center by the distance from the projection plane, the latter being
the z-coordinate in the screen system (see "depth cuing" in Section 4.4).

Let *ambient* be $PAL\_SIZE - reduced\_palette$, let z_0 be the average distance
of the face from the projection plane (Figure 6), let $(z_0)_{min}$ be the minimum
z-coordinate of the scene in the screen system and let *total_depth* be the
depth of the scene in the screen system. Finally, the shade value is

$$s \rightarrow s + ambient \underbrace{\frac{z_0 - (z_0)_{min}}{total\_depth}}_{\leq 1}. \tag{5}$$

Now we have

$$0 \leq s \leq PAL\_SIZE, \tag{6}$$

which means that we use the whole palette.

——— • ———

Now let us introduce n *different light sources*. Let I_1, $I_2,\ldots,I_n$ be their
intensities[13] and let the n shade values of a face, corresponding to each indi-

---

[13]In our simplified model, the colors of the light sources are all white.

vidual light source, be s_1, s_2,..., s_n. (The additional depth cuing (5) must not be introduced yet.) Then we have

$$s_{total} = I_1\,s_1 + I_2\,s_2 + \ldots + I_n\,s_n. \tag{7}$$

The value s_{total} should still fulfill Equation 3. This can easily be achieved by the condition $I_k \leq 1/n$, $k = 1, \ldots, n$. Such a strong restriction, however, implies that s_{total} is unlikely to ever reach its theoretical maximum value *reduced_palette* and that we will lose parts of the color palette. On the other hand, if I_{total} is too large, this may sometimes cause the shade value to exceed its maximum.

If we want to produce an optimum image of the scene, we have to precalculate the shade values s_{total} for all the facets and to determine their maximum value s_{max}. If we now scale all the light intensities by the factor $\lambda = reduced\_palette/s_{max}$ ($I_k \rightarrow \lambda\,I_k$), we can be sure that s_{total} will indeed fulfill condition (3). Finally, we modify s_{total} by additional depth cuing (5). Thus, the entire palette size will be used for the shade values. But be careful: once you animate the scene and recalculate the light intensities for each frame, the movie will flicker. Therefore, it is better not to change the intensities for each frame and to take the risk that from time to time a shade value may exceed the palette (take the maximum value in that case).

To put the theory into practice, let us now have a look at a function *calc_shade_of_face*().

Bool *Solid;*   ($\rightarrow$ Globals.h)
  /* This variable indicates whether the object the face belongs to is solid. */
float *Intensity[MAX_SYST]*;   ($\rightarrow$ Globals.h)
float *Full_width[MAX_SYST], Half_width[MAX_SYST]*;   ($\rightarrow$ Globals.h)
  /* Default values for the intensities of the light sources may be

>   **for** $(syst = 1;\ syst < Total\_systems;\ syst++)$
> $Intensity[syst] = 1/sqrt(($**double**$)\ No\_of\_lights)$;

>   (Other values $0 < Intensity[syst] < 1$ can be read from the data file.)
>   The variables *Full_width, Half_width* are initialized by

#define *AMBIENT (PAL_SIZE/5)*   ($\rightarrow$ Macros.h)
#define *REDUCED_PAL (PAL_SIZE - AMBIENT)*   ($\rightarrow$ Macros.h)

>   **for** $(syst = 1;\ syst < Total\_systems;\ syst++)$ {
> $Full\_width[syst] = REDUCED\_PAL * Intensity[syst]$;
> $Half\_width[syst] = 0.5 * Full\_width[syst]$;
>   }
  */
/* We add two members to **struct Face**. */

>   **Ubyte** *darkface[MAX_SYST]*;
>   **Ubyte** *shade[MAX_SYST]*;

#**define** *Backface(f)* (*f→darkface[SCREEN_SYST]*)   (→ `Macros.h`)
#**define** *Backlit(f, syst)* (*f→darkface[syst]*)   (→ `Macros.h`)

float *Average_z*;   (→ `Globals.h`)
Bool *Init(Smooth_shading, FALSE)*;   (→ `Globals.h`)
  /* In the case of smooth shading *Dim* must equal 3. */
Ubyte *Cur_shade*;   (→ `Globals.h`)
Ubyte *Shade_of_vertex[MAX_POLY_SIZE]*;   (→ `Globals.h`)
  /* For smooth shading (Section 4.6). */

```
float shade(f, syst)                                          (→ Proto.h)
   Face * f;
   short syst;
{   /* begin shade() */
   register  float cosine, s;
   Vector light_ray;

   /* Lambert's law. */
   Subt_vec(light_ray, *f→barycenter, Proj_center[syst]);
   cosine = Dot_product(f→normal, light_ray)/Length(light_ray);
   if (Solid) {
      if (cosine > 0) {
         s = cosine * Full_width[syst];
         Backlit(f, syst) = FALSE;
      } else {
         s = −Half_width[syst] * cosine;
         Backlit(f, syst) = TRUE;
      } /* end if (cosine > 0) */
   } else {  /* Light source and eye on the same side of the plane? */
      if (cosine * (0.5 − Backface(f)) > 0) {
         if (cosine < 0) cosine = −cosine;
         s = cosine * Full_width[syst];
         Backlit(f, syst) = FALSE;
      } else {
         if (cosine < 0) cosine = −cosine;
         s = cosine * Half_width[syst];
         Backlit(f, syst) = TRUE;
      } /* end if (cosine...) */
   } /* end if (Solid) */
   return s;
} /* end shade() */
```

#**define** $Z\_in\_screen(z, p)\backslash$ $(\rightarrow$ `Macros.h`$)$
     $Dot\_product(InvRot[SCREEN\_SYST][2], *p)^{14}$

---

void $calc\_shade\_of\_face(f)$ $(\rightarrow$ `Proto.h`$)$
     Face $* f$;
{ /* begin $calc\_shade\_of\_face()$ */
   register short $syst$;
   float s;
   register float $s0$;

   /* z-component for additional depth cuing. */
   $Z\_in\_screen(Average\_z, *f{\rightarrow}barycenter)$;
   $s0 = AMBIENT * (Average\_z - Min\_depth) / Total\_depth + 0.5$;
   for $(syst = 1; syst < Total\_systems; syst{+}{+})$ {
       $s0 {+}{=} (s = shade(f, syst))$;
       $f{\rightarrow}shade[syst] = s + 0.5$; /* Round value. */
   } /* end **for** $(syst)$ */
   $f{\rightarrow}shade[SCREEN\_SYST] = Cur\_shade = s0 =$
                              $Minimum(s0 + 0.5, PAL\_SIZE - 1)$;
   if $(Smooth\_shading)$ {
       Vector $**v = f{\rightarrow}vertices$;
       short $i = 0$;
       float z;
       for $(; i < f{\rightarrow}no\_of\_vertices; i{+}{+}, v{+}{+})$
           $Z\_in\_screen(z, *v), z {-}{=} Average\_z,$
           $Shade\_of\_vertex[i] = s0 + AMBIENT * (z/Total\_depth)$;
   } /* end **if** $(Smooth\_shading)$ */
} /* end $calc\_shade\_of\_face()$ */

4.6 Basic Graphics Output Algorithms

The Bresenham Algorithm for the Drawing of a Line

The most elementary feature a graphics programmer needs is the computer's
ability to draw a line by plotting pixels on the screen. Any compiler that supports
graphics output will also permit the drawing of a line on the screen. What it
might not support is the drawing of a "rubber band" (also called an "XOR line").
For this reason, we will list a function that sets the desired pixels in a very quick
manner because it only works with integer variables:

---

[14]Since *InvRot* is a global variable, *InvRot*[SCREEN_SYST][2] is a constant
address, which is evaluated during the compilation.

```
void plot_line(p, q)                                                  (→ Proto.h)
    Vector¹⁵ p, q;
{   /* begin plot_line() */
    register short x1 = p[X], y1 = p[Y], x2 = q[X], y2 = q[Y];
    short mod, dx, dy, sgn_dy, temp;

    if (x1 − x2)
        Swap(x1, x2), Swap(y1, y2);
    dx = x2 − x1;
    if (y2 − y1)
        dy = y2 − y1, sgn_dy = 1;
    else
        dy = y1 − y2, sgn_dy = −1;
    if (dy <= dx)
        for (mod = −((dx + 1) ≫ 1); ; x1++, mod += dy) {
            if (mod >= 0)
                y1 += sgn_dy, mod −= dx;
            G_set_pixel(x1, y1);
            if (x1 == x2)
                return ;
        } /* end for (mod...) */
    else
        for (mod = −((dy + 1) ≫ 1); ; y1 += sgn_dy, mod += dx) {
            if (mod >= 0)
                x1++, mod −= dy;
            G_set_pixel(x1, y1);
            if (y1 == y2)
                return ;
        } /* end for (mod...) */
} /* end plot_line() */
```

'Rubber Bands'

A function rubber_band() has almost the same code as the function plot_line(). We only have to replace the macro G_set_pixel() by the following macro:

```
#define Set_xor_pixel(x, y)\                                        (→ Macros.h)
    temp = G_get_pixel_color(x, y),\
    Cur_color ^= temp,\
    G_set_pixel(x, y),\
    Cur_color ^= temp
```

---

[15]With this function it does not make any difference whether p and q are of the type **Vector2** or of the type **Vector**. Both types are interpreted as pointers to a **float** and only the first two elements of the array are used.

The color of a pixel on the line now depends on the color the pixel had before. The two colors are connected by the XOR-assign, a fast bitwise operation that is undone if we apply it twice. Thus, if we write

$rubber\_band(p, q)$;

⋮

$rubber\_band(p, q)$;

the line is erased and the original background pixel is restored.

A Fill Algorithm for Convex Polygons

The task of filling polygons is one of the oldest in computer graphics, which is why many people have already solved the problem in various manners. We want to give the listing of an algorithm of our own for several reasons.

- Not all C compilers provide a function that fills polygons the way we need it. The so-called "floodfill"-command, for example, which needs a point in the interior of a closed area that is defined by a specific color, is not always able to fill polygons correctly for our purposes. (We want to erase other polygons. Therefore, parts of the interior of the polygon will usually have been filled with several colors before.)

- Imagine a face of our scene that is comparatively large (for example, the base plane of the scene). If we fill the image polygon of the face with one and the same color, it will look rather unrealistic. In such a case, we can fill our polygon line by line with slightly different colors (mainly according to the depth of the points in the screen system) in order to get the impression of smooth shading. This method is a special case of Gouraud shading ([GOUR71]).

- We will need a fill algorithm for polygons in a slightly modified form in Section 6.6, where we talk about transparency.

- The algorithm is essential for the so-called "depth buffering" and "shadow buffering" (Chapter 7).

Usually, a polygon is drawn by our function $fill\_poly()$. This function works with the macros $G\_move\_area(v)$, $G\_draw\_area(v)$ and $G\_close\_area()$. If the compiler does not support polygon filling routines, or if we want to do smooth shading or "depth buffering," the macros may call the following functions $poly\_move()$, $poly\_draw()$ and $poly\_close()$:

typedef struct {
    short x, y; /∗ Pixel coordinates. ∗/
    float $x0$; /∗ For more accuracy. ∗/

float z; /* For depth buffering. */
float *shade*; /* For smooth shading. */
short *prev*, *next*; /* Indices of neighboring vertices. */
} **Vertex**;[16] $(\rightarrow$ `Types.h`$)$

Vertex $Vtx[MAX\_POLY\_SIZE]$; $(\rightarrow$ `Globals.h`$)$
    /* Space for the vertices. This is especially necessary when the polygon has
       to be clipped before it is drawn. */
Vertex $* Cur\_vtx$, $*Min\_vtx$, $*Max\_vtx$; $(\rightarrow$ `Globals.h`$)$
    /* Cur_vtx points to the current vertex, Min_vtx and Max_vtx indicate the
       vertices with the minimum and the maximum $y-$values, respectively. */

---

void *poly_move*(a) $(\rightarrow$ `Proto.h`$)$
    Vector a;
{   /* begin *poly_move*() */
    $Cur\_vtx \ = \ Min\_vtx \ = \ Max\_vtx \ = \ Vtx$;
    $Cur\_vtx{\to}x \ = \ (Cur\_vtx{\to}x0 \ = \ a[X]) \ + \ 0.5$;
    $Cur\_vtx{\to}y \ = \ a[Y] \ + \ 0.5$;
    if $(Dim == 3) \ Cur\_vtx{\to}z \ = \ a[Z]$;
    $Cur\_vtx{+}{+}$;
}   /* end *poly_move*() */

---

void *poly_draw*(a) $(\rightarrow$ `Proto.h`$)$
    Vector a;
{   /* begin *poly_draw*() */
    register short $*x \ = \ \&Cur\_vtx{\to}x, *y \ = \ x \ + \ 1$;

    $*x \ = \ (Cur\_vtx{\to}x0 \ = \ a[X]) \ + \ 0.5; *y \ = \ a[Y] \ + \ 0.5$;
    /* The following question helps to avoid "double points" on a polygon (since
       the coordinates are round, this may happen even when the vertices are
       different). */
    if $(*x \ == \ (Cur\_vtx - 1){\to}x \ \&\& \ *y \ == \ (Cur\_vtx - 1){\to}y)$
        return ;
    if $(*y \ < \ Min\_vtx{\to}y)$
        $Min\_vtx \ = \ Cur\_vtx$;
    else if $(*y \ > \ Max\_vtx{\to}y)$
        $Max\_vtx \ = \ Cur\_vtx$;
    if $(Dim == 3) \ Cur\_vtx{\to}z \ = \ a[Z]$;
    $Cur\_vtx{+}{+}$;
}   /* end *poly_draw*() */

---

[16]It is also possible to use the type **Ubyte** for the shade. In this case, however,
sizeof(Vertex) will be 15 instead of 16. The program runs faster when the size
of the structure can be divided by 4.

```
void poly_close()                                              (→ Proto.h)
{   /* begin poly_close() */
    register  short  i, size;

    size  =  Cur_vtx  − Vtx;
    if  (size  <= 1) {
        G_set_pixel(Vtx−>x, Vtx−>y);
        return ;
    }
    /* Now all the vertices are concatenated. */
    for  (i = 0;  i <  size;  i++)
        Vtx[i].prev  =  i − 1, Vtx[i].next  =  i + 1;
    Vtx[0].prev  =  −−size;
    Vtx[size].next  =  0;
    flush_poly(); /* The actual fill routine. */
}   /* end poly_close() */
```

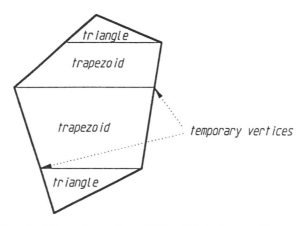

FIGURE 7. How to fill a polygon by splitting it into trapezoids.

The actual filling of the polygon is done by the function *flush_poly()*. This function splits the polygons into triangles and trapezoids with *x*-parallel sides. Figure 7 shows that, in general, each trapezoid will have two new (temporary) vertices.

```
void flush_poly()                                              (→ Proto.h)
{   /* begin flush_poly() */
    register  Vertex * a1, *a2, *b1, *b2;
    static Vertex reserve[2]; /* The temporary vertices. */
    Vertex *r  =  reserve;
    short  i;
    float t;
```

```
a1 = b1 = a2 = b2 = Min_vtx;
for ( ; a2 != Max_vtx || b2 != Max_vtx; a1 = a2, b1 = b2) {
    while (a2 != Max_vtx) { /* Next A₂ with greater y. */
        a2 = Vtx + a1->prev;
        if (a1->y == a2->y)
            a1 = a2;
        else break;
    } /* end while */
    while (b2 != Max_vtx) { /* Next B₂ with greater y. */
        b2 = Vtx + b1->next;
        if (b1->y == b2->y)
            b1 = b2;
        else break;
    } /* end while */
    if (a2->y > b2->y) { /* Interpolate new A₂. */
        t = ((float) b2->y - a1->y)) /(a2->y - a1->y);
        r->x0 = a1->x0 + t * (a2->x0 - a1->x0);
        r->y = b2->y; r->prev = a2 - Vtx; a2 = r;
        r++;
    } else if (a2->y < b2->y) { /* Interpolate new B₂. */
        t = ((float) a2->y - b1->y)) /(b2->y - b1->y);
        r->x0 = b1->x0 + t * (b2->x0 - b1->x0);
        r->y = a2->y; r->next = b2 - Vtx; b2 = r;
        r++;
    } /* end if (a2->y) */
    fill_trapezoid(a1, b1, a2, b2);
    if (r - reserve > 2)
        r = reserve;
} /* end for (a2...) */
} /* end flush_poly() */
```

Here is a code for the filling of a trapezoid:

```
void fill_trapezoid(a1, b1, a2, b2)                          (→ Proto.h)
    Vertex *a1, *b1, *a2, *b2;
{   /* begin fill_trapezoid() */
    register float x1, x2, dx1, dx2;
    short y, ymax, dy;

    y = a1->y, ymax = a2->y, dy = ymax - y;
    if (dy == 0) return ;
```

```
/* Increments on the lines A₁B₁ and A₂B₂. */
x1 = a1->x0; x2 = b1->x0;
dx1 = (a2->x0 - x1) /dy; dx2 = (b2->x0 - x2) /dy;
/* To round off the coordinates. */
if (x1 < x2 || a2->x0 < b2->x0)
      x2 += 0.5;
else
      x1 += 0.5;
if (Dim == 2) {
      for ( ; y < ymax; y++, x1 += dx1, x2 += dx2)
           G_move_xy(x1, y), G_draw_xy(x2, y);
      return ;
} /* end if (Dim == 2) */
} /* end fill_trapezoid() */
```

Smooth Shading (Gouraud Shading)

With a computer that is able to display palettes with many different shades, the objects (especially polygonized surfaces) can be shaded by means of Gouraud shading [GOUR71]. In the case of curved surfaces, this may even save time (in spite of the fact that the fill algorithm slows down the program), because we need much fewer polygons on the approximating polyhedron.

At the end of $fill\_trapezoid()$, we add the lines

```
if (Smooth_shading) {
    float s1, s2, ds1, ds2;
    short  *p = Map_color[Cur_palette];

    s1 = p[(short ) a1->shade] + 0.5;
    s2 = p[(short ) b1->shade] + 0.5,
    ds1 = (p[a2->shade] - s1) /dy;
    ds2 = (p[b2->shade] - s2) /dy;
    for ( ; y < ymax; y++,
                    x1 += dx1, x2 += dx2, s1 += ds1, s2 += ds2)
        if (x1 <= x2)
            shade_scan_line((short) x1, (short ) x2, y, s1, s2);
        else
            shade_scan_line((short) x2, (short ) x1, y, s2, s1);
} /* end if (Smooth_shading) */
```

The routine $shade\_scan\_line()$ may look like this:

```
void shade_scan_line(x1, x2, y, s1, s2)                    (→ Proto.h)
    register short  x1, x2, y;
    float s1, s2;
{   /* begin shade_scan_line() */
    float ds = s2 − s1;
    static short  j, dx, sign_s, k;

    if (x1 >= x2)
        return ;
    if (fabs(ds) < 0.5) {
        G_set_color(s1);
        G_move_xy(x1, y); G_draw_xy(x2, y);
        return ;
    } /* end if (ds) */
    if (ds < 0)
        ds = −ds, sign_s = −1;
    else
        sign_s = 1;
    dx = x2 − x1; k = 1;
    G_set_color(s1); G_move_xy(x1, y);
    for (j = −(dx >> 1); x1 <= x2; x1++, j += ds) {
        if (j >= 0) {
            G_draw_xy(x1, y);
            if (x1 == x2)
                return ;
            if (++k == ds) {
                G_set_color(s2); G_draw_xy(x2, y);
                return ;
            } /* end if (k) */
            j −= dx, s1 += sign_s, G_set_color(s1);
        } /* end if (j) */
    } /* end for (j) */
    G_draw_xy(x2, y);
} /* end shade_scan_line() */
```

5

A Fast Hidden-Surface Algorithm

Ever since the beginnings of computer graphics, many algorithms have been developed to remove those parts of the image of a scene that are obscured by other parts, and yet none of these algorithms seems to be entirely satisfactory. Among the general working algorithms, we have the "scan-line" algorithms, the "area subdivision" algorithms, "z-buffering," "ray tracing" and many others. If you want to read more about these algorithms, please refer to the following sources: [SUTH74/2], [THAL87], [GLAS90].

In this chapter we will talk about a rendering algorithm that in fact is already very well known: the *"painter's algorithm,"* also called the *depth sort* or *priority algorithm*. It processes polygons in a similar way as a painter might do it. The images of distant polygons are painted first, to be obscured partly or completely later on when the images of those polygons are painted that are closer to the viewer. The problem is to put the polygons into an order according to their priority.

This algorithm is extremely fast in removing hidden surfaces, but it has three enormous disadvantages.

- It is not a general algorithm – given an arbitrary set of polygons, it may happen that we cannot find a correct priority list. Especially when we deal with the intersection of objects, we have to split them up in a certain way.

- If we consider each polygon as an object in its own right, the calculation time for the priority tests will increase dramatically for scenes that consist of hundreds or thousands of polygons.

- The painter's algorithm only works on the screen and is not suitable for plotter drawings.

This may be the reason why many books on 3D-graphics mention the painter's algorithm only briefly and then go on to more general and more sophisticated rendering methods.

In this chapter, however, we will see that the painter's algorithm can be applied very effectively to almost any kind of scene (even if it has thousands of faces and intersecting objects) and to create *PostScript* images. Of course, this does not mean that it can replace all the other rendering algorithms, but it can be used as a powerful tool for

- the manipulation of rendered scenes on the screen.

- the fast creation of movies.

- the efficient creation of *PostScript*-images.[1]

FIGURE 1. Priority determination with the help of separating planes.

The secret of fast rendering is twofold:

1. We polygonize more complicated polyhedra in a special manner (for example, we cut them into "slices").

---

[1]Polygons that are painted in *PostScript*-mode on a laser printer will erase previously painted polygons.

2. We combine as many polygons as possible to primitives of different levels (this may be a "ring" or a "ribbon," a "slice," an "object" (polyhedron) or even an "object group"). In [NEWM84], such accumulations of polygons are called "clusters."

   These primitives can be separated by planes:

   A *"separating plane"* σ divides the space into two halfspaces (Figure 1). The plane σ itself may belong to both halfspaces. If we now have two primitives A and B, each of which is completely inside of one of the halfspaces (like two neighboring slices of a polyhedron), the priority between A and B can be determined quickly. If A is *not* inside the same halfspace as the projection center, it can *never* obscure B. Therefore, it will always be correct to draw the image of A before the image of B.[2]

The idea of the painter's algorithm can also be applied to the plotting of cast shadows. We can even introduce transparent objects and reflections (Chapter 6) without any major loss of speed.

For really complicated scenes or objects, which can neither be subdivided easily nor polygonized in the way we need it, we can still use other rendering algorithms (in Chapter 7 we will have a closer look at the above-mentioned "depth buffering," which will be extended to a "shadow buffering").

5.1 Objects with Convex Outlines

The most convenient objects by far are convex polyhedra. They have a convex outline, which is the image of the spatial contour polygon, for every projection. This is still true when we subtract some faces from a convex polyhedron (Figure 2). In many cases, the "object preprocessor" described in Chapter 3 will provide the computer with an object list where the non-convex polyhedra are split into convex parts.

Convex polyhedra are characterized by the fact that each face is either an invisible "backface" or a "frontface" that is not obscured by any other face of *the same* polyhedron. We can say that the face of a convex polyhedron is *locally* either completely visible or completely invisible. The criterion for the removal of the backfaces is very simple. The normal vector, which is oriented towards the outside of the polyhedron, includes an angle α with the vector from an arbitrary vertex of the face to the projection center. If $|\alpha| \leq \pi/2$, the face is visible, otherwise it is not.

Thus, we can render a convex polyhedron by ignoring the backfaces and by plotting all of the frontfaces in an arbitrary order. Furthermore, every (non-

---

[2]The negation of this statement is: it *may* be wrong to plot B before A (if the images of A and B do not overlap, the drawing order is of no importance).

solid) polyhedron with a convex outline can be displayed in two steps: first we render all the backfaces and then the rest of the faces.

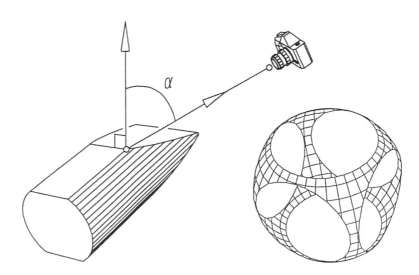

FIGURE 2. Polyhedra with convex outlines.

To determine the type of a face, we use the function

```
void face_types(obj, syst)                              (→ Proto.h)
   Polyhedron * obj;
   short syst;
{   /* begin face_types() */
   Vector proj_ray;
   register  Face * f  =  obj→faces;
   register  Vector * center  = (Vector *) Proj_center[syst];
   Face * hi_f  =  f +  obj→no_of_faces;

   for  ( ;  f <  hi_f; f + +) {
      Subt_vec(proj_ray, *f→vertices[0], *center);
      f→darkface[syst] =  (Dot_product(f→normal, proj_ray)  <=  0);
   } /* end for (f) */
} /* end face_types() */
```

The corresponding C code to plot a convex polyhedron looks like this:

```
void plot_convex_polyhedron(obj)                          (→ Proto.h)
    Polyhedron *obj;
{   /* begin plot_convex_polyhedron() */
    register  Face * f, *hi_f;

    face_types(obj, SCREEN_SYST);
    hi_f = (f = obj->faces) + obj->no_of_faces;
    for ( ; f < hi_f; f++)
        if (!Backface(f)) plot_face(f);
}   /* end plot_convex_polyhedron() */
```

```
void plot_polyhedron_with_convex_outline(obj)             (→ Proto.h)
    Polyhedron *obj;
{   /* begin plot_polyhedron_with_convex_outline() */
    register  Face * f, *hi_f;

    face_types(obj, SCREEN_SYST);
    hi_f = obj->faces + obj->no_of_faces;
    for (f = obj->faces; f < hi_f; f++)
        if (Backface(f)) plot_face(f);
    for (f = obj->faces; f < hi_f; f++)
        if (!Backface(f)) plot_face(f);
}   /* end plot_polyhedron_with_convex_outline() */
```

5.2 Surfaces of Revolution

We have already seen that convex polyhedra have some unique properties that can be used successfully. The same is true for another family of polyhedra Φ. In the following, we will simply call them "surfaces of revolution," but it should be kept in mind that they are, in fact, only approximations to surfaces of revolution.

Figure 3 shows how we have to plot the surface. Let us assume that the object preprocessor has "sliced" the polyhedron Φ and that the normals of the faces are oriented correctly (Section 3.6). Then each "slice" of Φ consists of one or more "rings" and we can render the slice as follows: from the outermost ring to the innermost ring, we plot all the backfaces and then, going from the innermost ring to the outermost ring, we plot the remaining frontfaces.

The only problem is in which order to plot the slices. For this purpose, we consider planes σ (Figure 3) that are perpendicular to the axis of the surface (polyhedron) Φ and that separate the slices of Φ. Additionally, we introduce a special separating plane σ_0 that coincides with the projection center. It may or may not cross Φ so that we distinguish between two different cases.

1. σ_0 does not cross the polyhedron Φ. Then the rendering is easy: we can render one slice after the other, beginning with the slice with the maximum distance from σ_0.

2. σ_0 crosses Φ. Then it splits Φ into two polyhedra Φ_1 and Φ_2 (each of which is completely in one of the two half spaces defined by σ_0) and a "critical slice" Σ_0, consisting of the faces that intersect σ_0. Since σ_0 coincides with the projection center, its image will be a line $s_0 = \sigma_0^c$, which separates the images of Φ_1 and Φ_2. Therefore, we can plot these images separately like in case 1. Only the image of the critical slice will obscure some parts of the images of Φ_1 and Φ_2, and that is why it has to be drawn after the rest.

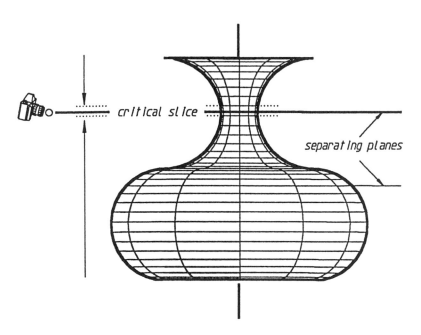

FIGURE 3. How to plot a simple "surface of revolution."

The rendering algorithm is extremely efficient. The computer will need only a short time for the determination of visibility. Thus, we can render and manipulate even complicated polyhedra.

5.3 Sliced Surfaces

In the previous section we sorted primitives with the help of separating planes. Each pair of neighboring slices of the surface of revolution Φ is separated by a plane that is normal to the axis of the polyhedron.

Thus, it should be possible to render even complicated surfaces in an equally fast manner, if we are able to polygonize them slice by slice. In [BLOO87], for example, such an algorithm is described in detail for polyhedra with known implicit equations.

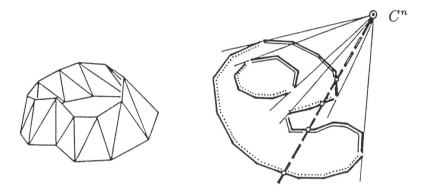

FIGURE 4. How to render a complicated slice by splitting it into "ribbons."

What we still need to know is how to render a general slice. First we determine the types of all the faces (backfaces or frontfaces) of the slice and combine adjoining faces of the same type to "ribbons" (Figure 4). It *should always* be possible to render the ribbons one after the other in the correct order (from the back to the front). The reason for this is that none of the ribbons can contain another ribbon (otherwise it would have been split into two ribbons).

The priorities among the ribbons can be determined as follows. Imagine an axis s that is perpendicular to the separating planes σ of the slices and that goes through the projection center C. It can be interpreted as the axis of a pencil of planes (ν). Each ribbon is confined by a sector that is defined by two planes of the pencil. For the determination of the priority between two ribbons R_i and R_j, we distinguish between two cases:

1. The two corresponding sectors do not overlap. Then the priority between R_i and R_j is of no importance.

2. The sectors overlap. Then both of the rings have a set of vertices *inside the common sector*. For these sets we determine the maximum distances from

FIGURE 5. Examples of sliced surfaces.

the projection center. The ring with greater maximum distance has to be plotted first.

When we check all the priorities between the ribbons, we can put them into an order. Even though this way of sorting seems to be similar to the algorithms for the sorting of numbers, it is different. If you sort numbers, the negation of $n_j < n_i$ is, of course, $n_j \geq n_i$. In priority lists, the negation of "R_j prior to R_i" can either be "R_i prior to R_j" or "no priority between R_i and R_j." (This makes the sorting easier. On the other hand, if we have an array of sorted primitives it is no longer possible to reconstruct the priorities between them!) This is the reason why we occasionally get several priority lists, all of which are correct and which depend on the "starting position of the primitives" in the sorting algorithm.

Now that we know how to plot an individual slice, it is easy to render the whole surface. The plotting order of the slices is exactly the same as for the rendering of surfaces of revolution (Section 5.2).

5.4 Function Graphs

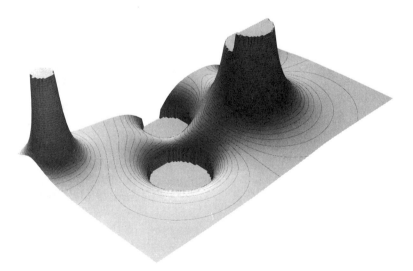

FIGURE 6. A function graph cut into slices that are parallel to the base plane.

As we mentioned in Section 3.6, function graphfunction graphs play an important part in the applied sciences. This is why many authors have dealt with the problem of the fast rendering of such surfaces. A frequent method of plotting the images of function graphs is to use the "floating horizon algorithm" ([ROGE85], [PLAS86]). However, this algorithm only works under certain conditions.

Function graphs can be cut into slices that are parallel to the base plane. This is a good idea, provided that the domain of definition is not a rectangle (Figure 6). It also depends on the kind of graph we want to render.

Let us assume that the domain of definition is a rectangle so that it is easy to slice the graph Γ by means of the planes σ and ψ, which are normal to the base plane β and parallel to the sides of the base rectangle. Now we will see how we can plot the image of the graph slice by slice in the correct order.

Let σ_0 and ψ_0 be the two "main normal planes" of the base plane and let them coincide with the projection center C (Figure 7). We have to distinguish between three different cases:

1. σ_0 and ψ_0 do not intersect the graph Γ. Then the image of Γ can be plotted as follows:

   The surface is cut into slices Σ which are separated by our planes σ. Thus, the drawing order for the slices is clear: we plot one slice after the other, starting off with the slice that has maximum distance from the plane σ_0. Each slice consists of a number of patches Ψ. These patches are separated by our planes ψ. Thus, the patches can also be plotted one after the other, starting off with the one that has the greatest distance from ψ_0.

   Each patch consists of two triangles, separated by a "diagonal plane" δ, which is orthogonal to the base plane β. (It is of no importance which of the two diagonal planes is chosen. The patch may even consist of more than two triangles.) The triangle that is not in the same halfspace as the projection center has to be plotted first.

   Since the separating planes σ, ψ and δ appear as straight lines in the normal projection on the base plane β, the priority determination is only two-dimensional. Therefore, it can be done very fast.

2. One of the two planes (σ_0 or ψ_0) intersects Γ. Then Γ is divided into two parts Γ_1 and Γ_2 plus a "critical slice" Σ_0 (i.e., the slice that is intersected by σ_0 or ψ_0). The plane acts as a separating plane between Γ_1 and Γ_2. Because its image is a straight line, the images of Γ_1 and Γ_2 will not intersect each other and each of the two parts of the graphs can be rendered separately like in case 1. At the end, we render Σ_0. Its image will obscure some parts of Γ_1 and Γ_2.

3. The two main normal planes σ_0 and ψ_0 intersect the graph Γ. Now Γ is split into four graphs Γ_i ($i = 1, \ldots, 4$) plus four critical slices Σ_i plus a critical patch Ψ_0. The images of Γ_i will never overlap because σ_0 and ψ_0 are separating planes, the images of which are straight lines. Thus, we can render the images of Γ_i separately like in case 1. Then we render the critical

slices Σ_i in an arbitrary order (their images will not overlap either, even though they will obscure some parts of the graphs Γ_i). Finally, we plot the patch Ψ_0, which may obscure some parts of Σ_i.

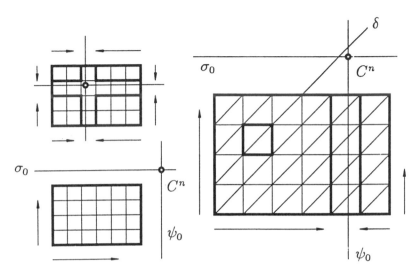

FIGURE 7. How to plot a function graph that is sliced perpendicularly to the base plane.

5.5 Priority Among Objects

Up to now, we have dealt with single polyhedra, which may consist of an arbitrary number of faces. In this section, we will learn how to determine the priority between two polyhedra (if this is possible). In Section 5.6, we will determine the priority lists of several objects.

Let A and B be two polyhedra that can be separated by a plane σ. (This means that A and B do not intersect and that neither of them surrounds the other one). We want to know which polyhedron has to be plotted first in order to get correct visibility.

For reasons of speed, the priority test will be made in several steps:

Step 1: Check the bounding rectangles (Figure 8).

Do the bounding rectangles overlap? If not, it does not matter whether we plot A first or B. (This is the easiest priority decision possible and the most convenient result for the priority list.) If the bounding rectangles overlap, continue with Step 2.

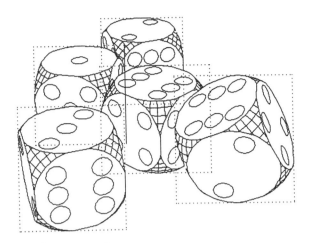

FIGURE 8. Bounding rectangles.

Step 2: Determine the priority by means of depth-comparisons or separating planes.

Is the maximum z-value of A smaller than the minimum z-value of B so that A has to be plotted first?

If not, it is a good idea to check whether specific spheres that contain the objects intersect (Figure 9). Such a "soap bubble" around an object may be a sphere with the barycenter of the object M as its center and with the greatest distance from M to the vertices as its minimal radius r. The two soap bubbles around A and B do not intersect if $\overline{M_A M_B} > r_A + r_B$. In this case, the priority between A and B is the same as the priority between their soap bubbles, which can be determined simply by comparing the depths (the z-values in the corresponding systems) of their centers.

If the soap bubble test does not work because the distance between the centers is too small, we try to use a separating plane that divides the space into two halfspaces, one of them containing A, the other one containing B (Figure 1). The existence of at least one separating plane σ is a fundamental condition for the use of the painter's algorithm. (In Section 5.8, we will see how we can find σ.) The polyhedron that is completely in the halfspace that does not contain the projection center has to be plotted first.

The methods we discussed in Step 2 are very useful for the quick determination of priority. They have, however, some disadvantages:

– Sometimes it is hard to find a separating plane (Section 5.8).

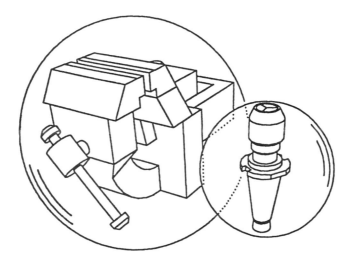

FIGURE 9. "Soap bubble test."

– When the outlines of the polyhedra do not really intersect (which may occur even when the bounding rectangles overlap), the result may be useless for the priority list. This means that if the images of A and B do not overlap, and if we assign a priority between A and B in spite of that, this may lead to a contradiction in the priority list ("Gordian knot" – see Section 5.6).

– Even though the above-mentioned tests are fast in checking the priority, they can produce longer computation times later on (especially when we plot shadows). Consider the following (rather common) case: the object A is completely obscured by B. The priority test in Step 2 only tells you that A has to be plotted first. Therefore, the computer will spend some time plotting A, but in the end, the image of A will be erased!

Thus, in the following three cases, we have to go one step further:

– We were not able to find a separating plane between A and B.

– A "Gordian knot" has occurred during a first test.

– The second object that is to be plotted is solid and may obscure the one that is plotted first.

Step 3: Intersect the outlines (the images of the contour polygon).

When intersecting the outlines, we have to distinguish between three different cases:

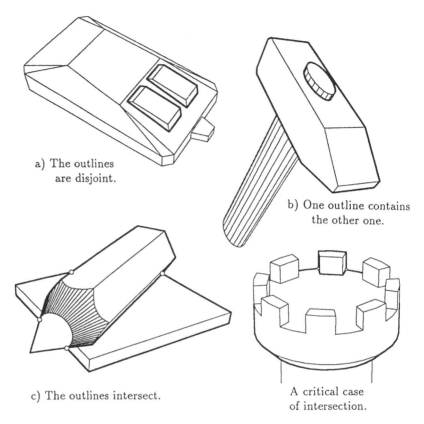

a) The outlines
are disjoint.

b) One outline contains
the other one.

c) The outlines intersect.

A critical case
of intersection.

FIGURE 10. Intersection of the outlines of two polyhedra.

1. The outlines are disjoint (Figure 10a), so that the drawing order of A and B is of no importance.

2. The outlines intersect (Figure 10b). Any of the intersection points in the image plane π can be interpreted as the image of a point P on the spatial contour of A or as the image of a point Q on the spatial contour of B. The distances of the two space points from the image plane π (the z-values in the screen system) may be p_z and q_z. According to the considerations in Section 2.3 (Equation 21), we transform these values into

$$p_z^* = \frac{p_z}{d - p_z}, q_z^* = \frac{q_z}{d - q_z}. \tag{1}$$

If $p_z^* < q_z^*$, the object A has to be plotted first, otherwise B has to be plotted before A.

3. The outline of A contains the outline of B or vice versa (Figure 10c). If we were not able to make a priority decision in Step 2, this case is

a bit inconvenient. (One might think that it is enough to compare the z-values of the barycenters of the objects. In most cases this will work, and yet there are examples where it won't.)

Consider a plane δ that is determined by the projection center C, an arbitrary vertex P on the spatial contour polygon of A and an arbitrary vertex Q on the contour polygon of B. This plane will intersect the spatial contour of A in a second intersection point $\overline{P}$. The line $P\overline{P}$ and the projection ray CQ both lie on δ and they will intersect in a point $\overline{Q}$. If we compare the z-values q_z^*, $\overline{q}_z^*$ of Q and $\overline{Q}$ (modified by Equation 21), we can determine the priority (if we have $q_z^* > \overline{q}_z^*$, the image of B has to be plotted first).

If the outline of the second object that is to be plotted contains the outline of the other one and if this obscuring object is convex (and therefore, solid), the priority between A and B is of no importance. This will simplify the generation of the priority list and, what is more, the obscured object does not have to be plotted at all!

Before we list the code for a C function that returns the priority of two objects A and B, we have to give the definition of a "halfspace":

```
#define NOT_FOUND 0
#define USE_SOAP_BUBBLES 2
typedef struct { /* Halfspace*/
    Vector normal; /* Normal to defining plane. */
    float cnst;
            /* Dot product of the normal vector and the position vector of the
            point on the plane. */
    short info;
        /* This structure member contains some additional information: info =
            NOT_FOUND: The plane was not to be found.
            info = ±1: The first of the two objects that are to be compared lies
                on the positive/negative side of the plane.
            info = USE_SOAP_BUBBLES: Do not use the halfspace for priority
                decisions. The distance between the objects is big enough for
                the "soap bubble test" (Figure 9), which – in this case – will
                also be more reliable.
        */
} Halfspace;                                                    (→ Types.h)
```

Now we extend the definition of a **Polyhedron** by some additional variables:

```
    Halfspace *sep_plane;
        /* Separating planes are used as an efficient tool for the determination
            of the priority of two objects when their images overlap. */
    short sep_start;
        /* Indicates the first separating plane of the object. */
```

float *max_rad*;

> /* This variable equals the radius of the smallest possible sphere that circumscribes the polyhedron (with the barycenter as its center). */

Vector *∗bounding_box*;

> /* This array of vectors stores the coordinates of the eight vertices of a rectangular box that circumscribes the polyhedron in the world system (usually the sides of the box are parallel with the coordinate planes, but this does not always have to be the case). */

Vector *∗box_min, ∗box_max*;

> /* Every image of an object (polyhedron) has a so-called "bounding rectangle," which is determined by the minimum screen coordinates and the maximum screen coordinates. The first two coordinates of *box_min*[*SCREEN_SYST*] and *box_max*[*SCREEN_SYST*] are reserved for these values. The z-values equal the minimum and the maximum distances from the projection plane in the screen system. What we said about the "bounding box" in the screen system is also true for bounding boxes in the various light systems. Thus, *box_min*[*LIGHT_SYST* 1] and *box_max*[*LIGHT_SYST* 1] store the minimum and the maximum values of this box in the first light system, and so forth. */

short *∗size_of_contour*;

> /* The polyhedron has a (spatial) contour in the screen system and in the light systems. The number of the vertices on each contour is stored in this array. */

Vector *∗∗∗contour*;

> /* Relax. It's just three stars, that's all. *∗contour*[k] is an array of pointers to the vertices on the (spatial) contour line of the polyhedron in the k-th system (*SCREEN_SYST*,...). Thus, *∗∗*(*contour*[k] + n) is the n-th point on the contour line in the same system. */

Ubyte *obscured*[*MAX_SYSTEMS*];

> /* When an object is completely hidden (shadowed) by other objects in the k-th system, we let *obscured*[k] = *TRUE*. */

Now to the desired function: it can be used for priority tests in the screen system as well as in the light systems. (Priority in a light system means: does A cast a shadow on B, or B cast a shadow on A, or do neither of them cast shadows?)

#**define** *NOT_FOUND* 0		(→ `Macros.h`)
#**define** *USE_SOAP_BUBBLES* 2		(→ `Macros.h`)
#**define** *NONE* *MAX_UBYTE*		(→ `Macros.h`)

```
#define Is_closer(obj) {\                                    (local macro)
    first = obj->index;\
    if (critical) goto intersect_outlines;\³
    else return first;\
}
#define DISJOINT 1                                         (→ Macros.h)
#define INTERSECTION 2                                     (→ Macros.h)
#define POLY2_INSIDE_POLY1 3                               (→ Macros.h)
#define POLY1_INSIDE_POLY2 4                               (→ Macros.h)
```

```
Ubyte which_obj_is_first(obj1, obj2, syst, critical)        (→ Proto.h)
    register Polyhedron * obj1, *obj2;
    short syst; /* Screen system or light systems. */
    Bool critical; /* Without or with separating planes. */
{   /* begin which_obj_is_first() */
    register Vector * min1, *max1, *min2, *max2;
    float z[2];
    Halfspace * sep_plane;
    Ubyte first = NONE;

    if (obj1->obscured[syst] || obj2->obscured[syst])
        return NONE;
    /* Do the bounding rectangles overlap? */
    min1 = obj1->box_min + syst; max1 = obj1->box_max + syst;
    min2 = obj2->box_min + syst; max2 = obj2->box_max + syst;

    if (!overlap(min1, max1, min2, max2))
        return NONE; /* Bounding rectangles do not overlap! */

    if ((*min1)[Z] > (*max2)[Z])
        { Is_closer(obj1); }
    else if ((*min2)[Z] > (*max1)[Z])
        { Is_closer(obj2); }


    /* Next step: try with separating planes. */
```

---

[3]The use of statement labels is generally frowned upon in high-level programming languages because they make programs hard to maintain. Of course, one does not have to use them. Sometimes, however, it is both easier and faster to use the **goto**-statement because it can help to avoid a lot of conditional branching in a routine.

```
sep_plane  =  obj1->sep_plane + obj2->index;
if (sep_plane->info == USE_SOAP_BUBBLES) {
    if (average_dist(obj1, syst) < average_dist(obj2, syst))
        { Is_closer(obj1); }
    else
        { Is_closer(obj2); }
} else  if (sep_plane->side! = NOT_FOUND) {
    if (Which_side(Proj_center[syst], *sep_plane) == sep_plane->info)
        { Is_closer(obj1); }
    else
        { Is_closer(obj2); }
}  /* end if (sep_plane) */
```

/* Final decision: we intersect the convex hulls and compare the z-values of
    the two space points that correspond to the first intersection point. */

intersect_outlines :

```
switch (relative_pos_of_hulls(z,
            obj1->size_of_contour[syst], obj1->contour[syst],
            obj2->size_of_contour[syst], obj2->contour[syst], syst)) {
    case INTERSECTION : /* Take the nearest point. */
        if (z[0] > z[1]) return obj1->index;
        else return obj2->index;
    case POLY2_INSIDE_POLY1 :
        if (first == obj1->index && Is_convex(obj1)) {
            obj2->obscured[syst] = TRUE;
            if (syst == SCREEN_SYST)
                return NONE;
            else return first;
        }
        if (first == NONE) {
            if (point_behind_polygon) return obj1->index;
            else return obj2->index;
        }
        return first;
    case POLY1_INSIDE_POLY2 :
        if (first == obj2->index && Is_convex(obj2)) {
            obj1->obscured[syst] = TRUE;
            if (syst == SCREEN_SYST)
                return NONE;
            else return first;
        } /* end if (first) */
        if (first == NONE) {
            if (point_behind_polygon) return obj2->index;
            else return obj1->index;
        } /* end if (first) */
        return first;
    case DISJOINT :
        return NONE;
} /* end switch() */
} /* end which_obj_is_first() */
```

Bool *overlap*(*min*1, *max*1, *min*2, *max*2)   ($\rightarrow$ Proto.h)
   register Vector $*min1, *max1, *min2, *max2$;
{   /* begin *overlap*() */
   if (($*min1$)[X] > ($*max2$)[X] || ($*max1$)[X] < ($*min2$)[X] ||
      ($*min1$)[Y] > ($*max2$)[Y] || ($*max1$)[Y] < ($*min2$)[Y])
        return *FALSE*;
   else return *TRUE*;
}   /* end *overlap*() */

---

float *average_dist*(*obj*, *syst*)   ($\rightarrow$ Proto.h)
   Polyhedron $* obj$;
   short *syst*;
{   /* begin *average_dist*() */
   Vector *r*;

   Subt_vec(*r*, $*obj \rightarrow barycenter$, *Proj_center*[*syst*]);
   return *Dot_product*(*r*, *r*);   /* We do not need the *sqrt*(). */
}   /* end *average_dist*() */

5.6 Final Priority List

In Section 5.3, we developed a sorting algorithm for "ribbons." This algorithm can also be used for the sorting of objects. First we determine the priorities among our n objects with the indices $0, \ldots, n-1$, which takes $\frac{n(n-1)}{2}$ comparisons. Our goal is now to create a list *order*$[0 .. n-1]$, in which we store the indices of the objects in the same order in which they have to be plotted. This list need not be unequivocal.

To create the list quickly, we start the recursive "mikado algorithm",[4] which resolves the scene in quite a natural manner. We select those k objects that are not obscured by any other objects (the "front objects") and add them at the end of our list. Now the number of objects to be sorted is reduced to $\overline{n} = n - k$. If it is impossible to select an object, we have a "Gordian knot" and priority sorting is impossible, too. In such a case, we have to split up some of the critical objects. If sorting is possible, we lower the end of the list to *order*$[\overline{n}]$. Among the residual

---

[4]Named after the "Mikado" game: several dozens of thin, painted sticks are thrown in a random pile on a table. The players have to pick up as many sticks as possible without moving any of the other sticks.

objects, we will again find objects that are not obscured by any other residual objects. Their indices have to be put at the lowered end of the priority list, etc. The algorithm is repeated until no more objects are to be sorted.

The mikado algorithm can be accelerated when we apply it twice (from the front and from the back):

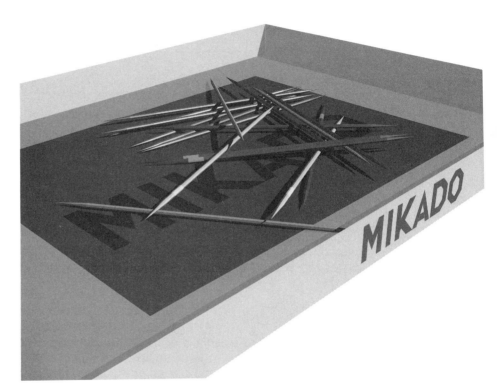

FIGURE 11. When we try to solve the "mikado"-puzzle we first remove the sticks that have no influence on the scene. Thus, we simplify the scene in a similar manner as the "mikado algorithm."

We select the k_1 front objects that are not obscured by any other objects. As usual, we place these objects at the end of our priority list. Furthermore, we pick those k_2 objects that do not obscure any other objects. These "back objects" come first on the list. Now there are only $\bar{n} = n - k_1 - k_2$ residual objects to be sorted. The recursion is finished when no more residual objects are to be sorted. It has to be stopped when no front objects or back objects can be found among the residual objects. In this case, we get a certain number of objects with a Gordian knot. (Imagine a scene of 50 objects where sorting is impossible just because three of the objects form a Gordian knot. The mikado algorithm will most probably stop when we only have a few residual objects, among which are the critical ones. Thus, it will be easy to isolate the critical objects and to split them. A message like "Cannot sort your 50 objects – try to split the scene!" would not be very helpful...)

A pseudo-code of the algorithm may look like this:

Determine priorities among the n given objects
Residual objects := given objects
i_min := 0, i_max := n

repeat
   select k_1 front objects and k_2 back objects among residual objects
   if $k_1 > 0 \land k_2 > 0$
       store indices of front objects at
                $order[i\_max - k_2] \ldots order[i\_max - 1]$
       store indices of back objects at
                $order[i\_min] \ldots order[i\_min + k_1 - 1]$
       i_min := $i\_min + k_1$
       i_max := $i\_max - k_2$
       residual objects := residual objects minus
                front objects minus back objects
   else
       error message "Gordian knot"
   endif
until no more residual objects $\lor$ Gordian knot

Before we can do the sorting, we have to determine all the priorities among the objects. The function *priorities()* is written in a flexible manner so that it can be used for different systems (screen system, light systems) and for arbitrary sets of objects (e.g., object groups).

```
void priorities(n, given_obj, syst, critical)                    (→ Proto.h)
    short  n; /* Number of objects. */
    Polyhedron *given_obj[ ]; /* Array of pointers to objects. */
    short  syst; /* Screen system, light systems. */
    Bool critical; /* Can we rely on separating planes? */
{   /* begin priorities() */
    register Polyhedron **obj1, **obj2;
    Polyhedron **hi_obj = given_obj + n;
    register Ubyte *pr1;
    register short  i1;
    staticBool priority_allocated = FALSE;
    if (!priority_allocated) {
        Polyhedron *obj;
        short i; /* Used within macro. */
        for (obj = Object_pool;  obj < Object_pool + n;  obj1++)
            Alloc_2d_array(Ubyte, obj->priority, Total_systems, Total_objects);
        priority_allocated = TRUE;
    } /* end if (priority_allocated) */
```

```
        for (obj1 = given_obj;  obj1 < hi_obj;  obj1++) {
          i1 = (*obj1)->index;
          pr1 = (*obj1)->priority[syst];
          for (obj2 = obj1 + 1;  obj2 < hi_obj;  obj2++) {
            pr1[(*obj2)->index] = (*obj2)->priority[syst][i1] =
                which_obj_is_first(*obj1, *obj2, syst, critical);
          } /* end for (obj2...) */
        } /* end for (obj1...) */
      } /* end priorities() */
```

Now we can sort the objects by means of the mikado algorithm.

Bool *sort_objects*(*order*, *n*, *given_obj*, *critical*)

($\rightarrow$ `Proto.h`)

register Ubyte *order*[ ]; /* Probable result (indices of objects). */
short   *n*; /* Number of objects. Note that the sorting algorithm runs in
            quadratic time with *n*. */
Polyhedron **given_obj*[ ]; /* Array of pointers to objects. */
Bool *critical*; /* Can we rely on separating planes? */
{   /* begin *sort_objects*() */
register short *i*, *j*;
register Polyhedron ***obj*;
static Ubyte ***prior* = *NULL*;[5]
        /* This is an array of pointers in which we store all the priorities. Because
          it may vary in size, we allocate it dynamically with its maximum size.
          */
static Polyhedron ***res_obj*;
        /* This is an array of pointers to the residual objects. It is allocated at
          the same time as *prior*. */
static Bool **is_in_front*, **is_in_back*;
        /* Arrays that indicate whether an object is a front object, a back object
          or neither of the two. */
Ubyte *i_min*, *i_max*, *i1*, *i2*, *k*;
if (*prior* == *NULL*) {
    Alloc_ptr_array(**Ubyte**, *prior*, *Total_objects*, "prior");
    Alloc_ptr_array(**Polyhedron**, *res_obj*, *Total_objects*, "res");
    Alloc_array(**Bool**, *is_in_front*, *Total_objects*, "front";
    Alloc_array(**Bool**, *is_in_back*, *Total_objects*, "back";
}
for (*i* = 0, *obj* = *given_obj*; *i* < *n*; *i*++, *obj*++) {
    prior[(*obj*)->*index*] = (*obj*)->*priority*[*SCREEN_SYST*];
    res_obj[*i*] = *obj*;
}

[5]**Static** variables help to avoid unnecessary global variables. A trick to declare
the size of arrays dynamically is to preinitialize the pointer to the array by *NULL*.

```
/* Mikado algorithm. */
i_min = 0;  i_max = k = n;
while (k) {
    if (!mikado_select(is_in_front, is_in_back, k, res_obj, prior)) {
        if (critical) {
            Print("Gordian knot while sorting the objects\n");
            for (i = 0;  i < k;  i++) {
                order[i_min + i] = res_obj[i]->index;
                fprintf(Output, "%s ", res_obj[i]->name);
            }  /* end for (i) */
            Print("Next time try to split some of these objects");
        }  /* end if (critical) */
        return FALSE; /* If not critical, we have another try! */
    }  /* end if (mikado_select) */
    k = 0;  i1 = i_min;  i2 = i_max;
    for (i = i1, obj = res_obj;  i < i2;  i++, obj++) {
        j = (*obj)->index;
        if (is_in_back[j])
            order[i_min++] = j;
        else if  (is_in_front[j])
            order[--i_max] = j;
        else
            res_obj[k++] = *obj;
    }  /* end for (i) */
}  /* end while (k) */
return TRUE;
}  /* end sort_objects() */
```

The Boolean function *mikado_select*() determines all the objects that either do not obscure any other objects or that are not obscured by any other objects. It returns *FALSE* if sorting is not possible.

```
Bool mikado_select(is_in_front, is_in_back, n, res_obj, prior)   (→ Proto.h)
    Bool is_in_front[ ], is_in_back[ ];
    short n; /* Number of objects. */
    Polyhedron * res_obj[ ]; /* Pointer to objects. */
    Ubyte * prior[ ]; /* Pointers to priority list. */
{   /* begin mikado_select() */
    register Polyhedron **obj, **obj2, **hi_obj  = res_obj + n;
    Ubyte * prior1;
    Ubyte i, j;
    for (obj = res_obj;  obj < hi_obj;  obj ++) {
```

```
            i = (*obj)->index;
            is_in_front[i] = is_in_back[i] = TRUE;
    }
    for (obj = res_obj;  obj < hi_obj;  obj ++) {
        i = (*obj)->index;
        prior1  = prior[i];
        for (obj2 = res_obj;  obj2 < hi_obj;  obj2 ++) {
            if (*obj == *obj2) continue;
            j = (*obj2)->index;
            if (prior1[j] == i) {
                is_in_back[i] = FALSE;
                if (!is_in_front[i]) break;
            } else if (prior1[j] == j) {
                is_in_front[i] = FALSE;
                if (!is_in_back[i]) break;
            }  /* end if (prior1) */
        }  /* end for (obj2) */
    }  /* end for (obj) */
    /* Check whether search was successful. */
    for (obj = res_obj;  obj < hi_obj;  obj ++) {
        i = (*obj)->index;
        if (is_in_front[i] || is_in_back[i])
            return  TRUE;
    }  /* end for (obj) */
    return FALSE;
}  /* end mikado_select() */
```

For the correct rendering of the scene, we now simply have to call the function

```
void sort_and_render_objects()                              (→ Proto.h)
{   /* begin sort_and_render_objects() */
    short  i;
    static Ubyte *order = NULL;
    static Polyhedron **obj_ptr;
        /* Array of pointers to objects. */
    Bool critical, success;
    if (order == NULL) { /* Initialize before drawings. */
        Alloc_array(Ubyte, order, Total_objects, "sort");
        Alloc_ptr_array(Polyhedron, obj_ptr, Total_objects, "ptr");
        for (i = 0; i < Total_objects; i++)
            obj_ptr[i] = &Object_pool[i];
    }
```

```
  for (critical = FALSE; ; critical = TRUE) {
      priorities(Total_objects, obj_ptr, SCREEN_SYST, critical);
      success = sort_objects(order, Total_objects, obj_ptr, critical);
      if (success || critical)
          break;
  }
  if (!success) {
      Print("Bad visibility test!\n");
      Print("The drawing order may be wrong!\n");
  }
  /* Plot entire scene. */
  for (i = 0;  i < Total_objects;  i++)
      plot_object(obj_ptr[order[i]]);
}   /* end sort_and_render_objects() */
```

5.7 The Creation of Object Groups

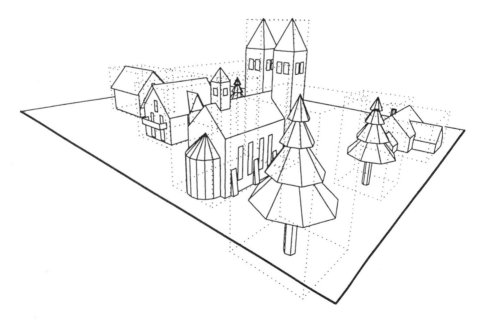

FIGURE 12. A scene that consists of several object groups.

The algorithm we described in Section 5.6 only works for "objects," i.e., polyhedra. Once a scene gets more complicated, the number of objects will of course
increase. The sorting time, however, runs in quadratic time with the number of

objects. Therefore, it is a good idea to check whether it is possible to combine several objects in an "object group."

The scene in Figure 12, for example, consists of several groups of simple polyhedra. Instead of checking the priority of each pair of polyhedra, we can determine a priority list of the groups and then plot the scene group by group. For scenes with lots of objects ($Total\_objects > 50$), this can mean an enormous increase of speed in the sort algorithm.

Two questions, however, remain:

1. Is it always possible to arrange the objects in groups that can be separated by planes? (Which is the prerequisite for the painter's algorithm.)

2. Is it always possible to sort the groups?

The answer to the first question is yes, if we allow a group to consist of only one object as well (in the worst case, we declare each object as a new group). Nevertheless, the creation of object groups will only reduce calculation time when there is a reasonable proportion between the number of groups and the number of objects.

The answer to the second question is no. Even if we have arranged the objects of our scene in groups that can be separated from each other, it may happen that we have to undo a "Gordian knot." The reason for this is that it is hard to find out whether the images of two groups are disjoint, even if their bounding rectangles overlap. The creation of object groups can still be a great advantage in such a case. If the polyhedra $\{A_i\}$ are elements of one group and the polyhedra $\{B_j\}$ elements of another group, and if we know the priority between these two groups, all the priorities (A_i, B_j) are determined automatically. In a few cases, however, this can be a dead end. As we have said, it is sometimes necessary to make use of the fact that between two objects there is *no* priority because their images are disjoint. (Otherwise we might try to undo a "Gordian knot.") In these few cases, we have to do the sorting without the use of object groups.

5.8   Bounding Boxes and Separating Planes

Throughout this chapter we have seen that "bounding boxes" and "separating planes" play an important part in the determination of priority lists. In this section, we want to describe in detail how bounding boxes and separating planes between disjoint convex sets can be found. Because the objects of our scene will generally keep their relative positions, these calculations can be done before starting the animator and have to be adapted once an object of the scene is animated separately.

Let us develop a code for the determination of a bounding box. This array of vectors stores the coordinates of the eight vertices of a rectangular box that circumscribes the object in the world system. In the most convenient case, the sides of the box are parallel to the coordinate axes. To keep the volume of the box as small as possible, it is a good idea to calculate the box immediately after the object has been defined and before it is manipulated by means of rotations:

#define *EPS1* 1e-4 ($\rightarrow$ Macros.h)

```
void bounding_box(box, n, v)                           (→ Proto.h)
    Vector box[8]; /* Into this array we write the result. */
    short  n; /* Number of points. */
    register Vector v[ ]; /* Arbitrary set of points. */
{   /* begin bounding_box() */
    Vector m[2]; /* Space for two Vectors. */
    Vector *min = m, *max = m + 1; /* For the argument lists. */
    short  i;
    min_max_vec_of_pool(min, max, n, v);
    /* Make sure that none of the coordinate differences is too small. This can
        only happen when all the points are on a plane that is parallel to a
        coordinate plane. The result could be an ambiguity in the priority test
        and – in the worst case – a division by zero later on. */
    for (i = 0; i < 3; i++)
        if (Is_zero((*max)[i] − (*min)[i])) {
            (*min)[i] −= EPS1; (*max)[i] += EPS1;
        } /* end if */
    create_coord_box(box, min, max);
}   /* end bounding_box() */
```

For the result, we needed two functions that are useful in other parts of the code as well. First we calculate the minimum and maximum coordinates.

```
#define Min_max(min, max, x)\                          (→ Macros.h)
    if (x < min) min = x;\
    else if (x > max) max = x;
#define Min_max_vec(min_v, max_v, v) {\                (→ Macros.h)
    Min_max((min_v)[X], (max_v)[X], (v)[X]);\
    Min_max((min_v)[Y], (max_v)[Y], (v)[Y]);\
    Min_max((min_v)[Z], (max_v)[Z], (v)[Z]);\
}
```

```
void min_max_vec_of_pool(min, max, n, v)               (→ Proto.h)
    register Vector *min, *max; /* Pointers[6] to the result. */
```

[6]The first two arguments of the function are **pointers** to **Vectors**. We can also pass **Vectors**, because the corresponding function only takes the *address* of the first element in the array. For superior style, however, we should pass a **Vector** *v* as (**Vector** *) *v* in this case.

```
        short  n; /* Number of vectors. */
        register Vector *v; /* Array of vectors. */
{   /* begin min_max_vec_of_pool() */
        register Vector *hi_v = v + n;
        Copy_vec(*min, *v); Copy_vec(*max, *v);
        for (v++; v < hi_v; v++)
            Min_max_vec(*min, *max, *v);
}   /* end min_max_vec_of_pool() */
```

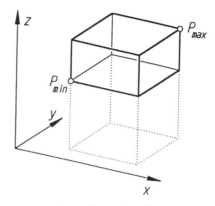

FIGURE 13. How to create a "coordinate box."

Next we create a box, the sides of which are parallel to the coordinate axes. It is given by the minimum and the maximum coordinates, i.e., the coordinates of two opposite vertices of the box (Figure 13):

```
void create_coord_box(box, min, max)                           (→ Proto.h)
        register Vector box[8];
        register Vector *min, *max;
{   /* begin create_coord_box() */
        register Vector *hi_box = box + 8;
        staticUbytecorner[8][3] = { 0,0,0, 1,0,0, 1,1,0, 0,1,0, 0,0,1, 1,0,1, 1,1,1,
        0,1,1};
        register Ubyte *c = (Ubyte *) corner;
        for ( ; box < hi_box; box++) }
            (*box)[X] = (*c++ ? (*max) : (*min))[X];
            (*box)[Y] = (*c++ ? (*max) : (*min))[Y];
            (*box)[Z] = (*c++ ? (*max) : (*min))[Z];
        } /* end for */
}   /* end create_coord_box() */
```

Now let us see how we can use bounding boxes for the determination of a separating plane between two objects:

Let O_1 and O_2 be two (convex or not convex) objects with the bounding boxes B_1 and B_2. Each box has eight vertices and six faces. The planes of each face will not intersect the corresponding object and are, therefore, potential separating planes. Thus, we will do the following:

We take the first face of B_1 and find out on which side of the face the object O_1 lies. (This is done by checking *one* vertex of O_1 that is not on the plane of the face.) If all the vertices of O_2 are on the opposite side of O_1, we have found a separating plane. Otherwise we continue the search with the other faces of B_1.[7] If none of the faces of B_1 is a separating plane, we continue the search with the faces of B_2.

If that does not work either and if none of the objects are convex, we give up. (Separating planes are a good tool to speed up the program, but they are not necessary for the priority algorithm.) If O_1 and/or O_2 are convex, we may continue our search for a separating plane. Each plane of a face of a convex object is a potential separating plane!

```
void sep_plane_between_obj(s, obj1, obj2)                        (→ Proto.h)
    Halfspace * s;
    Polyhedron * obj1, *obj2;
{   /* begin sep_plane_between_obj() */
    Halfspace * plane, *hi_plane;
    Vector dist, *normal;
    short side;
    float cnst;
    Polyhedron * temp; /* Used in the Swap macro. */
    Face * f, *hi_f;
    register Vector * v;
    Vector * lo_vec, *hi_v;


    /*  When the soap bubbles that contain the objects do not intersect, it is
        neither necessary nor useful to calculate a separating plane. */

    Subt_vec(dist, *obj1->barycenter, *obj2->barycenter);
    if  (Length(dist) > (obj1->max_rad + obj2->max_rad)) {
        s->info = USE_SOAP_BUBBLES;
        return ;
    }
```

[7]Note that the test also works for objects with only one face (i.e., simple polygons), because the bounding box is a little removed from the polygon's plane.

/* In many cases, the faces of the bounding boxes are themselves separating planes. */

```
for  (side  =  1; side  >=  −1; side − = 2) {
    hi_plane = (plane = Sep_pool + obj1−>sep_start) + 6;
    hi_v = (lo_vec = obj2−>bounding_box) + 8;
    for( ; plane < hi_plane; plane++) {
        normal  = (Vector ∗) plane−>normal;
        cnst  =  plane−>cnst + 0.005 ∗ fabs(plane−>cnst);
            /∗  This is a certain tolerance we should admit for inaccurate
                calculations that might occur. ∗/
        for  (v =  lo_vec; v < hi_v; v++)
            if  (Dot_product(∗normal, ∗v)  >  cnst) break;
        if  (v == hi_v) {
            ∗ s  = ∗plane;
            s−>info =  side;
            return ;
        }  /∗ end if (v) ∗/
    }  /∗ end for (plane) ∗/
    Swap(obj1,  obj2);
}  /∗ end for (side) ∗/
```

/* We still have a chance of finding separating planes, but only if at least one of the two objects has a convex outline! Then any of its faces might be a separating plane. */

```
for  (side  =  −1; side  <=  1; side + = 2) {
    if  ((Is_convex(obj1) || obj1−>geom_property  ==  HOLLOW)
            && obj1−>no_of_faces  >  1) {
        hi_f  =  (f = obj1−>faces) + obj1−>no_of_faces;
        hi_v = (lo_vec = obj2−>vertices) + obj2−>no_of_vertices;
        for  ( ; f < hi_f; f++) {
            normal  = (Vector ∗) f−>normal;
            cnst  =  f−>cnst;
            for  (v = lo_vec; v < hi_v; v++)
                if  (Dot_product(∗normal, ∗v)  <  cnst) break;
            if  (v  ==  hi_v) {
                Copy_vec(s−>normal, ∗normal);
                s−>cnst =  cnst;
                s−>info =  side;
                return ;
            }  /∗ end if (v) ∗/
        }  /∗ end for (f) ∗/
    } /∗ end if (Is_convex) ∗/
    Swap(obj1,  obj2);
}  /∗ end for  (side) ∗/
s−>info  =  NOT_FOUND;
}  /∗ end sep_plane_between_obj() ∗/
```

6

Advanced Features

Nowadays, people are used to seeing perfect computer-generated images and even computer-generated movies of incredible realism. The gap between the products of professional computer graphics studios and the possibilities of less sophisticated graphics computers is enormous. Therefore, it is important to put an emphasis on the acceleration of programs that produce an acceptably realistic output.

In Chapter 5, we saw that the painter's algorithm is a powerful tool for the quick rendering of even complicated scenes. This algorithm must, of course, be used with our special object preprocessor, which splits objects according to their type.

One of the first to extend the painter's algorithm to the plotting of cast shadows was Crow [CROW77]. His ideas turned out to be very useful for scenes with comparatively few faces. In recent times, however, most people have preferred different algorithms like ray tracing or the radiosity method [GORA84, ROGE90] for this purpose. These algorithms work for any kind of scene and are also capable of doing reflections and transparencies (refractions). They have only one great disadvantage: they take a lot of computation time.

In this chapter, we will see that the painter's algorithm can be used to add shadows, simple reflections and refractions, without any major loss of time. To get perfect images of a scene, we can still use more sophisticated algorithms and shading models. We can call this program a "movie maker."

To fulfill our task in an efficient manner, we have to insert two important sections about convex hulls.

6.1 Convex Hulls

In Section 5.5, we had to intersect the outlines of two objects in order to determine which one was to be plotted first. An outline is nothing but the projection of the *contour polygon* of the object onto the image plane.

Let us first develop a function *spatial_hull*(), which determines all the contour edges of a polyhedron with convex outline.

Usually, a contour edge is the side that a frontface and a backface have in common. (When the object consists only of one single face, each side of the face is a contour edge.) Because we know the neighboring faces of each face, for each backface of the polyhedron, we just have to check whether it has neighboring frontfaces. If this is the case, the common edge of the two faces is stored. Note that the function works both in the screen system and in the light systems.

#define *Screen_to_light(v, n)* (*Light_pool*[n] + (v − *Screen_pool*))

($\rightarrow$ `Macros.h`)

```
void spatial_hull(obj, syst)                              (→ Proto.h)
    Polyhedron * obj; /* Polyhedron with convex outline. */
    short  syst; /* Screen system and light systems. */
{   /* begin spatial_hull() */
    register  short  i;
    register  Face  * f, *f1, *hi_f;
    static Edge edge_pool[MAX_POLY_SIZE];
    Edge * edge  =  edge_pool;
    Vector  * *contour[1]; /* Space for one pointer. */
    short  n, size;

    face_types(obj, syst);
    hi_f  =  (f =  obj->faces) + obj->no_of_faces;
    for  ( ; f < hi_f; f + +) {
        if  (f->darkface[syst]) continue;
        n  =  f->no_of_vertices;
        for  (i =  0; i <  n; i + +) {
            f1  =  (Face *) f->neighbor_faces[i];
            if  (f1  ==  NULL || f1->darkface[syst]) {
                edge->v1 =  Screen_to_light(f->vertices[i], syst);
                edge->v2 =  Screen_to_light(f->vertices[(i + 1)% n], syst);
                edge + +;
            }  /* end if (f1...) */
        }  /* end for (i...) */
    }  /* end for (f...) */
    n  =  edge − edge_pool;
    contour[0]  =  obj->contour[syst];
    concat_to_polygons(&n, &size, contour, n, edge_pool, TRUE);
    obj->size_of_contour[syst]  =  n  =  size − 1;
    orient_ptr_poly(n, contour[0]);
}   /* end spatial_hull() */
```

The function *spatial_hull*() calls a routine that connects the edges to a (closed) polygon. More generally, it is also able to connect sets of edges to several polygons. For example, the contour polygon of a polyhedron that is an approximation to a torus will consist of two (closed) branches.

```
Bool concat_to_polygons(no_of_branches, branch_size, branch,
                n, edge_pool, is_a_convex_contour)          (→ Proto.h)
    short   * no_of_branches;
    short   * branch_size;     /* Size of each solution curve. */
    Vector * * *branch;
    /* Pointer to an array of pointers to the vertices of the polygon. branch[0]
        has to be allocated outside the function! */

    short   n; /* Number of edges. */
    Edge *edge_pool; /* Given edges. */
    Bool is_a_convex_contour;
{   /* begin concat_to_polygons() */
    register  Edge  * edge;
    register  Vector  * succ;
    register  short  i, j;
    Vector * *v  =  branch[0], * * hi_v;
    Vector * start_point;
    short  side, k  =  0;

    * no_of_branches  =  1;
    if (n  ==  0) {
        branch_size[0]  =  0;
        return  FALSE;
    }  /* end if (n == 0) */
    while (n) {
        branch[k]  =  v;
        edge  =  edge_pool;
        * v + +  =  edge–>v1;
        * v + +  =  edge–>v2;
        edge_pool[0]  =  edge_pool[– –n];
            /* Replace first edge by last one. */
        branch_size[k]  =  2;
        hi_v  =  v +  2  * n;
        succ  =  branch[k][1];
        for (side  =  0; side  <  2; side + +) {
            start_point  =  branch[k][0];
            do {
                for (i = 0, edge  =  edge_pool; i <  n; i + +, edge + +)
                    if (edge–>v1 ==  succ) {
                        succ  =  edge–>v2;
                        break; /* Quit the loop for (i...). */
                    } else  if (edge–>v2 ==  succ) {
                        succ  =  edge–>v1;
                        break; /* Quit the loop for (i...). */
                    }  /* end if (edge–>v1...) */
                if (i ==  n)
                    succ  =  NULL;
```

```
            else  {
                if  (v >=  hi_v) {
                    Print("branch too long");
                    break; /* Quit the loop while (n). */
                } /* end if (v...) */
                *v++  =  succ;
                edge_pool[i]  =  edge_pool[--n];
                        /* Replace edge that has been found by last one. */
            } /* end if (i == n) */
        } while  (succ && n  >  0 && succ ! =  start_point);
        branch_size[k]  =  v - branch[k];
        if  (succ  ==  start_point) {    /* Closed polygon. */
            if  (is_a_convex_contour)
                return  TRUE;
            else
                break; /* Quit the loop for (side...). */
        } else  if  (is_a_convex_contour) {
            Print("Warning: contour is not closed");
            return  FALSE;
        } /* end if (succ == start_point) */

        if  (side  ==  0) {
            Vector  *temp, **b1, **b2;

            /* Since we will now search in the other direction we store the
                branch 'upside down.' */
            succ  =  start_point;
            b1  =  branch[k]; b2  =  b1  +  (branch_size[k] − 1);
            for  ( ;  b1  <  b2; b1++, b2 −−)
                Swap(*b1, *b2);
        } /* end if (side) */
    } /* end for (side) */
    k++;
} /* end while (n) */
*no_of_branches = k;
return  TRUE;
} /* end concat_to_polygons() */
```

For the intersection of two convex hulls, it is necessary that the contour polygon is oriented counterclockwise. This can be achieved by a routine *orient_ptr_poly*(). We check whether the area of a triangle that is given by three points of the polygon (with the indices $i_1 < i_2 < i_3$) is positive or not. If it is negative, we change the order of the vertices of the polygon.

```
#define  Area_of_2d_triangle(a, b, c)\                    (→ Macros.h)
    (a)[X] * (b)[Y] − (a)[Y] * (b)[X] + \
    (b)[X] * (c)[Y] − (b)[Y] * (c)[X] + \
    (c)[X] * (a)[Y] − (c)[Y] * (a)[X]
#define  SMALL_AREA 1e − 2                                (local macro)
```

```
void orient_ptr_poly(n, poly)                                    (→ Proto.h)
    short  n;
    register  Vector  * *poly;  /* Array of pointers. */
{   /* begin orient_ptr_poly() */
    register  Vector  * *p1  =  poly + 1, * * p2  =  poly + 2;
    Vector  * temp, * * hi_p2  =  poly + n − 1;
    float  area;
    short  orientation  =  0;

    for  (; p2 <= hi_p2; p1 + +, p2 + +)   {
        area  =  Area_of_2d_triangle(* * poly, * * p1, * * p2);
        if  (area >  SMALL_AREA)
            return ;   /* Polygon is oriented correctly (i.e., ccw). */
        else  if  (area < −SMALL_AREA)
            break;     /* Orientation must be switched. */
        else  {  /* Delay decision. */
            orientation + =  Sign(area);
            if  (p2  ==  hi_p2 && orientation  >= 0)
                return ; /* Obviously the polygon is very small.
                            However, it seems to be oriented correctly. */
        }  /* end if (area...) */
    }  /* end for (p2...) */
    /* Switch orientation. */
    p1  =  poly;  p2  =  hi_p2;
    for  (; p1 < p2; p1 + +, p2 −−)
        Swap(*p1, *p2);
}  /* end orient_ptr_poly() */
```

#**undef** *SMALL_AREA*

Of course, the determination of the spatial hull of an object works much faster than a general routine for the determination of the convex hull of an arbitrary set of points. Sometimes, however, such a routine can be useful. For this reason, we include the listing of a function *hull*(), which takes an array of n given points (**Vectors** or **Vector2**s) and which calculates the oriented convex outline.

In fact, such an algorithm is needed so frequently that many different approaches have been tried (some of them are described in [PURG89]). The algorithm we use is based on a recursive algorithm by Bykat [BYKA78]. Calculation time increases only linearly with the number of points, provided that the points are distributed homogeneously. We will not need any trigonometric functions.

Figure 1 illustrates the idea. In a) we determine the leftmost point L and the rightmost point R of all the given points. The connection LR between these two points divides the hull into two convex parts. For both these parts, we now start a

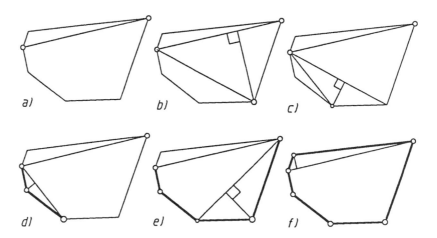

FIGURE 1. How to determine the convex hull of a set of points.

recursion: in *b*) we identify A with L and B with R and we determine the point C that has the maximum positive distance from the side AB (see Equation 1). The point C clearly belongs to the hull. Now C assumes the part of B. In *c*) the search for a point C is repeated until no other point with a positive distance is found. In *d*) the ultimate point C is concatenated with A and C assumes the part of A. In *e*) the recursion is started again. The algorithm comes to an end when there is no point left between B and R that has a positive distance. Now the lower chain is closed and in *f*) the algorithm is repeated for the upper chain.

Here is the code of the function *hull*():

typedef float Vec [ ];   ($\rightarrow$ `Types.h`)
    /* This is a "pseudo-type" which indicates that the variable can be either a **Vector** or a **Vector2**. Pointer arithmetic is not possible with this type, since **sizeof(Vec)** = 0! */
typedef struct {
    Vec *p; /* Pointer into *given_points*. */
    short *next*; /* Index of next point in *Point_chain*. */
} **P_ptr**;   ($\rightarrow$ `Types.h`)

                                                              (local macro)

#define *MAXP* 1000
static P_ptr *$*Point_chain[MAXP]$;

/* Local macros to make the code readable. */
#define $Idx(p)$ $(p - Point\_chain)$
#define $Next(p)$ $(Point\_chain[p\rightarrow next])$
#define $Is\_in\_chain(p)$ $(p >= Point\_chain)$
#define NO_MORE -1

```
void hull(size, result, n, given_points, dim)                    (→ Proto.h)
    short  *size; /* Number of points on the hull. */
    Vec  *result[ ]; /* Array of pointers to the vertices of the hull. The hull is
            oriented ccw.*/
    short  n; /* Number of given points. */
    Vec given_points[ ]; /* Vector2s or Vectors. */
    short  dim; /* 2D or 3D? */
{   /* begin hull() */
    register  float  *gp = (float *) given_points;
    register  short  i;
    float xmax, xmin, ymax, ymin;
    P_ptr *min, *max;
    P_ptr *residual;


    if (n > MAXP)
        Print("Too many points for convex hull\n"),
        n = MAXP;
    min = max = residual = Point_chain;
    for (i = 0; i < n; i++, gp += dim)
        Point_chain[i].next = i + 1,
        Point_chain[i].p    = (Vec *) gp;
    Point_chain[n − 1].next = NO_MORE;
    gp = (float *) given_points;
    /* Determine min and max. */
    xmax = xmin = gp[X]; ymax = ymin = gp[Y];
    for (i = 1, gp += dim; i < n; i++, gp += dim) {
        if (gp[X] < xmin)
            xmin = gp[X], min = &Point_chain[i];
        if (gp[X] > xmax)
            xmax = gp[X], max = &Point_chain[i];
        if (gp[Y] < ymin)
            ymin = gp[Y];
        if (gp[Y] > ymax)
            ymax = gp[Y];
    } /* end for (i) */
    /* Remove min and max. */
    if (Idx(min) == 0)
        residual++;
    else
        (min − 1)−>next = (Idx(min + 1) < n ?
                            Idx(min + 1) : (Idx(max) == 0 ? 1 : 0));
    if (max == min + 1) {
        if (Idx(min) == 0)
```

```
                    residual++;
            else
                    (max − 2)−>next = max−>next;
        } else  if  (Idx(max) == 0)
            residual++;
        else
                (max − 1)−>next = max−>next;
            *size = 0;
            divide_points(min, max, &residual, size, result, 2);
    }  /* end hull() */
```

This is the listing of the recursive function *divide_points*():

```
void divide_points(min, max, residual, size, result, sides)
                                                    (→ Proto.h)
    P_ptr *min, *max;
    P_ptr **residual;
    short  *size;
    Vec *result[ ];
    short  sides; /* Trace one or two sides. */
{   /* begin divide_points() */
    float max_neg_dist = 0, max_pos_dist = 0;
    P_ptr *lo, *hi;   /* Left and right points in residual. */
    P_ptr *p_min, *p_max; /* Points with max. (min.) distance. */
    P_ptr *p, *next_p;
    register float ax, ay, nx, ny, dist;

    lo = hi = p_min = p_max = NULL;
    p = *residual;
    /* Left or right? */
    nx = (*max−>p)[Y] − (ay = (*min−>p)[Y]);
    ny = (ax = (*min−>p)[X]) − (*max−>p)[X];
    while  (Is_in_chain(p)) {
        /* Distance of p from side. */
        dist = ((*p−>p)[X] − ax) * nx + ((*p−>p)[Y] − ay) * ny;
        next_p = Next(p);
        if (dist < EPS)  {
            if (dist < max_neg_dist)
                max_neg_dist = dist,
                p_min = p;
            p−>next = Idx(lo);
            lo = p;
        } else  {
            if (dist > max_pos_dist)
                max_pos_dist = dist,
                p_max = p;
            p−>next = Idx(hi);
            hi = p;
        }  /* end if (dist) */
        p = next_p;
    }  /* end while */
```

```
if  (!Is_in_chain(lo)) {
    /* No point on this side. */
    min->next  =  Idx(max);
    result[(*size)++]  =  max->p;
} else  if  (lo->next  ==  NO_MORE) {
    /* Insert the only point lo. */
    min->next  =  Idx(lo);
    lo->next  =  Idx(max);
    result[(*size)++]  =  lo->p;
    result[(*size)++]  =  max->p;
} else  {
    /* We are not ready yet (more than one point). */
    if  (lo  ==  p_min)
        lo  =  Next(lo);
    else  {
        p  =  lo;
        while  (Next(p) != p_min)
            p  =  Next(p);
        p->next  =  Next(p)->next;
    }  /* end if (lo) */
    p_min->next  =  NO_MORE;
    divide_points(min, p_min, &lo, size, result, 1);
    divide_points(p_min, max, &lo, size, result, 1);
    p  =  lo;
}  /* end if (Is_in_chain) */


if  (sides == 2) {
    if  (!Is_in_chain(hi)) {
        /* No points to insert. Concatenate min with max. */
        result[(*size)++]  =  max->p;
    } else  if  (hi->next  ==  NO_MORE) {
        /* Only hi found. */
        max->next =  Idx(hi);
        result[(*size)++]  =  hi->p;
        result[(*size)++]  =  max->p;
    } else  {
        if (hi  ==  p_max) {
            hi  =  Next(hi);
        } else  {
            p  =  hi;
            while  (Next(p) != p_max)
                p  =  Next(p);
            p->next  =  Next(p)->next;
        }  /* end if (hi) */
        p_max->next  =  NO_MORE;
        divide_points(max, p_max, &hi, size, result, 1);
```

```
        divide_points(p_max, min, &hi, size, result, 1);
        p = p_max;
        while  (p->next != Idx(min))
            p = Next(p);
        p->next = NO_MORE;
        p = hi;
      }  /* end if (Is_in_chain) */
      hi = NULL;
    }  /* end if (sides == 2) */
    *residual = hi;
  }  /* end divide_points() */
```

6.2 The Intersection of Convex Hulls

For depth comparisons, we have to intersect the convex hulls of two objects. Given these two hulls, we look for at least one of the (up to four) intersection points (Figure 10).

The function *relative_pos_of_hulls*() checks whether two hulls overlap or intersect. Additionally, it stores the z-values (modified by Equation 1.38) of two space points, the images of which coincide with an intersection point of the outlines of the polygons.

#define *Is_large_enough*(x) $(fabs(x) > 1e-2)$ ($\rightarrow$ `Macros.h`)
#define *Between_zero_and_one*(t) $(t > 0$ && $t < 1)$ ($\rightarrow$ `Macros.h`)

```
 short relative_pos_of_hulls(z, n1, hull1, n2, hull2, syst)     (→ Proto.h)
     float z[2]; /* z-values of two space points with the same image. */
     short n1, n2; /* Number of vertices of the hulls. */
     Vector *hull1[ ], *hull2[ ]; /* Arrays of pointers. */
     short syst;
 {  /* begin relative_pos_of_hulls() */
 register Vector **a1, **b1;
 register Vector **a2, **b2;
        /* We will try to intersect two sides (a1b1), (a2b2) of the polygons. An
           intersection point will only be taken into account when it belongs to
           both sides. */
 Vector **hi_1 = hull1 + n1, **hi2 = hull2 + n2;
 float t1, t2; /* Parameter values of the intersection point. */
 float dz, previous_dz; /* Distance of corresponding points. */
 Bool delay_decision = FALSE;
        /* If the z-values of the corresponding points differ only slightly (i.e.,
           when dz is small), we will not rely on the result. (After all, we are
           talking about the priority between two entire polyhedra!) In such a
           case, we will continue our search for intersection points. */
 Vector2 d1, d2; /* Direction vectors of two edges. */
```

```
for (a1 = hull1, b1 = a1 + 1; a1 < hi1; a1++, b1++) {
    if (b1 == hi1) b1 = hull1;
    Subt_vec2(d1, **a1, **b1);
    for (a2 = hull2, b2 = a2 + 1; a2 < hi2; a2++, b2++) {
        Bool parallel; /* In this case only a "dummy." */
        Vector2 s1; /* In this case only a "dummy." */

        if (b2 == hi2) b2 = hull2;
        Subt_vec2(d2, **a2, **b2);
        intersect_lines(s1, &t1, &parallel, **a1, d1, **a2, d2, 2);
        if (!Between_zero_and_one(t1))
            continue;

        if (!Is_zero(d2[X]))
            t2 = ((**a1)[X] + t1 * d1[X] - (**a2)[X])/d2[X];
        else if (!Is_zero(d2[Y]))
            t2 = ((**a1)[Y] + t1 * d1[Y] - (**a2)[Y])/d2[Y];
        else continue; /* Edge goes through projection center. */
        if (!Between_zero_and_one(t2))
            continue;
        z[0] = (**a1)[Z] + t1 * ((**b1)[Z] - (**a1)[Z]);
        z[1] = (**a2)[Z] + t2 * ((**b2)[Z] - (**a2)[Z]);
        if (Dist[syst] < 1000) {/* Projection rays not parallel. */
            T2(z[0], z[0], syst); T2(z[1], z[1], syst);
        } /* end if (Dist) */

        dz = z[1] - z[0];
        if (Is_large_enough(dz)) {
            return INTERSECTION;
        } else {
            /* This is bad for the final priority decision. If such a case has
               occurred before, compare the results. If they are the same, it
               should be okay! */
            if (delay_decision) {
                if (Sign(dz) == Sign(previous_dz))
                    return INTERSECTION;
                else /* Rely on the better result. */
                    if (fabs(dz) > fabs(previous_dz))
                        previous_dz = dz;
            } else {
                delay_decision = TRUE;
                previous_dz = dz;
            } /* end if (delay_decision) */
        } /* end if (Is_large_enough...) */
    } /* end for (a2...) */
} /* end for (a1...) */
```

```
      if (delay_decision) {/* Still??? Tough luck! */
          Print("Critical intersection of polygons\n");
          return INTERSECTION;
                                  /* Keep your fingers crossed and continue! */
      }
      if (inside_poly(*(hull1[0]), n2, hull2, syst, z))
          return POLY1_INSIDE_POLY2;
      else if (inside_poly(*(hull2[0]), n1, hull1, syst, z))
          return POLY2_INSIDE_POLY1;
      else
          return DISJOINT;
  }   /* end relative_pos_of_hulls() */
```

The last function calls another function *inside_polygon*(), which determines whether a point is inside the *image* of a closed spatial polygon or not.

Figure 2 shows how the problem can be solved. Let $\vec{n}$ be the *normalized* normal vector of a line PQ. With the implicit equation of PQ $\vec{n}\,\vec{x} = \vec{n}\,\vec{p} = const$ (see Equation 10), we can determine the *oriented* distance of a point R (position vector $\vec{r}$) from the line PQ:

$$d_R = \vec{n}\,\overrightarrow{PR} = \vec{n}\,(\vec{r} - \vec{p}) = \vec{n}\,\vec{r} - const. \tag{1}$$

If $\vec{n}$ is not normalized, the number d_R will be the distance scaled by the constant length of $\vec{n}$.

To determine whether a point Q is inside a given convex polygon **P** or not we do the following: we draw a line from the first point P of **P** through Q and check whether there is a residual intersection point $\overline{P}$ with the polygon **P**. Such a point exists when we can find two vertices R and S of **P** that lie on different sides of PQ ($sign(d_R) \neq sign(d_S)$). (Otherwise Q is outside the polygon.) The residual intersection can then be calculated by means of a linear interpolation:

$$\vec{\overline{p}} = \vec{r} + t\,(\vec{s} - \vec{r}) \quad \text{with} \quad t = d_R/(d_R - d_S). \tag{2}$$

Now the point Q is inside the polygon **P**, when it is inside the segment $P\overline{P}$ ($0 < \lambda = |PQ|/|P\overline{P}| < 1$), otherwise it is outside the polygon.

In our case, the given polygon **P** is the spatial hull of a convex object. Therefore, our function *inside_poly*() can also check whether the space point Q is *behind* that polygon or not: we just have to compare the z-value of Q with the interpolated z-value of a point $\overline{Q}$ that lies on $P\overline{P}$, and the image of which coincides with the image of Q.

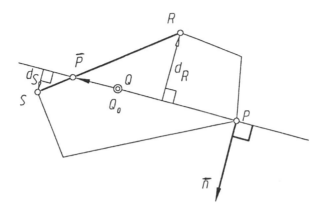

FIGURE 2. How to find out whether a point is inside a convex polygon or not.

Bool *inside_poly*(*q*, *n*, *poly*, *dist_syst*, *z*)

(→ Proto.h)

> **float** *q*[ ];   /* Point Q that is to be checked. */
> **short** *n*;   /* Size of polygon. */
> **Vec** **poly*; /* Array of pointers to the vertices of the polygon. */
> **float** *dist_syst*; /* Distance of proj. center (only for *dim* = 3). */
> **float** *z*[ ];   /* z-values of Q and Q_0. */

{ /* begin *inside_poly*() */
> **float** * *p* = **poly*;   /* First point P on polygon. */
> **float** * *r*, **s*;   /* Side RS of the polygon. */
> **float** *dist_r*, *dist_s*;   /* Distances of these points. */
> **float** *p0*[3];   /* Residual intersection point P_0 on PQ. */
> **float** *normal*[2], *cnst*; /* Implicit equation of PQ. */
> **register short** *i*;
> **register float** *t*; /* Parameter. */
>
>
> /* Implicit equation of PQ. */
> $normal[X] = q[Y] - p[Y]$; $normal[Y] = p[X] - q[X]$;
> $cnst = Dot\_product2(p, normal)$;
> /* Check distances of residual vertices on polygon. */
> $r = *(poly[1])$;   /* The second vertex of the polygon. */
> $dist\_r = Dot\_product2(r, normal) - cnst$;
> **for** $(i = 2; i < n; i{+}{+})$ {
> > $s = *(poly[i])$;   /* The $(i+1)$-th vertex of the polygon. */
> > $dist\_s = Dot\_product2(s, normal) - cnst$;
> > /* Are R and S on opposite sides of PQ? */
> > **if** $(Sign(dist\_r) != Sign(dist\_s))$

```
            break;
         r = s; dist_r = dist_s;
   }  /* end for (i) */
   if  (i == n)    /* All the points are on the same side. */
         return  FALSE;
   /* Interpolate intersection point P0. */
   t = dist_r /(dist_r − dist_s);
   for  (i = 0; i < Dim; i++)
         p0[i] = r[i] + t * (s[i] − r[i]);
   /* Calculate ratio PQ / PP0. */
   /* Which coordinate is more accurate? */
   i = fabs(p0[X] − p[X]) > fabs(p0[Y] − p[Y]) ? X : Y;
   t = (q[i] − p[i]) /(p0[i] − p[i] + EPS); /* No div. by zero! */
   if  (!Between_zero_and_one(t)) /* Q is outside the interval. */
         return  FALSE;
   if  (Dim == 3) {/* z-values of Q and Q0. */
         float w1, w2; /* Apply Transformation T2. */
         T2(z[0], q[Z], syst);
         T2(w1, p[Z], syst); T2(w2, p0[Z], syst);
         z[1] = (1 − t) * w1 + t * w2;
   }
   return  TRUE;
}  /* end inside_poly() */
```

The functions we have described so far in this chapter are quite useful for priority determinations and – as we will see in Chapter 7 – for hidden-line algorithms. For the clipping of filled polygons, we need another very important function *clip_convex*(), which determines the intersection polygon of two convex polygons. This function is one of the most frequent routines in our program. We need it, for example, every time we plot a shadow polygon or – as we will see in the following section – when we clip a polygon with a reflecting face. Therefore, it has to be perfectly optimized.

In Section 2.5, we explained the Hodgman-Sutherland algorithm for the clipping of an arbitrary polygon with the drawing window. The rectangular drawing area is just the special case of a convex polygon. The obvious thing to do is to extend the algorithm to the clipping with general convex polygons.

Figure 3 shows how this can be done: we cut the given polygon **P** (which may be convex or not) with each side of the clipping polygon **C** (in an arbitrary order). A side PQ (position vectors $\vec{p}$ and $\vec{q}$) of **C** divides the image plane into two halfplanes. Let $\vec{n}$ be the *oriented* normal vector of $\overrightarrow{PQ}$ ($\vec{n}$ points to the outside of **C**). Then the implicit equation of PQ $\vec{n}\vec{x} = \vec{n}\vec{p} = const$ (see Equation 10) helps to determine whether a point R (position vector $\vec{r}$) is on the same side as **C** or not: if the sign of d_R (Equation 1) is positive, R is on the opposite side of **C**.

We now check on which side of PQ all the vertices of **P** are on. When all the vertices are on the same side as **C**, we do not have to clip. When all the vertices are on the opposite side, the polygons are disjoint and we are finished. When the vertices of **P** are scattered on both sides of PQ, we do the following for all sides RS of **P** (in ascending order): if d_R is not positive, the vertex R belongs to the new polygon; if $sign(d_R) \neq sign(d_S)$, we calculate the intersection point S_0 (position vector $\vec{s}_0$) of PQ and RS by means of a linear interpolation (Equation 2) and add S_0 to the new polygon.

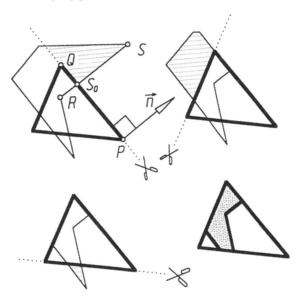

FIGURE 3. How to clip a polygon with a convex polygon.

If you take a closer look at the source code of *clip_convex*() you will see how this algorithm can be implemented by means of pointer arithmetic, which makes the function efficient and needs less memory.

#define *STATIC* **static**   ($\rightarrow$ Macros.h)
/* If the value of a local variable is only needed as long as the function is
    active, we will not declare the variable **static**, since this takes extra RAM.
    static variables speed up the code, however, because they do not have to be
    allocated at the stack each time the function is called. When your system has
    enough RAM left, you can accelerate functions that are needed frequently
    by declaring some temporary variables **static**. If you run out of RAM, write

#define *STATIC*
*/

short *clip_convex*(*n1*, *poly*, *n2*, *clipping_poly*, *inter*, *which*, *dim*)

($\rightarrow$ `Proto.h`)

/* This function returns the number of vertices of the intersection polygon.
*/

float *poly*[ ], *clipping_poly*[ ];

/* *clipping_poly* must be convex and should be oriented ccw. */

short *n1*, *n2*; /* Corresponding numbers of vertices. */

float *inter*[ ]; /* To make room for the intersection polygon. */

float **which;

/* This pointer to a polygon indicates whether *clipping_poly* is the intersection polygon. This will frequently be the case and can help to save time. (For example, if *poly* is a shadow polygon and *clipping_poly* the outline of a face, and if the intersection polygon is *clipping_poly*, the whole face will be dark and we do not have to calculate any further shadows.) */

short *dim*;

/* This function works both for **Vector2**s and **Vectors**. */

{   /* begin *clip_convex*() */

register Ubyte *j*;

STATIC **float** * *sp1*[*MAX_POLY_SIZE*], *sp2[*MAX_POLY_SIZE*];

/* Space for pointers to the vertices. */

register float **r;

float **r1 = *sp1*, * * *r2*; /* Switch between *sp1* and *sp2*. */

STATIC **float** *dist*[*MAX_POLY_SIZE*]; /* Distances. */

float *cnst*, *t*;

STATIC **float** *space*[2 * *MAX_POLY_SIZE* * **sizeof**(**Vector**)];

/* Space for intersection points. */

float * *new* = *space*; /* Coordinates of a new vertex. */

Ubyte *opposite*, *i*, *size* = *n2*;

float * *a*, *b;

Vector2 *n*; /* The normal vector. */

Bool *flip* = *FALSE*;

* *which* = *clipping_poly*;

/* We assume that *clipping_poly* is the intersection polygon. */

r = *r1*, *b* = *clipping_poly*;

for (*j* = 0; *j* < *size*; *j*++, *b* += *dim*)

r[*j*] = *b*;

for (*i* = 0; *i* < *n1*; *i*++) {

a = *poly* + *i* * *dim*;

b = (*i* + 1 < *n1* ? *a* + *dim* : *poly*);

n[*X*] = *b*[*Y*] − *a*[*Y*]; *n*[*Y*] = *a*[*X*] − *b*[*X*];

t = *fabs*(*n*[*X*]) + *fabs*(*n*[*Y*]);

if (*t* < *EPS*) **continue**;

n[*X*] /= *t*; *n*[*Y*] /= *t*;

```
    /*  Pseudo-normalizing for numerical reasons. */
cnst  =  Dot_product2(a,  n);
if  (i == 0) {   /* Check orientation of n⃗. */
    b += dim;   /* Test point poly[2]. */
    if  (Dot_product2(b, n)  − cnst  >  EPS)
        flip  =  TRUE;
}  /* end if (i == 0) */
if  (flip)
    cnst  =  −cnst, n[X]  =  −n[X], n[Y]  =  −n[Y];
r =  r1;  opposite  =  0;
for  (j  =  0;  j  <  size;  j++,  r++)
    if  ((dist[j]  =  Dot_product2(*r, n)  − cnst)  >  EPS)
        opposite++;
if  (opposite == size)
    return  0;   /* Polygons are disjoint. */
if  (!opposite)
    continue;   /* No clipping with this side. */
/*  We will find intersection points. */
dist[size]  =  dist[0];
r1[size]  =  r1[0];
r =  r2  =  (r1 == sp1 ? sp2  :  sp1);
for  (j  =  0;  j  <  size;  j++) {
    if  (dist[j]  <=  EPS)
        *r++  =  r1[j];
    if  (dist[j]  *  dist[j  +  1]  <  0) {
        /* Linear interpolation of the intersection point. */
        a  =  r1[j];  b =  r1[j  +  1];
        t  =  dist[j] /(dist[j]  − dist[j + 1]); /* 0 < t < 1 */
        new[X]  =  a[X]  +  t *  (b[X]  − a[X]);
        new[Y]  =  a[Y]  +  t *  (b[Y]  − a[Y]);
        if  (dim == 3)
            new[Z]  =  a[Z]  +  t *  (b[Z]  − a[Z]);
        *r++  =  new;
        new += dim;
        *which  =  inter;
    }  /* end if (dist[j]  *  dist[j  +  1]  <  0) */
}  /* end for (j < size) */
size  =  r − (r1  =  r2);
}  /* end for (i < n1) */
if  (*which  ==  clipping_poly)
    return  n2;
r =  r1;  a  =  inter;
if  (dim == 2)
    for  (j  =  0;  j  <  size;  j++)
        *a++  =  (*r)[X], *a++  =  (*r++)[Y];
else
    for  (j  =  0;  j  <  size;  j++)
        *a++  =  (*r)[X], *a++  =  (*r)[Y], *a++  =  (*r++)[Z];
return  size;
}  /* end clip_convex() */
```

6.3 Shadows

Shadows are very important for the realism of computer-generated images. Without shadows, the images appear two-dimensional, and depth comparisons can be misleading. Since shadows are projections from the light source, a scene with shadows can be interpreted as a multiple projection (in one and the same image). This allows human imagination to reconstruct the scene in space.

A "shadow" is defined as the darkness cast by an illuminated object. In nature, we are used to seeing images that are illuminated by one single light source that is at an "infinite distance" (provided that the weather is fine). Artificial light sources can be multiple and need not necessarily be point sources. In computer graphics, only few algorithms are known that produce the shadows of all kinds of objects. Of course, ray tracing [GLAS90] and the radiosity method [FOLE90] are among these algorithms. Another one ("shadow buffering" [THAL87, FOLE90]) will be discussed in detail in Section 7.4.

In this section, we will see how the shadows of polygons can be generated by means of a method that is based on convex polygon-clipping. Usually, it takes a lot of computation time to plot shadows. Under specific circumstances, however, this is not necessarily the case, as we will see in this section.

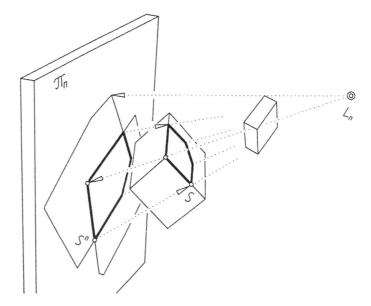

FIGURE 4. The clipping of shadow polygons.

Let L_n be the n-th light source and let P_1 and P_2 be two closed planar polygons (Figure 4) in space. From the geometrical point of view, the light system connected with L_n (Section 2.3) is the same as the screen system connected with the projection center C. In the screen system we say: when the images (i.e., the projections onto the image plane π) of the polygons P_1 and P_2 overlap, the one that is closer to the projection center obscures (parts of) the other polygon. When we apply the painter's algorithm, the obscured polygon has to be plotted first.

The analog in the n-th light system is: when the projections on the imaginary projection plane π_n of the light system of P_1 and P_2 overlap, the polygon that is closer to L_n casts shadows on the other polygon. When we apply the painter's algorithm, we add these shadows immediately after having plotted the shadowed polygon. Then we do not have to think about visibility.

The shadow polygon $\mathbf{S}$ can be added by means of 2D-clipping. The (convex) intersection polygon $\mathbf{S}^n$ (with the vertices S^n) of the *projections* P_1^n and P_2^n of the polygons has to be projected onto the plane ψ that carries the shadowed polygon. For this purpose, we intersect the light ray $L_n S^n$ with ψ, and we get the vertices S of the shadow polygon $\mathbf{S}$.

For a more accurate computation, this projection should be done in the *world* system. In the light system, a vertex S^n of the intersection polygon $\mathbf{S}^n$, which lies entirely on the projection plane π_n, may have the position vector $\vec{s}^n$. In the world system, we get the coordinates of points on π_n by transforming their light coordinates by means of a simple rotation, which is described by the matrix $R_n^{-1} \equiv InvRot[n]$ $(\vec{s}^{n^*} = \vec{s}^n\, R_n^{-1})$. We intersect the ray $L_n S^n$ with the plane ψ of the face and we get a vertex S of the shadow polygon in space. The projected point $S^c = \overline{CS} \cap \pi$ is a vertex of the *image* of the shadow polygon.

Which color should we choose for the shadow polygon? For sophisticated illumination models, this is a very difficult question because the color may vary for each pixel, depending on reflections from other objects, the colors of other light sources, etc. For our purposes, it will be enough to fill small shadow polygons with one and the same shade of a color, and, when the polygon is large, to vary the shade slightly, depending on its distance from the observer. Furthermore, the color of the shadow will only depend on the color of the face and it will not – as in more advanced models – be influenced by the colors of the light sources or by those of surrounding objects. This may seem to be a tremendous simplification, but in most cases, the images produced in this way are sufficiently realistic. In our simplified model, a shadow polygon is basically filled in the same manner as the image of the face, only with a darker shade.

How much darker the shade of a shadow has to be is not subject to any strict rules. Imagine two photographs of one and the same building with the same angle of incidence of the light rays, but with different light intensities (fog or dust in the atmosphere, etc.). The contrast between the shadows and the illuminated faces will be different. In general, pictures look realistic if we use approximately one-half the value of the variable *reduced_palette* in Formula (2).

Since in our illumination model the color of the shadow polygon only depends on the color and the depth of the corresponding face, we can plot several (convex)

FIGURE 5. Convex polyhedra only cast shadows on other polyhedra and not on themselves.

shadow polygons in an arbitrary order onto the face. The result will be a set of (convex or not convex) shadows (Figure 5).

This way of painting over existing polygons is very efficient, but it has a disadvantage that is due to the fill algorithm of polygons. Let P^c be the image polygon of a face and let S^c be the image of a shadow polygon that is not completely inside P^c. Then P^c and S^c will have part of the side $P\bar{P}$ of P^c in common (e.g., the line $S\bar{S}$). Even though from the mathematical point of view the line $S\bar{S}$ lies on $P\bar{P}$, the filling routine for S^c will not always cover all the pixels that $P\bar{P}$ and $S\bar{S}$ seem to have in common. (This has nothing to do with the screen resolution.) Some lighter pixels may be left at the border of S^c. The reason for this is that all the coordinates of the vertices are rounded off before the images of the polygons are drawn. One way to avoid such light pixels is to enlarge the shadow polygon at each vertex by one pixel. In most cases, this will work and the image will be improved. If your compiler has a routine *linewidth*() that allows to draw thicker lines, you can also draw the outline of a shadow polygon with a "linewidth of 2 pixels." If you choose a shade for this outline that is a bit brighter than the rest of the shadow polygon, you can create an "aura" around it. Artificial light sources (which are not perfect point sources) create such auras so that this trick is a simple method of simulating this effect without any complicated calculations.

So far we have only talked about one light source. What happens when we deal with several light sources? In this case, we will have shadow polygons of different "grade" (this idea is mentioned in [ANGE87]).

First, we plot the shadow polygons $\{S_i\}$ for all the light sources L_i. These polygons of grade 1 will appear comparatively light, depending on the intensities of the residual light sources. Then we clip all the shadow polygons of grade 1 that are cast by other light sources. Thus, we get shadow polygons of grade 2: $\{\mathbf{S}_{ij}\} = \{\mathbf{S}_i \cap \mathbf{S}_j \ (i \neq j)\}$. They have to be plotted in a darker shade because they are not illuminated by two light sources. If we have only two light sources, we are finished. Otherwise we have to check whether there are shadow polygons of grade 3: $\{\mathbf{S}_{ijk}\} = \{\mathbf{S}_{ij} \cap \mathbf{S}_{ik} \ (j \neq k)\}$, which will be even darker than the shadows of grade 2. The algorithm has to be continued until the grade of shadows equals the number of light sources.

What we have described so far is not very exciting. When we really check whether each polygon of the scene is shadowed by another polygon, complicated scenes will need a lot of computation time. To speed up the process, we use the same techniques as for the painter's algorithm:

By means of the object preprocessor, the faces of the scene are connected to primitives (objects, object groups, slices, etc.). Let a face belong to a primitive Ψ_1 and another face belong to a primitive Ψ_2. When the bounding rectangles of Ψ_1 and Ψ_2 do not overlap, we do not have to check anything. When the rectangles overlap, and when the result of the priority test in the n-th light system is that Ψ_1 is closer to the light source L_n than Ψ_2, all the faces of Ψ_1 potentially cast shadows on all the faces of Ψ_2. If in such a case Ψ_1 is convex, its outline in the light system is convex, too. This means that we only have to clip the outline of Ψ_1 with each face of Ψ_2. This is the reason why scenes that consist only of convex primitives can be rendered with shadows without any major loss of speed.

FIGURE 6. Several light sources illuminate convex polyhedra.

Convex polyhedra have the convenient property that they cannot cast shadows on *themselves* (Figure 5). This is why the shadow-test does not have to be applied to the other faces of the primitive the face belongs to. Non-convex polyhedra, however, *may* cast shadows on parts of themselves. The faces whose shadows can be seen must have their illuminated side turned to the viewer. (The viewer can see the illuminated side of a face when the projection center C and the light source L_n are on the same side of the plane of the face, otherwise the face is "dark.")

We have already dealt with important classes of non-convex polyhedra like function graphs and approximations to surfaces of revolution. All these surfaces are at least split up into slices. These slices are separated by parallel planes σ. The special separating plane σ_n, which coincides with the light source L_n, plays a similarly important role as the "critical planes" σ_0 played for the hidden-surface algorithm in the Sections 5.2–5.4. If Φ is a sliced surface and if σ_n intersects Φ, the two partial surfaces Φ_1 and Φ_2 on the different sides of σ_n cannot cast shadows on each other. A slice of a partial surface can only cast shadows on slices that are further away from σ_n. The "critical slice" that connects Φ_1 with Φ_2 may cast shadows on parts of any other slice.

The slices consist of two types of faces, which are analogous to the frontfaces and backfaces in the screen system (Figure 4).

The dot product of the normal vector of the face and the oriented light ray to the center of the face will be positive or zero for some faces and negative for others. Faces of the same type can be connected to "ribbons." The ribbons can be sorted like in Section 5.3. Faces of the same ribbon will never cast shadows on each other because in the light system their projections cannot overlap (otherwise the ribbon would have been split up). A ribbon can only cast shadows on another ribbon when it is closer to the axis a_n that is normal to the separating planes and that coincides with the light source. This is especially true for surfaces of revolution where each "ring" (Section 5.2) consists of one or two ribbons.

6.4 Reflections

Like shadows, reflections help to make spatial objects look more realistic. In combination with shadows, the effect is even more enhanced. However, this works only with a limited number of reflecting elements in a scene. Pictures with bouncing reflections are nice to look at and they are a test for really good algorithms (like ray tracing). On the other hand, such complicated images can be confusing.

In this section, we will only talk about simple reflections, i.e., reflections on one or several reflecting faces that cannot produce bouncing reflections (for example, the faces of individual convex objects). We will not talk about reflections on curved surfaces or about bouncing reflections, since the calculation of such images takes a lot of CPU time. Reflections on single "mirrors," however, can be done amazingly fast, provided that the scene consists of the primitives that are generated by our object preprocessor. In relation to the computation time, the quality of the result is satisfactory.

Consider a scene of objects, where only one face is reflecting (Figure 7). The mirror plane μ separates the space into two halfspaces. All the objects of the scene that are completely at the reflecting side of the mirror, or that are intersected by the plane μ, are potentially visible on the mirror's face.

We might also say that the imaginary object "doubles," which we get when we reflect the objects at the plane μ, can be seen through a "window" (the transparent reflecting face **R**) from the projection center.

Consequently, the painter's algorithm can also be applied to the plotting of reflections. We plot the images of the faces of our scene in the above-mentioned order, until we have plotted the image of the reflecting face. Before we plot the rest of the image, we do the following:

First we reflect all the objects that coincide (completely or partly) with the halfspace that is determined by the reflecting side of the mirror plane μ. When the

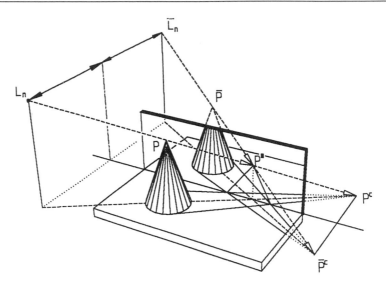

FIGURE 7. When we look into a mirror, we can see the "doubles" of our objects through the "mirror window."

scene is static (i.e., the objects remain in their relative positions), this calculation can be done before any drawings. Otherwise the "reflection pool" (where we store the coordinates of the reflected vertices) has to be recalculated for each frame.

Among the reflected objects, we select those that can be seen through the mirror window $\mathbf{R}$. We can check this with the help of bounding rectangles. (Do the bounding rectangles of the reflected objects overlap with the image $\mathbf{R}^c$ of the reflecting face $\mathbf{R}$?) With convex objects, we can find out which position the outlines of the objects have with respect to the outline of the clipping window. By means of this test, we can find out which of the selected doubles are partly visible and which are completely visible.

Now we sort the selected objects with the help of our priority test and then we plot them as usual, one after the other, according to the priority list. The images of the faces of objects that are only partly visible have to be clipped with the clipping window $\mathbf{R}^c$.

The shade of a reflected face is basically the same as that of the real face. The reflected face will appear a bit darker, however, because the light rays that are reflected from the original face make a detour over the mirror. (In all reflections the light rays are split up. In addition to that, the virtual distance from the viewer increases.)

This simplified shading model works fast and is satisfactory for many kinds of animations. Things get more complicated when the reflecting face itself illuminates the scene indirectly, i.e., with reflected light. (This occurs when its reflecting side is turned towards a light source and when the reflecting face is not in the shadow of an object.) This kind of illumination is in fact the same as the illumination by an additional light source L_n^*. Thus, if we plot a scene with reflections on a reflecting face, each light source that illuminates the reflecting side of the face **R** increases the number of light sources by one.

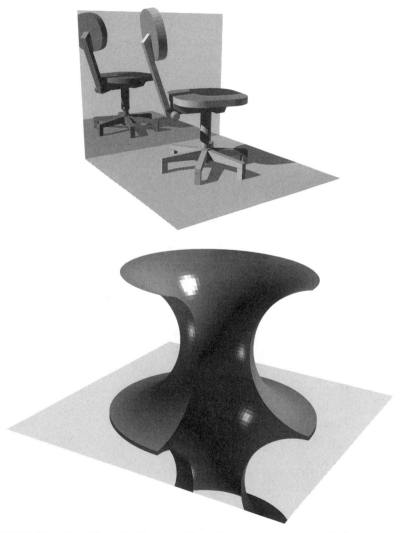

FIGURE 8. The simplified shading model works very fast, especially for scenes with only one reflecting face.

We get the coordinates of L_n^* when we reflect the given light source L_n. Of course, the intensity of the point source L_n^* is less than the intensity of L_n (because reflections reduce the light intensity). Furthermore, the reflected light can only come through the mirror window **R**.

If we go one step further and calculate cast shadows, the reflected light may be additionally obscured by shadow polygons cast from the objects in front of the reflecting face, which will happen when the light comes from L_n. We get the same shadow polygons when we cast shadows from the object doubles and when the light comes from L_n^*. Consequently, we may say that *the reflected light is additionally obscured by the reflected objects*.

These considerations show that difficulties will increase dramatically when we have several reflecting faces. As long as the faces are in such a position as to not allow any bouncing reflections, the simplified shading model (Figure 8) works fine (and comparatively fast). We plot the scene one face after the other. Every time we plot a reflecting face, we paint the corresponding reflected scene on it. Once we calculate shadows, however, each reflecting face that is turned towards an existing light source will produce a new light source. Therefore, we should leave such complicated scenes to really sophisticated programs like ray tracing.

6.5 Patterns

Consider an object with patterns like the one in either Figure 6 or Figure 9. The patterns are polygons painted on different faces. Of course, it would not be wise to declare these polygons as objects in their own right. In this case, the computer might have trouble with the priority list because the patterns touch the object. In addition to that, the number of objects would increase, so that the processing would be slowed down unnecessarily.

For this reason, we combine each pattern with the corresponding face. After the face has been plotted, its patterns are added. A face can have any number of patterns. The patterns should be split into convex polygons.

If we want to add shadows, we first plot the shadows on the face. The images of the shadow polygons of different degree (Section 6.3) are stored temporarily. Then we plot the patterns in the following way: If the whole face is "dark" (i.e., if it is a backface in all the light systems), all its patterns can be plotted in a darker shade. If the face is lit by at least one light source, we clip the images of all the patterns with the precalculated shadows of different degree (starting with degree 1).

This method is very efficient in terms of computation time. In general, we can say that the number of patterns has much less influence on the CPU time than the number of faces.

General patterns (polygons) can be described by two-dimensional coordinates in a data file (Figure 10):

```
CUBE gray box voll 10 10 10
    patterns face 1 polygon LEFT  white  -1 -1, 1 -1, 1 1, -1 1
             face 2 polygon FRONT yellow -2 -2, 2 -2, 2 2, -2 2
             face 3 polygon RIGHT black  -3 -3, 3 -3, 3 3, -3 3
```

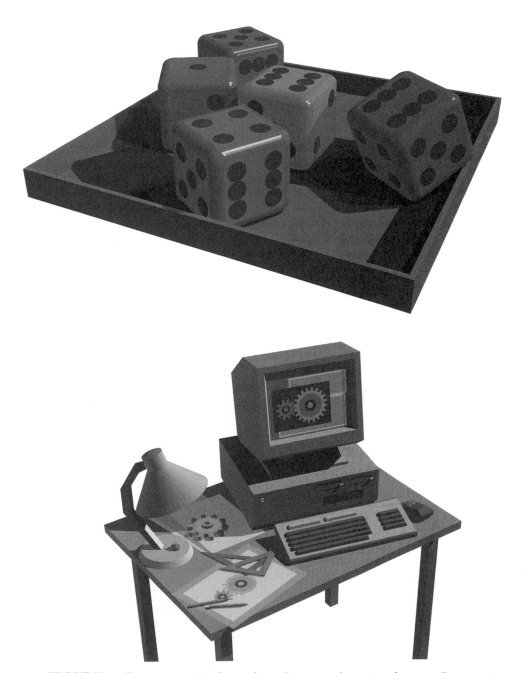

FIGURE 9. Patterns on the faces of an object can be a nice feature. Computation times increase only a little.

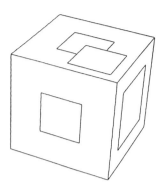

FIGURE 10. Cube with patterns.

```
face 4 polygon BACK   red     -4 -4, 4 -4, 4 4, -4 4
face 6 polygon TOP1   cyan    -2 -2, 2 -2, 2 2, -2 2
           polygon TOP2   black   0 0, 4 0, 4 4, 0 4
```

In the sample data files on your disk, you can find several other examples for patterns.

6.6 Refraction, Transparent Objects

In Section 6.4, we saw that the painter's algorithm can be applied successfully to a simplified reflection model. On the other hand, we had to realize that when we include shadows the fast algorithms soon reach their limits.

The same is true for transparency models. Usually, the images of transparent polyhedra or transparent solids with curved surfaces are drawn by ray tracing programs. Such programs work perfectly for the calculation of refractions on transparent material because they trace both the projection rays and the light rays.

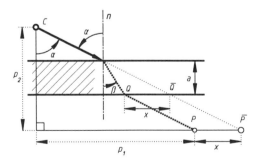

FIGURE 11. The refraction of light rays on parallel plane surfaces.

In this section, we will show that the painter's algorithm can still produce acceptable results (at least for computer animations) for transparent plane surfaces and transparent solid polyhedra. This simplified model can easily be extended to single reflections and shadows.

Figure 11 illustrates that the refraction of light rays on a transparent material with parallel surfaces depends on the angle of incidence α, as well as on the thickness a and the kind of the material given by a constant c for the refraction, which is given by

$$c = \frac{\sin \alpha}{\sin \beta}. \tag{3}$$

For very thin material, the refraction is even negligible.

To solve the problem we can use the following trick. We plot our scene face by face. Whenever a face is transparent (and not colorless), we do not fill the polygon completely, but we set only every second (third, fourth) pixel. This implies that the face will be slightly visible in its given color. On the other hand, the background color is only partly erased and will "shine through." The better the screen resolution is, the closer the pixels will stick together. Thus, for the human eye, the different colors will more or less melt together to a new color. (This trick is also used in various printing techniques.)

When we plot the shadow of a transparent face, we do not fill the shadow polygon with a darker shade of the color of the obscured face, but we set every second (third, fourth) pixel in a darker shade of the color of the transparent face. Moreover, the shadow polygons of the transparent faces have to be drawn *after* the "normal" shadows! (In fact, the pixels that are filled with the color of the transparent face are not shadows but illuminated spots, which must not be erased!).

Once we deal with transparent solid polyhedra Θ (prisms, pyramids, etc.), refractions have to be taken into account. In this case, we refract the projection rays through the vertices of the transparent frontfaces $\mathbf{F}_i$. This leads to new polygons $\mathbf{F}_i^c$ in the image plane. The intersections of $\mathbf{F}_i^c$ with the image polygon of Θ are polygons $\mathbf{R}_i$. All the faces the image polygons of that intersect $\mathbf{R}_i$ are subject to refraction. We calculate their intersection polygons $\{\mathbf{I}_{ik}\}$ with $\mathbf{R}_i$. Now we start to plot our scene. When we come to the transparent polyhedron Θ, we do the following:

- We paint the contour polygon of Θ in the background color.
- We calculate all the intersection polygons $\{\mathbf{I}_{ik}\}$ and refract them inversely.
- We fill these polygons with a shade that is a bit darker than that of the corresponding faces.
- When the material the polyhedron Θ consists of is not colorless, we plot the frontfaces of Θ as transparent faces.

A simple application is illustrated in Figure 12. The inversion of the refraction can be solved using 3 ($c \approx 4/3$) as follows (Figure 11):

Because of $x = Q\overline{Q} = P\overline{P}$ we have

$$a \left(\tan \alpha - \tan \beta \right) = a \left(\tan \alpha - \frac{\sin \alpha}{\sqrt{c^2 - sin^2 \alpha}} \right) = p_2 \tan \alpha - p_1. \tag{4}$$

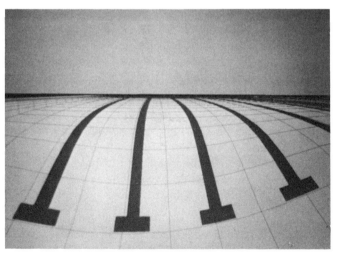

FIGURE 12. A swimming pool with constant depth from two different point of views.

This leads to the trancendent implicit equation

$$f(\alpha) \equiv (p_2 - a)\tan\alpha + \frac{a\sin\alpha}{\sqrt{c^2 - \sin^2\alpha}} - p1 = 0. \tag{5}$$

When the projection center is outside the water ($p_2 > a$, $\frac{-\pi}{2} \le \alpha \le \frac{\pi}{2}$), the only real solution of this equation can be found by means of NEWTON's iteration (see Section 8.2).

7

Hidden-Line Removal

For technical drawings and publications, we often have to produce line drawings, mainly because they are easier to handle and to reproduce. Sometimes it is also easier to demonstrate specific facts by means of line drawings than by means of painted images. For this reason, we dedicate this chapter to the removal of hidden lines. We will distinguish between algorithms that are screen-oriented and algorithms that can be used for plotter drawings.

7.1 A Quick Screen-Oriented Method

In Chapter 5, we talked about a fast hidden-*surface* algorithm: the painter's algorithm. This algorithm can also be used for the quick removal of hidden *lines*. When we plot the image of a scene, we do not fill the images of the faces with the color of the faces but with the color of the background. In this manner, the image polygons of the faces are erased. Immediately after an image polygon has been erased, we redraw its outline and, if necessary, other lines (like the outlines of patterns) in the color of the face.

The adapted painter's algorithm works efficiently and removes hidden lines very fast, especially when we deal with objects, the images of which can easily be rendered by a simple shading model. (In addition to objects with convex outlines, these are the surfaces of revolution, function graphs and sliced surfaces like in Chapter 5).

Since this method is screen-oriented, it can be used to make hard copies or photographs from the screen. If your screen has a good resolution (in Figure 1 the resolution is 1280×1024), this poses no problems. For lower screen resolutions we will either use algorithms that can be used for plotter drawings[1] or we will create *Postscript* images that work in the same manner as the painter's algorithm.

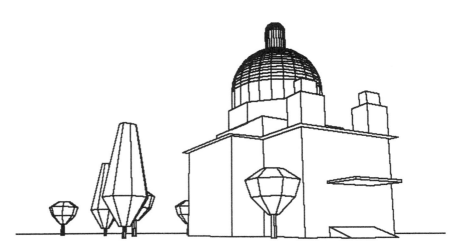

FIGURE 1. The adapted painter's algorithm removes hidden lines very quickly, but is dependent on the screen resolution. However, it is perfectly suited to create *PostScript* files.

7.2   Hidden-Line Removal on Objects with Convex Outlines

As for almost every application in computer graphics, convex objects play an important part in the speed of a graphics program: convex polyhedra are perfectly suitable for fast and precise hidden-line removal.

Let a scene consist only of convex (solid) polyhedra. Let the priority list of the objects be already determined (Section 5.6). Now we plot the images of the edges of the individual objects. (We may plot the objects from the back to the front, according to the priority list, although this is not necessary.) Instead of filling the images of the frontfaces, we only plot their outlines and – if necessary – other lines on them like the outlines of patterns.

Each line PQ in a frontface is potentially visible, because the whole frontface is locally visible (Section 5.1). However, it can be partly or completely hidden by the convex outlines of the images of the other objects, which may obscure the

---

[1]With the appropriate software, the drawings can also be done by printers, especially by laser printers like the illustrations in this book. In this case, the accuracy of the image is not dependent on the screen resolution!

the convex outlines of the images of the other objects, which may obscure the object according to the priority list (Figure 2).

In order to find out whether the outline O_k^c of the k-th object obscures $\overline{P^cQ^c}$ we can check whether or not the bounding rectangles of the image line $\overline{P^cQ^c}$ and of O_k^c overlap. If the rectangles overlap, we try to intersect $\overline{P^cQ^c}$ with O_k^c. When we get two intersection points S_{k_1} and S_{k_2}, we store the parameters λ_{k_1}, λ_{k_2}, which lead to their position vectors $\vec{s}_{k_1}$ and $\vec{s}_{k_2}$ ($\vec{s}_{ki} = \vec{p^c} + \lambda_{ki}(\vec{q^c} - \vec{p^c})$). We sort the parameters ($\lambda_{k_1} < \lambda_{k_2}$) and modify them by

$$\lambda_{ki} = \begin{cases} 0, & \text{if } \lambda_{ki} \leq 0 \ (\Rightarrow S_{ki} = P); \\ \lambda_{ki}, & \text{if } 0 < \lambda_{ki} < 1; \\ 1, & \text{if } \lambda_{ki} \geq 1 \ (\Rightarrow S_{ki} = Q); \end{cases} \qquad (i = 1, 2). \qquad (1)$$

If $\lambda_{k_1} = 0$ and $\lambda_{k_2} = 1$, the edge is completely hidden and we can turn to the next image line. Otherwise the "zone" $[\lambda_{k_1}, \lambda_{k_2}]$ on $\overline{P^cQ^c}$ is hidden.

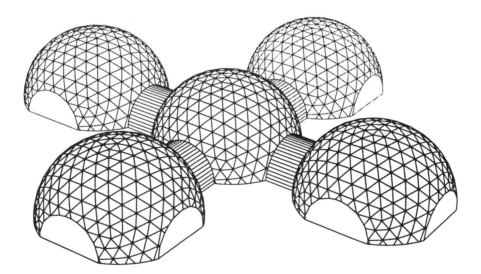

FIGURE 2. The image of the edge of a convex object can only be hidden by the outlines of other polyhedra. Note that the primitives do not intersect, even if it looks as if they did.

Here is the C code for the determination of the hidden zones for convex objects:

```
void invisible_zones(k, zones, p, q, obj)                    (→ Proto.h)
    short  *k; /* Number of zones. */
    Vector2 zones[ ]; /* Has to be allocated outside the function. */
    register Vector p, q; /* The vertices of the edge. */
    Polyhedron *obj; /* The object the edge belongs to. */
```

```
    register  Polyhedron  * obj2  =  Object_pool,
                         * hi_obj2  =  obj2  +  Total_objects;
Vector min, max;
short  i, n;
register  Vector2 * zone  =  zones;
Vector **poly;
float z[2]; /* Dummy. */


/*  Bounding box of edge. */
for  (i =  0;  i <  3;  i++)
    if  (q[i]  <  p[i])    min[i]  =  q[i],  max[i]  =  p[i];
    else  min[i]  =  p[i],  max[i]  =  q[i];
/*  Clip with the outlines of all the other objects. */
for  ( ; obj2  <  hi_obj2;  obj2++) {
    if  (obj→priority[SCREEN_SYST][obj2→index] ! =  obj2→index)
        continue;
    if  (!overlap((Vector *) min, (Vector *) max,
              obj2→box_min,  obj2→box_max)) continue;
    n  =  obj2→size_of_contour[SCREEN_SYST];
    poly  =  obj2→contour[SCREEN_SYST];
    if  (!segment_cuts_poly(zone, p, q, n, poly)) {
        if  (inside_poly(p, n, poly, SCREEN_SYST, z))
            return ; /* Completely hidden. */
        else  continue;
    }
    /* Modify zone. */
    for  (i =  0;  i <  2;  i++) {
        if  ((*zone)[i]  <  EPS) (*zone)[i]  =  0;
        else  if  ((*zone)[i]  >  (1 − EPS)) (*zone)[i]  =  1;
    }
    if  ((*zone)[0]  ==  0 && (*zone)[1]  ==  1) {
        *k  = 0; return ;    /* Completely hidden! */
    }
    else  if  ((*zone)[0]  <  (*zone)[1]) zone++;
} /* end for (obj2) */
*k  =  zone − zones;
}  /* end invisible_zones() */
```

The function *segment_cuts_poly*() calculates the parameter values to the intersection points of an edge with a convex polyhedron. If the edge is completely out of or completely inside the polygon, the function returns *FALSE*, else it returns *TRUE*.

```
Bool segment_cuts_poly(lambda, p, q, k, poly)                    (→ Proto.h)
    float lambda[ ];
    Vector p, q;
    short  k;
    Vector **poly;
{   /* begin segment_cuts_poly() */
    register  Vector **a = poly, **b = a + 1, **hi_poly = a + k;
    short  n = 0;
    float t1, t2;
    float temp;

    while (a < hi_poly) {
        if (b == hi_poly) b = poly;
        if (intersect_segments(&t1, &t2, p, q, **a, **b)) {
            if (t2 >= 0 && t2 <= 1) {
                lambda[n++] = t1;
                if (n == 2) {
                    if (fabs((double) lambda[0] − lambda[1]) < EPS)
                        return  FALSE;
                    if (lambda[0] > lambda[1])
                        Swap (lambda[0], lambda[1]);
                    return  TRUE;
                } /* end if (n) */
            } /* end if (t2) */
        } /* end if (intersect) */
        a++; b++;
    } /* end while (a) */
    return  FALSE;
} /* end segment_cuts_poly() */
```

After having calculated n hidden zones on $\overline{P^cQ^c}$ we have to determine which zones of $\overline{P^cQ^c}$ are still visible. If no hidden zones were found ($n = 0$), $\overline{P^cQ^c}$ is not obscured at all. If only one hidden zone was found ($n = 1$), the edges given by the parameter intervals $[0, \lambda_{k_1}]$ (if $\lambda_{k_1} > 0$) and $[\lambda_{k_2}, 1]$ (if $\lambda_{k_2} < 1$) are visible. For $n > 1$, we have to sort the zones as follows (Figure 3):

Let μ_1 and μ_2 be the parameter values that lead to a visible zone. We let $\mu_1 = 0$ and start a loop:

First, for all the hidden zones, we check whether μ_1 is inside a hidden zone. If this is the case, we transfer the beginning of the visible zone to the end of the hidden zone:

$$\lambda_{k_1} \leq \mu_1 < \lambda_{k_2} \Rightarrow \mu_1 = \lambda_{k_2} \quad (k = 1, \ldots, n). \tag{2}$$

Now we come to μ_2. We start with $\mu_2 = 1$ and, for all the hidden zones, check whether μ_2 is inside a hidden zone. If this is the case, we transfer μ_2 to the beginning of the respective zone:

$$\lambda_{k_1} < \mu_2 \leq \lambda_{k_2} \Rightarrow \mu_2 = \lambda_{k_1} \quad (k = 1, \ldots, n). \tag{3}$$

Now we plot the part of $\overline{P^c Q^c}$ that is given by the interval $[\mu_1, \mu_2]$. To enhance the three-dimensional aspect of the image, it is a good idea to shorten the line "a little bit,"[2] if μ_i is not 0 or 1 (Figure 4). At the same time, we store the upper limit of the zone $\mu_0 = \lambda_{k_2}$ of the hidden zone.

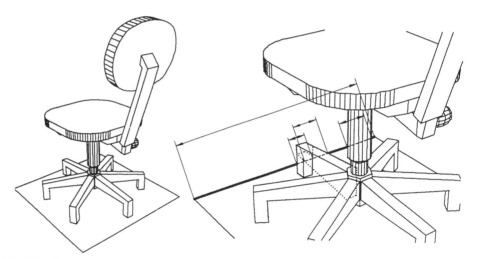

FIGURE 3. How to get the visible zones on the image of an edge.

For the next visible zone, we let $\mu_1 = \mu_0$. If $\mu_1 = 1$, we are finished, otherwise we have to reenter the loop.

The corresponding C code looks like this:

```
void plot_visible_zones(p, q, n, pool)                    (→ Proto.h)
    Vector p, q; /* The line segment (screen coordinates). */
    short  n; /* Number of hidden zones. */
    Vector2 pool[ ]; /* n hidden zones. */
```

---

[2]By approximately the size of a pixel. Because we do not think in terms of screen resolution, it is better to say: to shorten the line by a constant length s that is approximately 1% to 2% of the total diameter of the image of the scene. For really perfect images, we better create an "aura" of constant width s around the visible objects by enlarging the outlines Φ_k^c like in Figure 4. This shortens the lines automatically.

FIGURE 4. Objects with an "aura."

```
{   /* begin plot_visible_zones() */
    Vector a, b, pq;
    Vector2 *lambda = pool, *hi_lambda = lambda + n;
    register float m1, m2, t_help;
    Bool go_up, go_down;

    if (n == 0) { /* No hidden zones. */
        draw_line(p, q);
        return ;
    }
    if (n == 1) {
        /* One hidden zone and, therefore, up to two visible zones. */
        Subt_vec(pq, p, q);
        if ((m1 = (*lambda)[0]) > 0)
            Linear_comb(a, p, pq, m1),
            draw_line(a, p);
        if ((m2 = (*lambda)[1]) < 1)
            Linear_comb(b, p, pq, m2),
            draw_line(b, q);
        return ;
    }  /* end if (n == 1) */
    Subt_vec(pq, p, q);
    t_help = 0;
    do {
        m1 = t_help;     /* Determine lower parameter m1. */
        do {
            go_up = FALSE;
            for (lambda = pool; lambda < hi_lambda; lambda + +)
```

```
            if ((*lambda)[0] <= m1 && (*lambda)[1] > m1) {
                m1 = (*lambda)[1] + EPS; go_up = TRUE;
            }
        } while (go_up);
        m2 = 1;    /* Determine upper parameter m2. */
        do {
            go_down = FALSE;
            for (lambda = pool; lambda < hi_lambda; lambda ++) {
                if ((*lambda)[0] > m1 && (*lambda)[0] < m2) {
                    m2 = (*lambda)[0] − EPS; go_down = TRUE;
                    t_help = (*lambda)[1];
                }
            } /* end for (lambda) */
        } while (go_down);
        if (m2 − m1 > EPS) { /* Draw segment from m1 to m2. */
            Linear_comb(a, p, pq, m1);
            Linear_comb(b, p, pq, m2);
            if (m1 > EPS && m2 < (1 − EPS))
                draw_line(a, b);
            else if (m1 > EPS)
                draw_line(a, b);
            else if (m2 < (1 − EPS))
                draw_line(b, a);
        } /* end if (m2 − m1) */
    } while (m2 < (1 − EPS));
} /* end plot_visible_zones() */
```

In which order do we draw the images of the edges? When we plot them according to the edge list, we first have to eliminate the edges on the backfaces, which is not always easy. Therefore, it is best to plot the edges as sides of the faces. (We know the drawing order of the faces.)

We only have to make sure that we do not plot the images of some edges twice because an edge is always the intersection line of two faces. (The only edges, the images of which will never be plotted twice, are the contour edges, because they are the intersection lines of a frontface and a backface, and we ignore the backfaces.)

One idea to prevent double drawing is the following: let Φ be the object, the image of which we intend to plot. Now we copy the edge list of Φ into a temporary table. Before we draw the image $\overline{P^c Q^c}$ of an edge PQ, we check whether we can find the edge PQ (or QP) in the table. When we can find it, we plot $\overline{P^c Q^c}$ and eliminate the edge PQ from the temporary table.

When we remove the frontface of a convex polyhedron Φ, we can look into the polyhedron. In this case, we also have to check the edges on the back of Φ, to

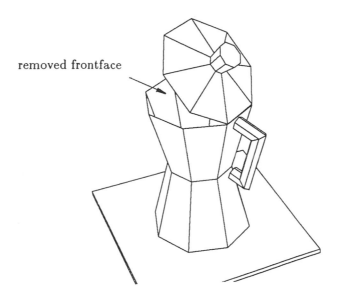

removed frontface

FIGURE 5. How to modify hidden zones when they are overlapped by the image of a removed frontface.

clip their images with all the outlines of the other objects that obscure Φ and to intersect the hidden zones $\overline{S_{k_1} S_{k_2}}$ with the image F^c of the *removed* frontface. Whenever a hidden zone is overlapped by the polygon F^c, it has to be modified or even to be split into two zones (Figure 5).

When we remove more than one face of Φ, things get more complicated. First, we have to modify all the hidden zones by means of the images of all the removed frontfaces. Secondly, it may be possible that we can "look through" the polyhedron. To find out whether this is the case, we do the following (Figure 6):

- If all the removed faces are backfaces, the object can be treated like a convex object.

- If all the removed faces are frontfaces, we cannot look through the polyhedron. In this case, we can treat the object like a convex object when we compare it with the other objects.

- If there **are** frontfaces *and* backfaces among the removed faces, we clip the image of each removed backface with the images of all the removed frontfaces. Thus, we get a set $\{S_j\}$ of (mostly convex) intersection polygons through which we can look through the polyhedron. If this set is empty, there is no "hole" in the image of Φ. If it is not empty, we have to store it as a part of the outline of Φ.

If the image of Φ has holes (given by the set $\{S_j\}$ of convex polygons), we have to modify the hidden zones that are produced by the convex outline of the image of Φ like in Figure 6.

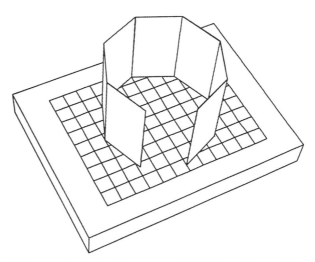

FIGURE 6. How to check whether we can look through a polyhedron with convex outline.

As we can see, the precise hidden-line algorithm for objects with convex outlines is still reasonably fast, even if the objects are hollow.

7.3 Depth Buffering for Visibility

In Chapters 5 and 6, we described a rendering algorithm that works very efficiently for scenes that consist of non-intersecting primitives with convex outlines. Admittedly, it is sometimes hard to split scenes in this way (even though in many cases it is worthwhile!). In the previous sections, we discussed a special hidden-line algorithm. In this section, we will develop a screen-oriented rendering algorithm that works for any kind of objects.

Two major advantages of the following algorithm are that it is easy to implement and it works comparatively fast. A disadvantage, however, is that in its genuine implementation, it needs a lot of memory (up to several Megabytes), which makes it necessary to split the scenes up in a certain way — at the cost of computation time.

——— • ———

The scene is interpreted as a set of polygons (it is of no importance to which objects the polygons belong[3]). Each polygon $\mathbf{P}$ has a picture $\mathbf{P}^c$ on the image plane π (the screen). We apply the linear transformation $\mathbf{T}_2 \; : \; P(x,\,y,\,z) \rightarrow$

---

[3]However, to be able to apply "backface removal" we should know whether the polygon we are plotting is the face of a convex polyhedron or not.

$P^*(x^* = x,\, y^* = y,\, z^* = z/(d-z))$ of Section 2.3 to all the vertices of the polygons. If we project the new set of polygons orthogonally from the infinite point of the positive $z^* - axis$ onto the image plane, we will get the genuine image of our scene again (Figure 7).

Now consider a grid $[0, M-1] \times [0, N-1]$ that is placed over the screen. We initialize each field value of a two-dimensional array $Zbuf[M][N]$ by the smallest z^*-value. Then we "buffer" each polygon of the scene in the following way: for each grid point $X^c(i,\, j)$ at the inside of the image polygon $\mathbf{P}^c = \mathbf{P}^{*c}$, we have a space point X^* on the normal to the projection plane π on the plane of $\mathbf{P}^*$. This "depth" z^* is stored if and only if $z^* > Zbuf[i][j]$. By doing this for each polygon of the scene, we store the *visible parts* of our polygons.

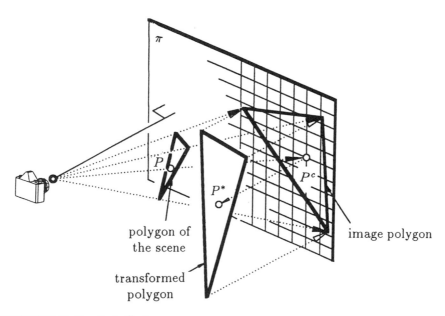

FIGURE 7. Depth buffering.

At any time of the rendering of the scene, the visibility test is simple: an arbitrary space point $P(x,\, y,\, z)$ is visible (at the moment when the image pixel is drawn) if and only if the corresponding field value contains the value $z^* = z/(d-z)$ ($\pm$ a certain tolerance, depending on the width of the grid).

In the simplest case, the grid dimensions M and N are the dimensions of the screen (measured in pixels). Then a point $P(x,\, y,\, z)$ corresponds to the field value $Zbuf[round(x)][round(y)]$. If we want to have control over the two-dimensional field of **float** variables, we need $4\,M\,N$ bytes, i.e., 3 Megabytes for a screen with a resolution of 1024×768 or 1 Megabyte for a screen with a resolution of 640×400! Because we have to admit a certain tolerance anyway, it will be enough to store the z^*-values as **short** numbers, where we assign the smallest z^*-value to 0 and the greatest z^*-value to the largest **unsigned short** number (≈ 65000). This reduces the necessary memory to 50% ($2\,M\,N$ bytes).

As long as we have enough RAM memory at our disposal, we prefer this kind of storage. Otherwise, we divide the screen into several horizontal zones and display the scene in several steps – at the cost of computation time, because many polygons will have to be proceeded two or even more times if they overlap two or more zones.[4]

The allocation and the freeing of the two-dimensional grid can be done by a function

#define *Alloc_huge_2d_array*(*type*, *array*, *n*, *m*) $\{^5$ \   ($\rightarrow$ `Macros.h`)
    array = (*type* **) *mem_alloc*(*n*, **sizeof**(*type* *), `"pointers"`);\
    for ($i = 0$; $i < n$; i++)\
        array[*i*] = (*type* *) *mem_alloc*(*m*, **sizeof**(*type*), `"2D-array"`);\
}

typedef **unsigned short Ushort**;   ($\rightarrow$ `Types.h`)

Ushort *Init*(* * *Zbuf*, *NULL*),
        Init(*Max_x_grid*, 100), *Init*(*Max_y_grid*, 50);   ($\rightarrow$ `Globals.h`)
Bool *Init*(*Z_buffering*, *FALSE*);   ($\rightarrow$ `Globals.h`)

Global Init_fptr(*move_scan*, *quickmove*);   ($\rightarrow$ `Proto.h`)

Global Init_fptr(*draw_scan*, *quickdraw*);   ($\rightarrow$ `Proto.h`)

---

void *z_buffer*(*on*)   ($\rightarrow$ `Proto.h`)
    Bool *on*;
{ /* begin *z_buffer*() */
    register short *i*;

    Z_buffering = *on*;
    if (*on*) {
        move_scan = *move_buffer*;
        draw_scan = *quick_draw_buffer*;
        Max_x_grid = *Max_x* − *Min_x* + 1;
        Max_y_grid = *Max_y* − *Min_y* + 1;
        if (*Zbuf* == *NULL*)
            Alloc_huge_2d_array(**Ushort**, *Zbuf*, *Max_y_grid*, *Max_x_grid*);

---

[4]In an extreme case, each line of the screen can be considered as a zone. Usually this is done in connection with scan-line algorithms [FOLE90].

[5]In Chapter 3, we developed a very similar macro *Alloc_2d_array*(*type*, *array*, *n*, *m*). This macro allocates memory allocation all the space for the array at the same time. On computers with less memory, this might cause an "out of memory error," even though there is enough memory left. Thus, we split the memory into *n* sectors. This will have no influence on the access to the variable *Zbuf*[*i*][*j*], which is transformed into the expression *(*(*Zbuf* + *i*) + *j*) by the compiler.

```
    } else {
        move_scan = quick_move, draw_scan = quick_scan;
        Free_huge_2d_array(Zbuf, Max_y_grid); Zbuf = NULL;
    }
}   /* end z_buffer() */
```

(The functions $move\_buffer()$ and $quick\_draw\_buffer()$ will be developed later on.) The initialization of the array is done by the function

void $clear\_z\_buffer()$ $(\rightarrow$ Proto.h$)$

```
{   /* begin clear_z_buffer() */
    register Ushort * grid, *hi_grid, i;

    if (!Zbuf) safe_exit("Use z_buffer(TRUE) first");
    for (i = 0; i < Max_y_grid; i++) {
        hi_grid = (grid = Zbuf[i]) + Max_x_grid;
        while (grid < hi_grid)
            * grid++ = 0;
    }
}   /* end clear_z_buffer() */
```

When we proceed a polygon, we first clip it with the clip volume (Section 2.5). The clipped polygon is then proceeded as usual. At the end of the function $poly\_move()$ (Section 4.6), we add the lines

```
        if (Z_buffering)
            set_plane_point(0, a);
```

and at the end of the function $poly\_draw()$ (Section 4.6), we add the lines

```
        if (Z_buffering && Cur_vtx − Vtx < 3)
            set_plane_point(i, a);
```

The function $set\_plane\_point()$ transforms the z-value of the point a to the interval $0 < z_{trans} < 2^{16} = 65536$, i.e., to the range of an **unsigned short** number. When it comes to the third point, we can determine the constants of the plane of the polygon:

Plane $Buffered\_plane;$ $(\rightarrow$ Globals.h$)$

#define $Float\_to\_Ushort(\text{u, f})\backslash$ $(\rightarrow$ Macros.h$)$
    $u = 1000 + 64000 * (f − Min\_z) / (Max\_z − Min\_z)$

```
void set_plane_point(i, p)                           (→ Proto.h)
    short  i;
    Vector p;
{   /* begin set_plane_point() */
    static Vector tri[3];

    if  (i > 2) return ;
    Copy_vec2(tri[i], p);
    /* Transform the z-value into the range of a Ushort. */
    Float_to_Ushort(tri[i][Z], p[Z]);
    if  (i == 2)
        plane_constants(&Buffered_plane, tri[0], tri[1], tri[2]);
}   /* end set_plane_point() */
```

With the help of the plane constants, we can determine the z^*-values of all points
in the polygon's plane by means of the routine

```
float z_value(x, y)                                  (→ Proto.h)
    short  x, y;
{   /* begin z_value() */
    static float  *d  =  &Buffered_plane.cnst,
                  *a  =  &Buffered_plane.normal[X],
                  *b  =  &Buffered_plane.normal[Y],
                  *c  =  &Buffered_plane.normal[Z];
    return  (*d − *a * x − *b * y) / (*c + EPS);
}   /* end z_value() */
```

(The EPS helps to avoid a division by zero.)

Now we can write the desired functions
$move\_buffer()$ and $quick\_draw\_buffer()$:

short $X1\_grid$, $Y1\_grid$;   (→ Globals.h)

```
void move_buffer(x, y)                               (→ Proto.h)
    register  short  x, y;
{   /* begin move_buffer() */
    X1_grid  =  x;
    Y1_grid  =  y;
}   /* end move_buffer() */
```

```
void quick_draw_buffer(x, y)                                    (→ Proto.h)
   register short  x, y;
{  /* begin quick_draw_buffer() */
   register short  x1 = X1_grid;
   float z1, dz;
   register Ushort * xg = &Zbuf[y − Min_y][X1_grid − Min_x];

   z1 = z_value(X1_grid, y);
   dz = (x != x1) ? ((z_value(x, y) − z1) /(x − x1)) : 1;
   for  ( ; x1 <= x; x1 + +, z1 + = dz, xg + +) {
      if (*xg < z1)
           * xg = z1,
           G_set_pixel(x1, y);
   }  /* end for (x1) */
   X1_grid = x;
}  /* end quick_draw_buffer() */
```

To display the scene, we now use the function

```
void buffer_scene()                                            (→ Proto.h)
{  /* begin buffer_scene() */
   short  max_zones = 4;
       /* If you have enough RAM, let max_zones = 1; */
   float h = Window_height;
   float y1, y2, y0 = (short ) (h) /max_zones;

   for  (y1 = 0, y2 = y0; y1 < h; y1 + = y0, y2 + = y0) {
       z_buffer(FALSE);
       xy_region(0.0, Window_width, y1, Minimum(y2, h));
       z_buffer(TRUE);
       clear_z_buffer();
       < plot all the polygons of the scene in an arbitrary order >
   }  /* end for (y1) */
   G_swap_screens();
}  /* end buffer_scene() */
```

and we let $display\_scene = buffer\_scene$;

For a general hidden-line removal, we still need a general function $draw\_buffered$ $\_line()$, which connects two space points:

```
void draw_buffered_line(p, q)                                    (→ Proto.h)
   Vector p0, q0;
{   /* begin draw_buffered_line() */
   Vector p, q, delta;
   short i, i0;
   float t;
   register short x, y;
   Ushort *z;
   Vector g;
   Bool exists;
   if (!clip3d_line(&exists, p, q, p0, q0)) {
        Copy_vec(p, p0); Copy_vec(q, q0);
   } else if (!exists) return;
   Float_to_Ushort(p[Z], p0[Z]);
   Float_to_Ushort(q[Z], q0[Z]);
   i0 = Maximum(fabs(q[X] − p[X]), fabs(q[Y] − p[Y]));
   if (!i0) {
        x = p[X] + 0.5; y = p[Y] + 0.5;
        z = &Z_buffer.val[y − Min_y][x − Min_x];
        t = Maximum(p[Z], q[Z]);
        if (*z <= t) {
            *z = t;
            G_set_pixel(x, y);
        }
        return;
   }
   t = 1.0 / i0;
   Subt_vec(delta, p, q);
   Scale_vec(delta, delta, t);
   Copy_vec(g, p);
   for (i = 0; i <= i0; i++) {
        x = g[X]; y = g[Y];
        z = &Z_buffer.val[y − Min_y][x − Min_x];
        if (*z <= g[Z]) {
            *z = g[Z];
            G_sct_pixel(x, y);
        }
        Add_vec(g, g, delta);
   }
}   /* end draw_buffered_line() */
```

8
Mathematical Curves and Surfaces

In Chapters 8 and 9, we will talk about mathematical curves and surfaces and – as an approximation to them – spline curves and spline surfaces. Sometimes it is better to have line drawings as an output. The drawn images of such curves further support the human imagination, especially when we talk about the lines of intersection of such surfaces. For scientific purposes, the line of intersection is often of much more interest than the rest of the image.

If we want to draw the image of a surface by hand or with the plotter, we do it by drawing the images of curves on the surface, especially the parameter lines and the contour lines. These and, of course, many other curves on surfaces as well have always been of great interest to geometrists. With the help of computers, today we are able to do things that in the past would have meant a lot of work. This is especially true for the calculation of surfaces that are known only approximatively, which means that only a limited number of points on the surface are given.

Of course, from the geometrist's point of view, it is interesting and often necessary to approximate surfaces bit by bit with the help of mathematically seizable surfaces (spline surfaces). This is what is normally done and the results are by no means unsatisfactory. However, the price that has to be paid for interpolations of this kind are comparatively long periods of calculation. Furthermore, every interpolation is only a guess. This means that even though in some cases we get pictures that look perfect, they do not necessarily correspond to reality. One only has to think of a landscape, the shape of which can be completely arbitrary. In a reversal of this train of thought, one can approximate surfaces with the help of polyhedra. In this case, the computer does not have to distinguish between mathematically defined or empirically seizable surfaces. Certain kinds of problems, and intersections in particular, can be solved much more easily this way. Also, many fast algorithms for the rendering of certain types of polyhedra even permit an animation of the picture of the surface. An approximation by polyhedra may pose problems, particularly when one is forced to come back to the second differential form of the surface. In that case, a reasonable representation of osculating lines or lines of curvature without the use of mathematical formulas is simply impossible. Therefore, we want to discuss both kinds of surfaces, however, with an emphasis put on approximational polyhedra.

8.1 Parametrized Curves

A "mathematical curve" is a (planar or not planar) line in space. In our context, we will only talk about curves in 3D-space (a curve in 2D-space can be interpreted as a curve in 3D-space, where the third coordinate vanishes). If such a curve is given by a parametrized equation

$$\vec{x} = \vec{x}(u) = \begin{pmatrix} x(u) \\ y(u) \\ z(u) \end{pmatrix} \quad \text{with} \quad u \in [u_1, u_2] \tag{1}$$

(where $x(u)$, $y(u)$, $z(u)$ are arbitrary functions in the parameter u), it is quite easy to plot its image. We calculate a certain number n of space points, which belong to n different u-values, and submit their coordinates to a perspective or orthogonal projection. Then the image points are connected to a polygon that approximates the image of the curve. The number n of points depends on the application, but the more points we calculate, the better the approximation will be.

Example 1: The straight line is the simplest curve in space:

$$\vec{x} = \begin{pmatrix} p_x + u\,q_x \\ p_y + u\,q_y \\ p_z + u\,q_z \end{pmatrix}, \; u \in R. \tag{2}$$

$P(p_x,\, p_y,\, p_z)$ is a point on the line, $(q_x,\, q_y,\, q_z)$ is the direction vector. With straight lines, we can generate ruled surfaces like the ones shown in Figures 5, 6 and 7.

Example 2: A circle in 3D-space with the radius r, the center $M(m_x, m_y, m_z)$ and the normalized direction $\vec{a} = (a_x,\, a_y,\, a_z)$ of its axis can be described by

$$\vec{x} = \begin{pmatrix} m_x - \frac{r}{s}(a_y \cos u + a_x a_z \sin u) \\ m_y + \frac{r}{s}(a_x \cos u - a_y a_z \sin u) \\ m_z + rs \sin u \end{pmatrix} \text{ with } s = \sqrt{a_x^2 + a_y^2},\; u \in [0, 2\pi]. \tag{3}$$

or

$$\vec{x} = \begin{pmatrix} m_x + r\cos u \\ m_y + r\sin u \\ m_z \end{pmatrix} \quad u \in [0, 2\pi], \tag{4}$$

when the axis is parallel z $(a_x = a_y = 0)$.

Such circles can be used to generate tubular surfaces like the ones shown in Figures 5, 6 and 7.

Example 3: A loxodrome on a sphere (center O, radius r) that intersects all the meridian circles of the sphere at the constant angle α (Figure 1) is described by

$$\vec{x} = \begin{pmatrix} s\sin t\cos u \\ s\sin t\sin u \\ s\cos t - r \end{pmatrix} \quad \text{with } s = \frac{2r}{\sqrt{1 + e^{2u\cot\alpha}}}, \ t = \arctan e^{u\cot\alpha}, \ u \in R. \tag{5}$$

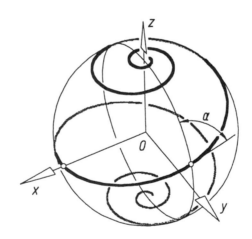

FIGURE 1. Loxodrome on a sphere.

Example 4: The line of intersection of two cylinders

$$x^2 + y^2 = r^2 \text{ and } (x - a)^2 + z^2 = s^2 \ (a \geq 0)$$

(Figure 2) can be parametrized as follows:

1. For $s < r - a$, the curve is split into two branches. One of them has the representation

$$\vec{x} = \begin{pmatrix} a + s\cos u \\ \sqrt{r^2 - (a + s\cos u)^2} \\ s\sin u \end{pmatrix}, \quad u \in [0, 2\pi], \tag{6}$$

the other one is symmetrical to the xz-plane.

2. The case $s > r + a$ (two branches as well) is covered by

$$\vec{x} = \begin{pmatrix} r \cos u \\ r \sin u \\ \sqrt{s^2 - (r \cos u - a)^2} \end{pmatrix}, \ u \in [0, 2\pi]. \tag{7}$$

(The other branch of the line is symmetrical to the xy-plane.)

3. In the third case ($s \in [r-a, r+a]$), the line of intersection is continuous and a possible parametric representation is

$$\vec{x} = \begin{pmatrix} t(u) \\ \pm\sqrt{r^2 - t(u)^2} \ (< 0 \ if \ u \in [2\pi, 4\pi]) \\ \pm\sqrt{s^2 - (t(u) - a)^2} \ (< 0 \ if \ u < [\pi, 3\pi]) \end{pmatrix}, \ u \in [0, 4\pi]. \tag{8}$$

The function

$$t(u) = \frac{1}{2}[r + s - a + (r - s + a) \cos u]$$

guarantees that all the coordinates are real ($t \in [a-s, r]$) and that the points on the curve are distributed homogeneously. Figure 2 shows the limiting case $s = r - a$ (treated as case 3).

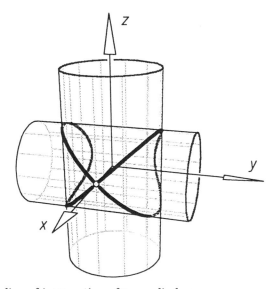

FIGURE 2. The line of intersection of two cylinders.

Other examples of parametrized curves can be derived from Equations 10 to 14 if u is constant and if v varies.

In practice, however, there are many cases in which curves are *not* given by a parametrized equation. As a matter of fact, many curves are seen in connection with the surfaces they lie on. This is not so amazing when we consider that on every surface there are ∞^2 lines (on a line there are "only" ∞^1 points).

8.2 Classes of Parametrized Surfaces

Analogously to Equation 1, a "mathematical surface" can be given by a parametrized equation

$$\vec{x} = \vec{x}(u,\, v) = \begin{pmatrix} x(u,\, v) \\ y(u,\, v) \\ z(u,\, v) \end{pmatrix} \quad \text{with} \quad u \in [u_1, u_2], v \in [v_1, v_2]. \tag{9}$$

For $v = const$, we get the so-called u-lines, and for $u = const$, we get the v-lines as the simplest curves on the surface.

Let $x_0(u)(u)$, $y_0(u)(u)$, $z_0(u)(u)$ be the parametric representation of a line g in space ($u \in [u_1,\, u_2]$). This "generating line" can now be submitted to arbitrary transformations in order to generate a surface. (A parametrized equation $\vec{x} = \vec{x}(t)$ of a general curve on the surface is defined by the functions $u = u(t), v = v(t)$.)

Example 1: Translation surfaces. The simplest way of generating a surface is to translate g along a line h (Figure 3) with the parametric representation $\bar{x}_0(v)$, $\bar{y}_0(v)$, $\bar{z}_0(v)$ ($v \in [v_1,\, v_2]$). Such a *"translation surface"* has the equation

$$\vec{x}(u,\, v) \;=\; \begin{pmatrix} x_0(u) + \bar{x}_0(v) \\ y_0(u) + \bar{y}_0(v) \\ z_0(u) + \bar{z}_0(v) \end{pmatrix} \quad . \tag{10}$$

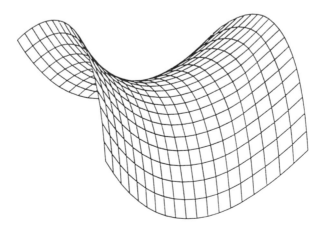

FIGURE 3. The hyperbolic paraboloid as a translation surface.

Example 2: Surfaces of revolution. When the generating line g is rotated about an axis a, we get a *surface of revolution* (Figure 4). When a is the z-axis, the general equation of such a surface is

$$\vec{x}(u,\,v) \;=\; \begin{pmatrix} x_0(u)\,\cos v - y_0(u)\,\sin v \\ x_0(u)\,\sin v + y_0(u)\,\cos v \\ z_0(u) \end{pmatrix} \quad v \in [0,\,2\pi]. \tag{11}$$

When g is planar and when its plane contains the axis a (e.g., for $y_0(u) \equiv 0$), g is also called the "meridian line."

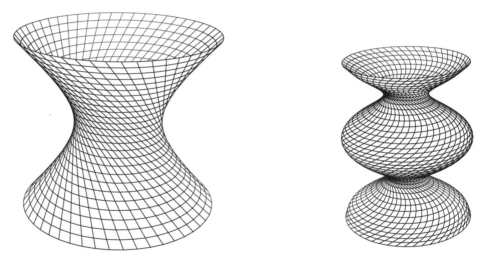

FIGURE 4. Surfaces of revolution: the surface on the left is a hyperboloid with a straight generating line. The surface on the right has a generating helix, and surprisingly, it is also a translation surface!

Example 3: Helical surfaces. When the generating line g is not only rotated about an axis a (the z-axis) but also translated proportionally along a, the generated surface is a *helical surface* (Figure 5):

$$\vec{x}(u,\,v) \;=\; \begin{pmatrix} x_0(u)\,\cos v - y_0(u)\,\sin v \\ x_0(u)\,\sin v + y_0(u)\,\cos v \\ z_0(u) + c\,v \end{pmatrix} \qquad (c\ldots\text{constant parameter}). \quad (12)$$

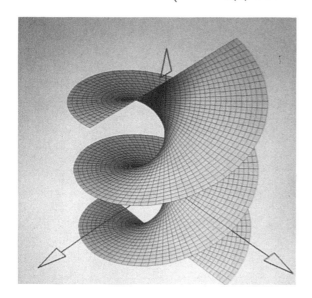

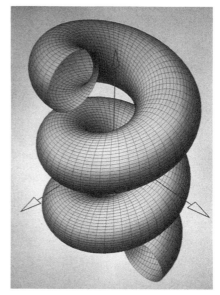

FIGURE 5. Ruled and tubular helical surfaces.

Example 4: Rotoidal surfaces. A possible generalization of the helical motion is the "*rotoidal motion*": we replace the proportional translation along the axis a by a proportional rotation about an axis b (ratio c). The axis b is skew and perpendicular to a and rotates around a (Figure 6).[1] The generated *rotoidal surfaces* have the equation

$$\vec{x}(u, v) = \begin{pmatrix} (x_0(u) - z_0(u) \cos cv) \cos v - y_0(u) \sin v \\ (x_0(u) - z_0(u) \cos cv) \sin v + y_0(u) \cos v \\ z_0(u) \sin cv \end{pmatrix} . \qquad (13)$$

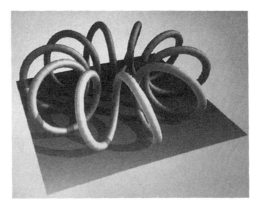

FIGURE 6. Ruled and tubular rotoidal surfaces.

[1]The motion converges to the helical motion when b converges to the infinite line ([GLAE81]).

Example 5: Spiral surfaces. At last an example of a family of surfaces where the generating line g is not only moved in space but scaled as well. We rotate g about an axis (the z-axis), and we apply a proportional scaling to g with a fixed point on the axis (e.g., the origin) as its center. The generated surfaces are then *spiral surfaces* (Figure 7, Figure 8 and Figure 20):

$$\vec{x}(u,\,v) \;=\; \begin{pmatrix} (x_0(u)\,\cos v - y_0(u)\,\sin v)\,e^{cv} \\ (x_0(u)\,\sin v + y_0(u)\,\cos v)\,e^{cv} \\ z_0(u)\,e^{cv} \end{pmatrix} \quad (c\ldots \text{constant}). \qquad (14)$$

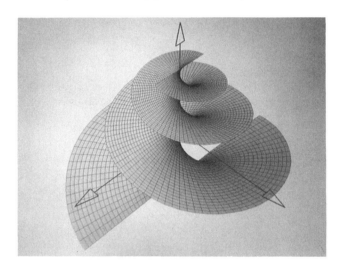

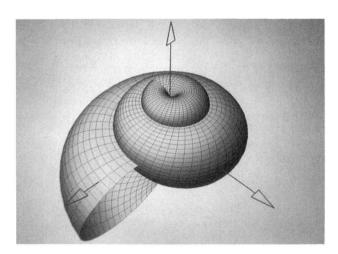

FIGURE 7. Ruled and tubular spiral surfaces.

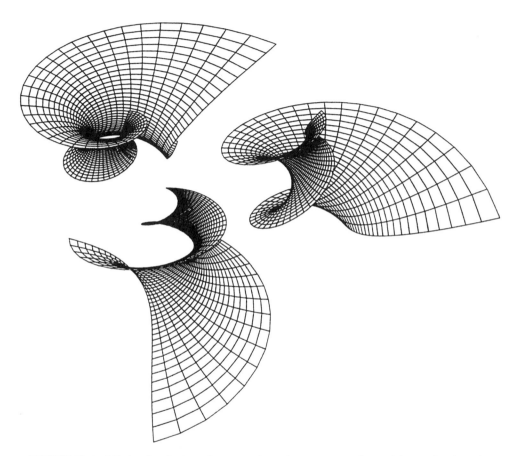

FIGURE 8. Minimal spiral surfaces are bent into one another without altering the metric of the surfaces (vanishing main curvature!) ([WUND54]). Similar bendings exist for any type of minimal surfaces, e.g., for the transformation of a helicoid into a catenoid ([GLAE88/2]).

8.3 Surfaces Given by Implicit Equations

The set of points $P(x, y, z)$ that fulfills a condition $F(x, y, z) = 0$ is also a surface Φ. The function $F(x, y, z)$ is called the "implicit equation" of Φ. If F is an algebraic function

$$F(x, y, z) \equiv \sum_{i+j+k \leq n} a_{ijk} x^i y^j z^k = 0 \quad (i, j, k \geq 0, \ a_{ijk} = \text{constant}) \tag{15}$$

in x, y and z, the surface is algebraic as well. The highest exponent n in Equation 15 is called the "degree" of an algebraic surface Φ. It can be interpreted as the highest possible number of intersection points of Φ with a straight line. For example, the surfaces given by the linear implicit equation

$$F(x, y, z) \equiv a_{100}x + a_{010}y + a_{001}z + a_{000} = 0 \tag{16}$$

are all identical with planes in space.

The general quadratic equation

$$\begin{aligned} F(x, y, z) \quad \equiv \quad & a_{200}\, x^2 + a_{020}\, y^2 + a_{002}\, z^2 + \\ & + a_{110}\, xy + a_{011}\, yz + a_{101}\, zx + \\ & + a_{100}\, x + a_{010}\, y + a_{001}\, z + a_{000} = 0 \end{aligned} \tag{17}$$

describes the surfaces of degree 2. Among these "quadrics", we have the spheres or, more generally, the ellipsoids, the paraboloids and the hyperboloids. Special cases are the elliptic (parabolic, hyperbolic) cylinders and the elliptic cones.

In simple cases, it will be possible to find the implicit equation of a surface when its parametrized equation is given and vice versa.

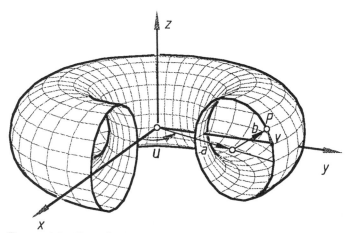

FIGURE 9. Parametrization of a torus.

A torus (Figure 9), for example, can be described by the parametrization

$$\vec{x}(u, v) = \begin{pmatrix} (a - b\cos v)\cos u, \\ (a - b\cos v)\sin u, \\ b\sin v \end{pmatrix} \quad (u \in [0, 2\pi],\ v \in [0, 2\pi]). \tag{18}$$

The parameters u, v can be eliminated, which leads to

$$F(x, y, z) \equiv (a - \sqrt{x^2 + y^2})^2 + z^2 - b^2 = 0 \tag{19}$$

or

$$F(x, y, z) \equiv (x^2 + y^2 + z^2 + a^2 - b^2)^2 - 4a^2(x^2 + y^2) = 0. \tag{20}$$

Thus, a torus turns out to be an algebraic surface of degree 4.

An interesting surface can be generated from a torus by "inverting" it with respect to a sphere (Figure 10). Let $C(x_0, 0, 0)$ be the center of the sphere and ϱ be its radius. Then the inversion is given by

$$\vec{x}^* = \frac{\varrho^2}{(\vec{x} - \vec{c})^2} (\vec{x} - \vec{c}). \tag{21}$$

Without proof, the surface is also of degree 4, and it is called "Dupin's cyclid" ([WUND66]).

FIGURE 10. The inverse surface of a torus with respect to a sphere is called "Dupin's cyclid."

8.4 Special Curves on Mathematical Surfaces

A line of intersection of two surfaces can only be parametrized in special cases. The same is true for the contour lines of surfaces or "integral curves" on surfaces

(Section 8.5). Furthermore, it often takes a lot of CPU time to calculate enough points on the line for a smooth image polygon.

Fortunately, many important classes of curves on surfaces Φ $(\vec{x}(u, v))$ can be characterized by a condition $f(u, v) = 0$.

We will now develop a subroutine $zero\_manifold\_of\_f\_uv()$, which can be used to trace curves that are characterized by an equation $f(u, v) = 0$. The result will be a contiguous (sorted) set of parameter pairs (u, v). Considering the importance of such a routine for geometrists, it is not surprising that a number of different solutions of the problem have been described (see, for example, [SEYB77], [PAUK86], [GLAE86]). The routine we will develop does the job comparatively fast, provided that the result does not have to be extremely accurate (there is no restriction to accuracy, however, if we do not mind longer periods of calculation time).

The idea is the following: if we interpret $w = f(u, v)$ as the third coordinate of a Cartesian (u, v, w) system, the solution of $f(u, v) = 0$ consists of all the intersection points of the graph $\Gamma : w = f(u, v)$ with the plane $\beta : w = 0$. The zero manifold of $f(u, v)$ can, thus, be interpreted as the planar line of intersection $s = \Gamma \cap \beta$, which may consist of several branches.

Equation 22 defines a one-to-one correlation between the surface and the base rectangle in the (u, v)-plane β. Therefore, we have a one-to-one correlation between those lines of intersection of function graphs and curves that fulfill a condition $f(u, v) = 0$ on a surface $\vec{x}(u, v)$. Every point $S(u_s, v_s)$ on the line of intersection s then corresponds to a point $P(x, y, z)$ on the desired space curve on the surface: $x = x(u_s, v_s)$, $y = y(u_s, v_s)$, $z = z(u_s, v_s)$.

It is easy to find a large set of intersection points of the graph. The problem, however, is to connect these points to polygons (this enables us to draw *line segments* instead of little dots on the screen). The key to the solution lies in the triangulation of the graph Γ.

We calculate a comparatively small number of points on Γ that are above a grid on the horizontal base rectangle ($u \in [u_1, u_2]$, $v \in [v_1, v_2]$) and triangulate this approximating polyhedron. In order to get the best triangulation possible, we use "average normals" in each point of the polyhedron.

Now we intersect each triangle with the base plane β. For all the triangles that have a line of intersection, we store the two pointers to the vertices of the respective segment of the line of intersection. This enables us to connect the line segments to polygons. Most of the intersection points will be reached twice, because, in general, two neighboring triangles have one side in common. Thus, we start the following algorithm:

We identify a first branch of s with an arbitrary line segment $\{a_0, a_1\}$. If there is a line segment $\{a_1, a_2\}$ (or $\{a_2, a_1\}$) among the residual segments, we enlarge the branch to $\{a_0, a_1, a_2\}$. This procedure is repeated until no further line segments can be added. The branch has now grown to $\{a_0, a_1, \ldots, a_{m-1}, a_m\}$. If $a_0 = a_m$, the branch is a closed line, otherwise we try to continue it from its other end. Without altering the branch, we swap its points to $\{a_m, a_{m-1}, \ldots, a_1, a_0\}$. If there is a line segment $\{a_0, a_{m+1}\}$ (or $\{a_{m+1}, a_0\}$) among the residual segments ($\{a_0, a_1\}$ has already been concatenated), we add it to the branch and so forth ($\Rightarrow \{a_0, a_{m+1}, \ldots, a_s\}$). The current ($k$-th) branch then consists of $s+1$ points.

We trace new branches until there are no residual segments left.

A C version ($concat\_to\_polygons()$) of the algorithm is listed in Section 6.1. Since it works almost exclusively with pointer arithmetic, we also list a pseudo-code for better understanding:

```
residual segments rs ≡ all line segments
n  := number of residual segments
k  := 0
repeat
    {branch[k][0], branch[k][1]}  :=  rs[0]
    n  :=  n − 1
    rs[0]  :=  rs[n]
    s  :=  1
    closed  :=  FALSE
    first_chain  :=  TRUE
    repeat
        repeat
            b := branch[k][s]
            if exists rs[i] with {b, succ} ∨ {succ, b}
                s  :=  s + 1
                branch[k][s]  :=  succ
                n  :=  n − 1
                rs[i]  :=  rs[n]
                if succ = branch[k][0]
                    closed  :=  TRUE
        until closed ∨ n = 0 ∨ no succ found
        size[k]  :=  s + 1
        if not closed ∧ first_chain
            for i  :=  0 to s/2
                swap(branch[k][i], branch[k][s − i])
            first_chain  :=  FALSE
    until closed ∨ ¬first_chain ∨ n = 0
    k  :=  k + 1
until n = 0
no_of_branches  :=  k
```

In this manner, the line of solution can be found very quickly. The result, however, is not as satisfactory as one might expect it to be. Because we replace the graph by a polyhedron, the line of intersection will hardly be very smooth, unless we drastically increase the number of the faces of the polyhedron.

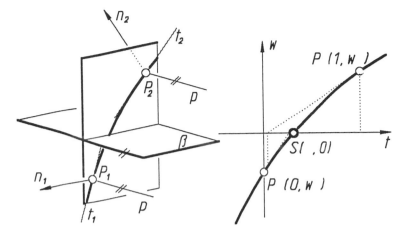

FIGURE 11. The parameter lines on the graph Γ are approximated piecewise by means of cubic parabolas. Such a parabola is determined by two "line elements."

To make the curve s smooth, we replace the sides of the intersecting triangles by planar cubic parabolas (Figure 11a). The plane ψ on which such a parabola lies is normal to the base plane β. The parabola itself is determined by the two end points P_1 and P_2 and by the "average" normals n_1 and n_2 in P_1 and P_2. The tangent t_i of the parabola in P_i is normal both to n_i and to the normal p of ψ.

Figure 11b illustrates the situation in ψ. We introduce a local two-dimensional coordinate system (t, w). The parabola will have the equation

$$w = a\,t^3 + b\,t^2 + c\,t + d. \tag{22}$$

The two given points may have the coordinates $P_1(0, w_1)$ and $P_2(1, w_2)$. Thus, we have $(1)\ldots w_1 = d$ and $(2)\ldots w_2 = a + b + c + d$. The slope of a general tangent of the parabola is given by the first derivation

$$\dot{w} = \frac{dw}{dt} = 3a\,t^2 + 2b\,t + c. \tag{23}$$

The slopes of the tangents t_1 and t_2 may be k_1 and k_2. Thus, we have $(3)\ldots k_1 = c$ and $(4)\ldots k_2 = 3a + 2b + c$. The equations $(1)\ldots(4)$ lead to the coefficients of the parabola:

$$a = k_1 + k_2 - 2(w_2 - w_1),\ \ b = 3(w_2 - w_1) - 2k_1 - k_2,\ \ c = k_1,\ \ d = w_1. \tag{24}$$

Now we have to intersect the parabola with $w = 0$. This can be done quickly by NEWTON's iteration ([FOLE90]). The solution point may have the local coordinates $S(\lambda, 0)$. In the (u, v)–coordinates, the point S is then described by $s_u = p_{1u} + \lambda(p_{2u} - p_{1u})$, $s_v = p_{1v} + \lambda(p_{2v} - p_{1v})$.

———— • ————

Let us now gradually develop the necessary code for the important function *zero_manifold_of_f_uv()*:

/* We need a pointer to a function $f(x)$. */

Global Init_fptr(f_x, cubic_parabola); ($\rightarrow$ Proto.h)

/* This is the initializing function. */

float *Coeff*[4];
    /* Global in the current module. */

```
float cubic_parabola(x)                              (→ Proto.h)
    float x;
{   /* begin cubic_parabola() */
    return  ((Coeff[0] * x + Coeff[1]) * x + Coeff[2]) * x + Coeff[3];
}   /* end cubic_parabola() */
```

/* The next function tries to find the zero of $f(x)$. */

```
float zero_of_f_x_with_newton(x, eps, ok)            (→ Proto.h)
    float x, eps;
    Bool * ok;
{   /* begin zero_of_f_x_with_newton() */
    float x0, y, dx = 1e − 4;
    short i = 0;

    do {
        x0 = x;
        y = f_x(x0);
        x = x0 − y /((f_x(x0 + dx) − y) /dx);
    } while (fabs(x − x0) > eps && ++i < 10);
    * ok = (i < 10 ? TRUE : FALSE);
    return x;
}   /* end zero_of_f_x_with_newton() */
```

/* The iteration by NEWTON works fast, but it does not converge in any
    case. Thus, we need another function for the determination of the zero of a
    function. */

```
float zero_of_f_x_with_bin_search(x1, dx, y1, eps)          (→ Proto.h)
    float x1, dx, y1, eps;
{   /* begin zero_of_f_x_with_bin_search() */
    float x0, y0, dx;

    if (dx < eps) return x1;
    dx /= 2;
    x0 = x1 + dx;
    y0 = f_x(x0);
    if (fabs(y0) < EPS) return x0;
    else if (y1 * y0 < 0)
        return zero_of_f_x_with_bin_search(x1, dx, y1, eps);
    else
        return zero_of_f_x_with_bin_search(x0, dx, y0, eps);
}   /* end zero_of_f_x_with_bin_search() */
```

/* Now we can find the zero of a cubic parabola. */

```
float zero_of_cubic_par(a, b, c, d, start_x)               (→ Proto.h)
    float a, b, c, d, start_x;
{   /* begin zero_of_cubic_par() */
    float x;
    Bool ok;

    Coeff[0] = a; Coeff[1] = b; Coeff[2] = c; Coeff[3] = d;
    f_x = cubic_parabola;
    x = zero_of_f_x_with_newton(start_x, 1e - 3, &ok);
    if (ok) return x;
    else return zero_of_f_x_with_bin_search(0.0, 1.0, d, 1e - 3);
}   /* end zero_of_cubic_par() */
```

/* The following function checks whether two vectors are (more or less) identical. */

```
Bool identical(a, b)                                        (→ Proto.h)
    Vector a, b;
{   /* begin identical() */
#define SMALL 1e - 4
    if (fabs(a[X] - b[X]) > SMALL
        || fabs(a[Y] - b[Y]) > SMALL
        || fabs(a[Z] - b[Z]) > SMALL) return FALSE;
    else return     TRUE;
#undef SMALL
}   /* end identical() */
```

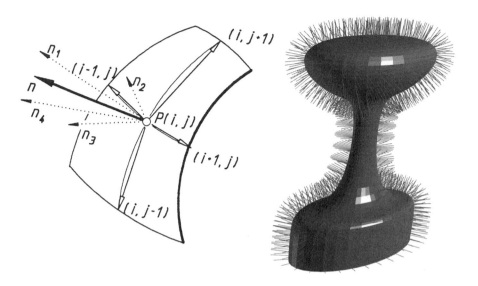

FIGURE 12. How to determine the "average normals" of a surface.

/* The next function takes a given *grid* of points on any surface and determines possible *normal*s of the surface in these grid points (Figure 12). */

```
void average_normals(normal, grid, imax, jmax)              (→ Proto.h)
    Vector **normal; /*  Average normals in grid points (2d). */
    Vector **grid; /*  Grid of basepoints (2-dimensional). */
    short imax, jmax;
        /*  Size of grid: 0 ≤ i < imax, 0 ≤ j < jmax. */
{   /* begin average_normals() */
    Vector n, diff[4];
    short i, j, k, k1;
    register Vector *p, *average_normal;
    Vector *v[4];
    Bool closed[2];

    closed[0] = identical(grid[0][0], grid[0][jmax − 1]);
    closed[1] = identical(grid[imax − 1][0], grid[0][0]);
    for (i = 0; i < imax; i++)
        for (j = 0; j < jmax; j++) {
            p = v[0] = v[1] = v[2] = v[3] = (Vector *) grid[i][j];
            if (i > 0) v[0] = (Vector *) grid[i − 1][j];
            else if (closed[1]) v[0] = (Vector *) grid[imax − 2][j];
```

```
        if (j > 0) v[1] = (Vector *) grid[i][j − 1];
        else if (closed[0]) v[1] = (Vector *) grid[i][jmax − 2];
        if (i + 1 < imax) v[2] = (Vector *) grid[i + 1][j];
        else if (closed[1]) v[2] = (Vector *) grid[1][j];
        if (j + 1 < jmax) v[3] = (Vector *) grid[i][j + 1];
        else if (closed[0]) v[3] = (Vector *) grid[i][1];

        for (k = 0; k < 4; k++)
            if (v[k] != p)
                Subt_vec(diff[k], *p, *v[k]);
        average_normal = (Vector *) normal[i][j];
        Zero_vec(*average_normal);
        for (k = 0, k1 = 1; k < 4; k++, k1 = (k1 + 1) % 4) {
            if (v[k] != p && v[k1] != p) {
                Cross_product(n, diff[k1], diff[k]);
                normalize_vec(n);
                Add_vec(*average_normal, *average_normal, n);
            } /* end if (v[k]) */
        } /* end for (k) */
        normalize_vec(*average_normal);
    } /* end for (j) */
} /* end average_normals() */
```

/* The following function checks whether the k-th side of the triangle tri intersects the base plane $w = 0$. The side is interpolated by a cubic parabola and
the point of intersection is calculated by means of NEWTON's iteration. */

typedef Vector Triangle [3];   ($\rightarrow$ **Types.h**)

```
Bool cut_line(sec, tri, k, grid, normal)                           (→ Proto.h)
    Vector sec;
    Triangle tri;
    short k;
    Vector **grid, **normal;
{ /* begin cut_line() */
    register Vector *p1 = tri[k], *p2 = tri[(k + 1)%3];
    register float t;
    Vector *temp;
    static Vector n = { 0, 0, 0 };
    Vector *n1, *n2, tg1, tg2;
    float y1, y2;
    float k1, k2;
    Vector2 diff;
    float scale;
    float h1, h2;
```

```
    if  (Sign((*p1)[Z]) == Sign((*p2)[Z])) return  FALSE;
    if  ((*p1)[Z]  >  0)
        Swap(p1, p2);
    /* Normal of projecting plane through side of triangle. */
    Subt_vec2(diff, *p1, *p2);
    Normal_vec2(n, diff);
    /* Idealized normals in p1 and p2. */
    n1  =  normal[0]  +  (p1 − grid[0]);
    n2  =  normal[0]  +  (p2 − grid[0]);
    /* Tangent vectors in p1 and p2. */
    Cross_product(tg1, *n1, n);
    Cross_product(tg2, *n2, n);
    /* The tangent vector must have the same direction. */
    if  (Dot_product2(tg1, diff)  <  0) Turn_vec(tg1, tg1);
    if  (Dot_product2(tg2, diff)  <  0) Turn_vec(tg2, tg2);

    y1  =  (*p1)[Z]; y2  =  (*p2)[Z];
    if  (y1 == − y2) t =  0.5;
    else  {
        scale  =  Length2(diff);
        k1  =  tg1[Z] /(Length2(tg1) /scale);
        k2  =  tg2[Z] /(Length2(tg2) /scale);
        h1  =  y2 − y1 − k1; h2  =  k1 − k2;
        t = zero_of_cubic_par(−2 * h1 − h2, h2 + 3 * h1,
                                              k1, y1, y1 / (y1 − y2));
    }
    sec[X]  =  (*p1)[X]  +  t * diff[X];
    sec[Y]  =  (*p1)[Y]  +  t * diff[Y];
    sec[Z]  =  0;
    return  TRUE;
}   /* end cut_line() */
```

/* The next function checks whether a point has already been stored in a pool
   of size n. */

```
Vector * ptr_to_section(p, pool, n)                        (→ Proto.h)
    Vector p;
    register  Vector  *pool;
    register  short  n;
{  /* begin ptr_to_section() */
    while  (n−−  > 0) {
        if  (identical(*pool, p))
            return  pool;
        pool++;
    }
    return  NULL;
}   /* end ptr_to_section() */
```

/* The following function "measures" how much the normal vector of a triangle differs from the desired normal vectors in its vertices: it returns the sum of all deviation angles. */

```
float deviation(tri, grid, normal, i1, j1, i2, j2, i3, j3)        (→ Proto.h)
    Triangle tri;
    Vector **grid, **normal;
    short  i1, j1, i2, j2, i3, j3;
{   /* begin deviation() */
    Vector face_normal;

    tri[0]  =  (Vector *) grid[i1][j1];
    tri[1]  =  (Vector *) grid[i2][j2];
    tri[2]  =  (Vector *) grid[i3][j3];
    normal_vector(face_normal, tri);
    return  acos(fabs(Dot_product(face_normal, normal[i1][j1]))) +
            acos(fabs(Dot_product(face_normal, normal[i2][j2]))) +
            acos(fabs(Dot_product(face_normal, normal[i3][j3])));
}   /* end deviation() */
```

#define *MAX_SECTIONS* 2000

/* The following function determines the optimized triangulation plus the optimized normals of a surface. Space for the variables *triangles* and *normal* is allocated in the routine and can be freed outside the function. */

```
void triangulate_surface(total_tri, triangles,
                 normal, surf, imax, jmax)                (→ Proto.h)
    short  * total_tri; /* Number of triangles. */
    Triangle **triangles; /* The optimized triangulation. */
    Vector ***normal; /* Pointer to all normals. */
    Vector **surf; /* Grid of points in the surface. */
    short  imax, jmax;
                 /* Size of grid on the surface: 0 ≤ i < imax, 0 ≤ j < jmax */
{   /* begin triangulate_surface() */
    short  i, j, k;
    static Triangle * tri_pool;
    register Triangle * tri;
    Triangle alt[2];
    static Vector **nrm;
```

```
Alloc_2d_array(Vector, nrm, imax, jmax);
average_normals(nrm, surf, imax, jmax);
*normal = nrm;
/* Triangulate graph. */
*total_tri = 2 * (imax − 1) * (jmax − 1);
*triangles = tri = Alloc_array(Triangle, tri_pool, *total_tri, "tri_pool");
for (i = 0; i < imax − 1; i++)
    for (j = 0; j < jmax − 1; j++, tri += 2)
        /* Create two pairs of test triangles and compare their
                    deviations. Choose the 'better' pair of triangles. */
    if (deviation(tri[0], surf, nrm, i, j, i + 1, j, i + 1, j + 1) +
        deviation(tri[1], surf, nrm, i + 1, j + 1, i, j + 1, i, j) >
        deviation(alt[0], surf, nrm, i, j + 1, i, j, i + 1, j) +
        deviation(alt[1], surf, nrm, i + 1, j, i + 1, j + 1, i, j + 1)) {
            for (k = 0; k < 3; k++)
                tri[0][k] = alt[0][k];
            for (k = 0; k < 3; k++)
                tri[1][k] = alt[1][k];
    }
} /* end triangulate_surface() */
```

/* This is the function that determines the line of intersection of the function graph $w = f(u, v)$. This line consists of a number of branches. As a side effect, this function determines the optimized triangulation plus the optimized normals of the surface. */

```
void zero_manifold_of_f_uv(section, triangles, nrm,
                           total_branches, branch_size, branch,
                           grid, imax, jmax)                    (→ Proto.h)
    Vector ***nrm; /* Pointer to all normals. */
    Vector **section; /* Address of the array of solution points. */
    Triangle **triangles; /* The optimized triangulation. */
    short * total_branches; /* How many solution curves. */
    short * branch_size; /* Size of each solution curve. */
    Vector ***branch; /* Array of array of pointers into section. */
    Vector **grid; /* Grid of basepoints (2-dimensional) */
    short imax, jmax;
                    /* Size of grid on the surface: 0 ≤ i < imax, 0 ≤ j < jmax */
{ /* begin zero_manifold_of_f_uv() */
    short j, k, n, total_tri;
    static Vector * space;
    static Triangle * tri_pool;
    short found;
    Vector * ptr;
    Edge * line_pool, *line;
    short total_sections; /* How many section points. */
    static Vector **normal;
```

```
triangulate_surface(&total_tri, &tri_pool, &normal, grid, imax, jmax);
*triangles = tri_pool; *nrm = normal;

/* Allocate section points */

*section = Alloc_array(Vector, space, MAX_SECTIONS, "space");
line = Alloc_array(Edge, line_pool, MAX_SECTIONS/2, "line_pool");
n = total_sections = 0;
for (j = 0; j < total_tri; j++) {
    found = 0;
    for (k = 0; k < 3; k++) {
        if (cut_line(*space, tri_pool[j], k, grid, normal)) {
            found++;
            ptr = ptr_to_section(*space, *section, total_sections);
            if (!ptr) {
                ptr = space++;
                if (++total_sections > MAX_SECTIONS)
                    safe_exit("too many sections");
            } /* end if (!prt) */
            if (found == 1)
                line->v1 = ptr;
            else {
                line->v2 = ptr;
                line++;
                break;
            }
        } /* end if cut_line */
    }  /* end for k */
}   /* end for j */
n = line - line_pool;
if (n == 0)
    *total_branches = 0;
else {
    Alloc_ptr_array(Vector, branch[0], 2 * n, "branch[0]");
    concat_to_polygons(total_branches, branch_size, branch,
            n, line_pool, FALSE);
}
Free_mem(line_pool, "line_pool");
}  /* end zero_manifold_of_f_uv() */
```

After these general considerations, we will now present three examples in order to give you an idea of what the function $f(u, v)$ may look like:

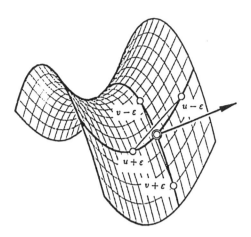

FIGURE 13. How to approximate the normal of a mathematical surface.

Example 1: Contour Lines. A point on a surface is considered to be a contour point if the corresponding tangent plane coincides with the projection center, that is to say, if the projection ray is orthogonal to the normal vector of the surface (Figure 13). Let us approximate the tangent vectors $\vec{x}_u$, $\vec{x}_v$ of the parameter lines:

$$\frac{\partial \vec{x}}{\partial u} = \vec{x}_u = (x_u, y_u, z_u) = \vec{x}(u+\varepsilon, v) - \vec{x}(u-\varepsilon, v), \tag{25}$$

$$\frac{\partial \vec{x}}{\partial v} = \vec{x}_v = (x_v, y_v, z_v) = \vec{x}(u, v+\varepsilon) - \vec{x}(u, v-\varepsilon), \ \varepsilon \text{ small.}$$

Then the normal vector $\vec{n}$ can be approximated by the vector product of these difference vectors:

$$\vec{n} = \vec{x}_u \times \vec{x}_v. \tag{26}$$

The condition for the existence of a contour point is that the dot product of the normal vector and the projection ray vanishes

$$f(u, v) \equiv \vec{n}(u, v) \cdot (\vec{x}(u, v) - \vec{c}) = 0, \tag{27}$$

where $\vec{c}$ is the position vector to the projection center.

A function *contour_condition*(u, v) may have the following code.

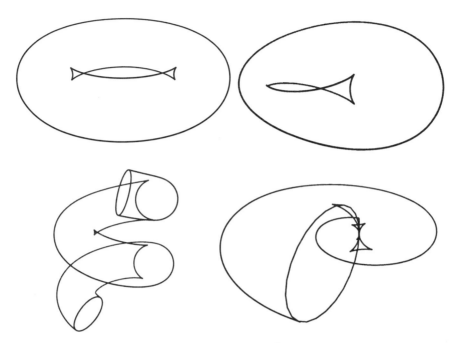

FIGURE 14. Contour lines on mathematical surfaces.

Global Init_fptr(xyz, xyz_torus);   ($\rightarrow$ `Proto.h`)

---

float *contour_condition(u, v)*   ($\rightarrow$ `Proto.h`)
    float *u, v;*

{   /* begin *contour_condition()* */
    Vector *p, n, proj_ray, pu1, pu2, pv1, pv2, tu, tv;*
    float *eps* = 1e − 2;

    xyz(p, u, v);
    xyz(pu1, u − eps, v);
    xyz(pu2, u + eps, v);
    xyz(pv1, u, v − eps);
    xyz(pv2, u, v + eps);
    Subt_vec(tu, pu1, pu2); Subt_vec(tv, pv1, pv2);
    Cross_product(n, tu, tv);
    normalize_vec(n);
    Subt_vec(proj_ray, p, Eye);
    normalize_vec(proj_ray);
    return *Dot_product(proj_ray, n);*
}   /* end *contour_condition()* */

/* This is the initializing function for $xyz()$. */

```
void xyz_torus(p, u, v)                              (→ Proto.h)
    Vector p;
    float u, v;
{   /* begin xyz_torus() */
    float cu, su, r;
    float a = 3, b = 2;
    cu = cos(u); su = sin(u);
    r =   a + b * cos(v);
    p[X]  = r * cu; p[Y]  = r * su; p[Z]  = b * sin(v);
}   /* end xyz_torus() */
```

Example 2: Isophotes. Isophotes are those curves on surfaces along which parallel light rays enclose a constant angle with the surface (Figure 15). For this reason, they are also called lines of equal illumination.[2] Consequently, the angle between the normal vector of the surface and the corresponding light ray is invariable for each point on such a line. This means that from the mathematical point of view, the dot product of the normalized normal vector $\vec{n}_0$ and the normalized light ray vector $\vec{l}_0$ equals the cosine of the given constant angle of incidence β (Equation 14). Thus, the condition for $f(u, v)$ is

$$f(u, v) \equiv \vec{n}_0(u, v) \cdot \vec{l}_0(u, v) - \cos\beta = 0. \tag{28}$$

Example 3: Lines of Intersection with Other Surfaces. We now want to intersect the surface Φ with another surface Ψ (e.g., with a plane, a sphere or a cylinder; Figure 16). In most cases, especially with algebraic intersecting surfaces, the implicit equation $G(x, y, z)$ of Ψ can be given. The coordinates of the points on the line of intersection have to fulfill this condition as well, and thus, we get

$$f(u, v) \equiv G\big(x(u, v), y(u, v), z(u, v)\big) = 0. \tag{29}$$

If the implicit equation of the surface cannot be calculated, we may try to parametrize the intersecting surface Ψ and find an implicit equation $F(x, y, z)$ of the surface Φ.

Note that this method is *not* appropriate for the calculation of the self-intersections of a surface. In this case, we would get $f(u, v) \equiv F(x, y, z) \equiv 0$, i.e., the graph Γ would be identical to the base plane β so that a line

---

[2]If the light rays were not parallel, we would have to take the distance from the light source into account as well.

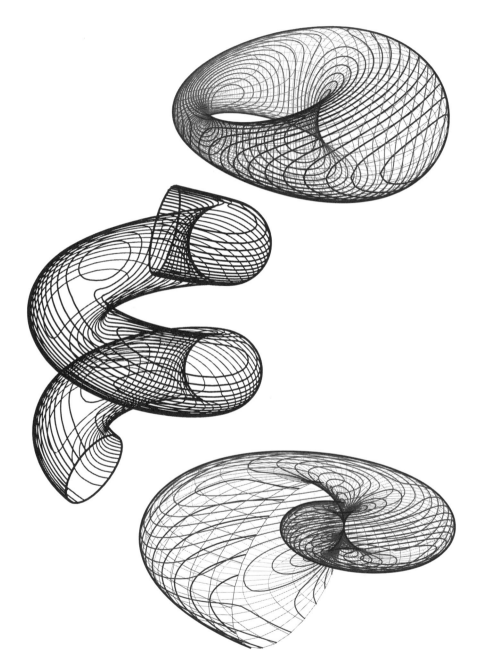

FIGURE 15. Isophotes on mathematical surfaces.

of intersection could not be detected! To calculate the self-intersections, we have to check for each face of the polygonized surface whether it intersects other faces or not. The intersection segments can be concatenated in the above-mentioned manner.

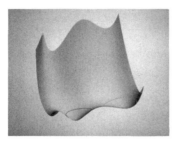

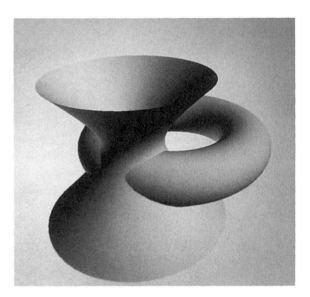

FIGURE 16. The intersection of a hyperboloid and a torus. The surfaces are given by their parametrized equations $\vec{x}_{hyp}(u, v)$ and $\vec{x}_{tor}(u, v)$. Furthermore, we know the implicit equation $G_{tor}(x, y, z)$ of the torus. The line of intersection corresponds to the zero manifold of the graph $z = G_{tor}(x_{hyp}, y_{hyp}, z_{hyp})$ (image on the left).

8.5 A More Sophisticated Illumination Model

In Section 4.5, we developed a simple shading model that is suitable for "ordinary" polyhedra like cubes. We also mentioned that it is not perfectly suitable for polyhedra that are approximations to smooth *reflecting* surfaces. Therefore, we want to extend our shading model according to the ideas of L. Phong [BUIT75].

It is a fact that shiny surfaces have highlighted spots. These spots do not only depend on the angle of incidence of the light rays – in each point of a shiny surface, the incoming light ray will be reflected according to the law of reflection (Figure 17): the incoming light ray, the reflected light ray and the normal of the surface lie on the same plane and the angle of incidence equals the angle of reflection. If the reflected light ray hits the eye point, the point on the surface is highlighted. Points that are close to the highlighted spot can also be considered to be highlighted, provided that the "perfect reflection ray" does not pass too far from the eye point. This is due to the consistency of the surface, which will never be perfectly smooth so that every spot will send out a bundle of non-parallel reflected light rays.

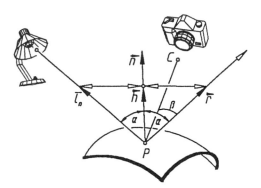

FIGURE 17. The law of reflection.

If $\vec{n}$ is the normalized normal vector in the point P of the surface and $\vec{l}_n$ the normalized direction vector of the light ray $\overrightarrow{PL_n}$ through the n-th light source, the reflected ray has the (normalized) direction

$$\vec{r} = \vec{h} + (\vec{h} - \vec{l}_n) = 2\vec{h} - \vec{l}_n \quad \text{with } \vec{h} = (\vec{n}\,\vec{l}_n)\,\vec{n}. \tag{30}$$

We now modify Equation (2) by means of the formula

$$s = reduced\_palette\,[k_1 \cos\alpha + k_2\,w(\alpha)\,\cos{}^m\beta]. \tag{31}$$

In this formula, β is the angle enclosed by the reflected light ray and by the projection ray PC; $w(\alpha)$ is a function that depends on the angle of incidence α of the light ray and on the material the surface consists of; m is a constant that is the higher, the more reflecting the surface is and k_1 and k_2 are also factors that depend on the material of the surface. Good values for reflecting surfaces are

$$2^1 < m < 2^{10},\ 0.2 < k_1 < 0.5,\ k_2 \approx \log{}_2 m = \log m / \log 2. \tag{32}$$

If $\vec{p}$ is the normalized direction vector of the projection ray, we have

$$\cos\beta = \vec{p}\,\vec{r}. \tag{33}$$

FIGURE 18. Four different shadings of one and the same surface: plastic, metallic, wooden coatings, normal shading.

The function $w(\alpha)$ can only be described by means of measured data ([PURG85]). The graph is described only by a few data and is then interpolated by cubic splines (Chapter [9]). Sometimes $w(\alpha)$ is simply set to a constant ([FOLE90]).

Equation (31) does not take the color of the light source into account (it assumes that the light source is white).[3] If the shade value s is larger than the palette size, we take the largest possible value instead.

Figure 18 shows a surface of revolution where the material-dependent constants are varied.

---

[3]Colored light sources produce highlighted spots of the same color on the surface. Since we only deal with lookup-tables for RGB colors, we cannot produce new RGB colors during the rendering. The only thing we can do is to create palettes of mixed colors. For example, if we deal with a gray surface and if the light source is red, we can create a small palette consisting of some light red-gray shades that replace the brighter shades of the red palette.

8.6   Shadow Buffering for Shadows

In Chapter 7, we talked about a very common and general working algorithm (depth buffering or z-buffering). In Chapter 6, we saw that, from the geometrical point of view, there is no difference between the light systems and the screen systems. For this reason, we can do the following:

FIGURE 19. Shadow buffering generally works and the algorithm is comparatively fast, but it requires large amounts of RAM to create images of good quality.

We transform the n-th light coordinates of all the vertices of the scene linearly into a box $M_n \times N_n \times 65000$. Before we do the depth buffering of our polygons, we buffer the scene completely in all the light systems.

If we then want to plot a visible pixel, we first transform the corresponding "space point" (actually it is a tiny box) to all the light systems and check whether the depth value w_n^* of the point corresponds approximately to the buffered value in the system. If w_n^* is smaller than the buffered value, the point is shadowed in the corresponding light system. Finally, the pixel is given a shade that depends on how often it has been shadowed, similar to the calculation of the shades for shadow polygons.

An estimation of memory requirements shows that again we will need 0.5 MB *RAM* for each light source, even if we use a comparatively small grid size of 500×500 in the light systems. It is no longer possible to split the grid into horizontal zones as we did in the ordinary depth buffering because, in general, the polygons, the n-th light coordinates of which are covered by the grid strip in the n-th light system, will not be covered by a strip in another system.

If we run out of memory, a compromise is the only solution. We transform the depth values to the interval $[0, 255]$. This interval can be covered by the type **Ubyte** which needs only one byte of storage space. Such a restriction also means that a narrow grid does not make sense any more, so that we reduce our grid size to about 250×250 in the n-th system.

Now the whole buffer in the n-th light system needs less than 64 Kbytes.[4] The price to be paid for this restriction is a loss of accuracy when we plot shadows (Figure 19).

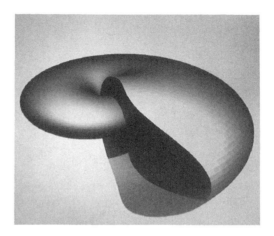

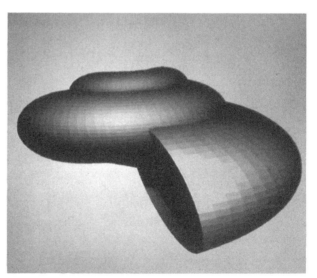

FIGURE 20. These images of a nautilus and a snail were created by means of shadow buffering. In nature, you can find a lot of spiral surfaces (Section 8.2, Example 5), because they are a result of continuous growth.

[4]In addition to that, blocks of a maximum of 64 Kbytes can be accessed much faster by some operating systems.

Spline Curves and Spline Surfaces

9.1 Interpolating Curves and Surfaces

In the previous chapter, we used cubic parabolas (Equation 22) to interpolate the line of intersection P_1P_2 of the graph Γ with a vertical plane ψ. Analogously, a patch Ψ on Γ, which is roughly approximated by two triangles, can be replaced by a cubic graph that consists of all the cubic parabolas we get when we vary the plane ψ. Such a graph is called an "interpolating surface."

If we concatenate several cubic parabola segments in the same plane ψ, the new line is called a "spline curve." The breakpoints are also called "knots." The arch between two knots is a "span." In each knot, the two neighboring spans touch each other because they have the same tangent. This is called C^1 continuity [FOLE90]. However, the local characteristics of each segment may be quite different, and the concatenated curve does not necessarily look very smooth.

All the parabolas described by Equation (22) have one thing in common: they never have vertical tangents ($\dot{w} = 0$ in Equation (23) occurs only for $t = \pm\infty$). Each parabola has its infinite point in the direction of the w-axis. This is no restriction as long as we only want to interpolate a function graph (which by definition must not have vertical tangents). For general surfaces, however, we have to generalize the cubic span p by means of a parametrized equation:

$$\vec{x} = (x,\, y,\, z) = \vec{a}\,t^3 + \vec{b}\,t^2 + \vec{c}\,t + \vec{d}. \tag{1}$$

Note that, in general, the infinite point of the parabola ($t = \pm\infty$) will not be the infinite point of an axis. Furthermore, the curve is really three-dimensional and not planar any more.

Let (P_1, t_1) and (P_2, t_2) be two "line elements" of the parabola p. They may fulfill Equation (1) for $t = 0$ and $t = 1$. By means of the first derivation

$$\dot{\vec{x}} = \frac{d\vec{x}}{dt} = (\frac{dx}{dt}, \frac{dy}{dt}, \frac{dz}{dt}) = (\dot{x}, \dot{y}, \dot{z}) = 3\vec{a}\,t^2 + 2\vec{b}\,t + \vec{c}, \tag{2}$$

we get the "coefficient vectors" almost in the same manner as in Section (8.2):

$$\begin{aligned}
\vec{a} &= \vec{t_1} + \vec{t_2} - 2\,(\vec{p_2} - \vec{p_1}), \\
\vec{b} &= 3\,(\vec{p_2} - \vec{p_1}) - 2\,\vec{t_1} - \vec{t_2}, \\
\vec{c} &= \vec{t_1}, \\
\vec{d} &= \vec{p_1}.
\end{aligned} \tag{3}$$

Any point on p between P_1 and P_2 can be calculated by evaluating Equation (2) with a t-value between 0 and 1.

Interpolating Splines

Now we have two line elements and are able to calculate an arbitrary number of points on the cubic span p. For many applications, however, we also have to solve the following problem: given a polygon $Q_0 Q_1, \ldots, Q_n$, we try to find a smooth curve that interpolates the polygon that is given by the $n + 1$ control points. In principle, we can "make up" $n + 1$ arbitrary tangent vectors $\vec{t_i}$ in Q_i. Then the n cubic spans between Q_i and Q_{i+1} are determined by two line elements each, and we have a set of parabola segments without any sharp bends (C^1 continuity). It turns out, however, that the visual impression of this interpolating spline curve is heavily dependent on the tangent vectors we choose. For many purposes, it is a good idea to let the tangent vector $\vec{t_i}$ in Q_i be dependent on two points before Q_i and two points after Q_i (Figure 1).

For the determination of the tangent vectors, several methods have been developed ([PURG85]). Good results can be achieved with the approach proposed by Akima. Since Q_{-1}, Q_{-2}, Q_{n+1} and Q_{n+2} are not given, we say

$$\begin{aligned}
\vec{q}_{-1} &= \vec{q}_2 + 3(\vec{q}_0 - \vec{q}_1) \\
\vec{q}_{-2} &= \vec{q}_1 + 3(\vec{q}_{-1} - \vec{q}_0) \\
\vec{q}_{n+1} &= \vec{q}_{n-2} + 3\,(\vec{q}_n - \vec{q}_{n-1}) \\
\vec{q}_{n+2} &= \vec{q}_{n-1} + 3\,(\vec{q}_{n+1} - \vec{q}_n).
\end{aligned} \tag{4}$$

Now we define

$$\vec{t_i}[j] = \lambda_1[j]\,\overrightarrow{Q_i Q_{i-1}}[j] + \lambda_2[j]\,\overrightarrow{Q_i Q_{i+1}}[j] \quad (j = 0, 1, 2) \tag{5}$$

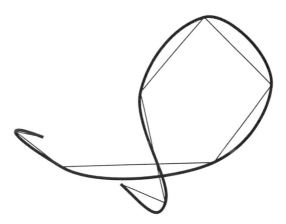

FIGURE 1. Spline interpolation (Akima).

and

$$\lambda_i[j] = \begin{cases} \frac{l_i}{l_1+l_2} & \text{if } l_1 + l_2 > 0; \\ 0.5 & \text{otherwise.} \end{cases} \quad (l_1 = |\overrightarrow{Q_iQ_{i-2}}[j]|, \ l_2 = \overrightarrow{Q_iQ_{i+2}}[j]|). \quad (6)$$

A set of points interpolated in this way will form an interpolating spline curve without any unwanted oscillations, which tend to occur especially at the end points of the curve. (This would be the case if we tried to force an algebraic curve of degree n to go through our $n + 1$ control points.)

Here is the C code for the calculation of an arbitrary set of points on an interpolating spline curve that is given by $n + 1$ control vertices Q_i. For each span Q_iQ_{i+1}, we calculate s_i points so that we have $m = s_0 + \ldots + s_{n-1}$ points on the spline curve at our disposal.

#**define** *AKIMA* 0   ($\rightarrow$ `Macros.h`)

```
void akima_spline_curve(m, vertices, n, ctrl_point, span_size)
                                                        (→ Proto.h)
    short   *m;  /* Number of points on the curve. */
    Vector vertices[ ]; /* Array of points on the curve. */
    short  n;   /* Number of control points. */
    Vector ctrl_point[ ]; /* Array of control points. */
    short  span_size[ ]; /* Number of points on each span. */
{   /* begin akima_spline_curve() */
    Vector coeff[4];
    register float *a, *b, *c, *d;
    Vector *tangent; /* Tangent vectors in the control points. */
    Vector *tg, *tg1;
    Vector *v = vertices, *hi_v,
           *q = ctrl_point, *hi_q = q + n - 1, *q1;
    short  j;
    float t, delta_t, h;
```

```
        Alloc_array(Vector, tangent, n, "tg");
        akima_tangents(tangent, n, ctrl_point);

      tg = tangent;
      for  ( ; q < hi_q; q++, tg++, span_size++) {
          q1 = q + 1; tg1 = tg + 1;
          a = &coeff[0][X]; b = a + 3; c = b + 3; d = c + 3;
          for (j = 0; j < 3; j++) {
              h = (*q1)[j] − (*q)[j];
              *a++ = (*tg)[j] + (*tg1)[j] − 2 * h;
              *b++ = 3 * h − 2 * (*tg)[j] − (*tg1)[j];
              *c++ = (*tg)[j];
              *d++ = (*q)[j];
          } /* end for (j) */
          Copy_vec(*v, *q);    /* Trivial first point. */
          t = delta_t = 1.0 / * span_size;
          hi_v = v++ + *span_size;
          for  ( ; v < hi_v; v++, t+ = delta_t) {
              a = &coeff[0][X]; b = a + 3; c = b + 3; d = c + 3;
              for (j = 0; j < 3; j++, a++, b++, c++, d++)
                  (*v)[j] = ((*a * t + *b) * t + *c) * t + *d;
          } /* end for (v) */
      } /* end for (q) */
      Copy_vec(*v, *q);    /* Trivial last point. */
      *m = (v − vertices) + 1;
      Free_mem(tangent, "tg");
  } /* end akima_spline_curve() */
```

```
  void akima_tangents(tangent, n, ctrl_point)                    (→ Proto.h)
      Vector tangent[ ];
      short n;
      Vector ctrl_point[ ];

  {   /* begin akima_tangents() */
      short i, imax = 3 * n;
      Vector * diff, *d, *v;
      float len1, len2, *result;
      register float * d0, *d1, *d2, *d3;

      Alloc_array(Vector, diff, n + 3, "diff");
      d = diff + 2;
      v = ctrl_point;
      for (i = 2; i <= n; i++, d++, v++)
          Subt_vec(*d, *v, *(v + 1));
  #define Invent_diff(diff_vec, a, b) \
      d = (Vector *) diff_vec, Add_vec(*d, a, a), Subt_vec(*d, b, *d)
```

```
Invent_diff(diff[1], diff[2], diff[3]);
Invent_diff(diff[0], diff[1], diff[2]);
Invent_diff(diff[n + 1], diff[n], diff[n − 1]);
Invent_diff(diff[n + 2], diff[n + 1], diff[n]);
```
#undef *Invent_diff*()

```
d0 = &diff[0][X]; d1 = &diff[1][X];
d2 = &diff[2][X]; d3 = &diff[3][X];
result = &tangent[0][X];
for (i = 0; i < imax; i++, d0++, d1++, d2++, d3++) {
    len1 = fabs(*d3 − *d2);
    len2 = fabs(*d1 − *d0);
    if (len1 + len2 < EPS)
        len1 = len2 = 1;
    *result++ = (len1 * (*d1) + len2 * (*d2)) /(len1 + len2);
}
Free_mem(diff, "diff");
} /* end akima_tangents() */
```

Interpolating splines with C^1 continuity do not always look very smooth. Curves with C^2 continuity (where even the first derivation of the spline has C^1 continuity) look more natural (Figure 2). Such interpolating spline curves are called "cubic splines." All of the n spans $Q_i Q_{i+1}$ $(i = 0, \ldots, n-1)$ of the spline are described by

$$\vec{x}_i(t) = \vec{a}_i(t-i)^3 + \vec{b}_i(t-i)^2 + \vec{c}_i(t-i) + \vec{d}_i \ (t \in [i, i+1]). \tag{7}$$

The conditions for C^2 continuity are

$$\begin{aligned}
\vec{x}_i(i) &= \vec{q}_i, & i &= 0, \ldots, n \\
\vec{x}_i(i) &= \vec{x}_{i-1}(i), & i &= 1, \ldots, n \\
\dot{\vec{x}}_i(i) &= \dot{\vec{x}}_{i-1}(i), & i &= 1, \ldots, n-1 \\
\ddot{\vec{x}}_i(i) &= \ddot{\vec{x}}_{i-1}(i), & i &= 1, \ldots, n-1.
\end{aligned} \tag{8}$$

For the end points, we let $\ddot{\vec{x}}(0) = \ddot{\vec{x}}(n) = 0$. First this leads to

$$\vec{d}_i = \vec{q}_i \ (i = 0, \ldots, n), \tag{9}$$

then to the linear system

$$\begin{aligned}
\vec{b}_0 &= \vec{b}_n = (0, 0, 0), \\
\vec{b}_{i-1} + 4\vec{b}_i + \vec{b}_{i+1} &= 3(\vec{d}_{i-1} - 2\vec{q}_i + \vec{d}_{i+1}) \ (i = 1, \ldots, n-1), \tag{10}
\end{aligned}$$

and finally to

$$\vec{c}_i = (\vec{d}_{i+1} - \vec{d}_i) - \frac{1}{3}(\vec{b}_{i+1} + 2\vec{b}_i)$$

$$\vec{a}_i = \frac{1}{3}(\vec{b}_{i+1} - \vec{b}_i) \quad (i = 0, \ldots, n-1). \tag{11}$$

Calculation time increases only linearly with the number of knots. Usually, cubic splines look very smooth, but they have a major drawback: every change of a control point will influence the appearance of the *whole* curve, so that unwanted oscillations may be produced.

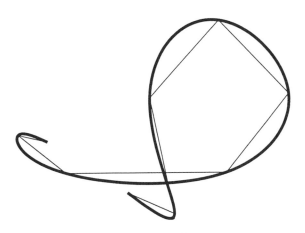

FIGURE 2. Interpolating cubic splines with C^2 continuity.

Here is the C code for the calculation of the coefficient vectors:

void *cubic_spline_curve*(*m, vertices, n, q, span_size*)

($\rightarrow$ Proto.h)

```
    short  *m;   /* Number of vertices on the spline. */
    Vector vertices[ ];   /* Vertices of the spline. */
    short  n;   /* Number of control vertices. */
    Vector q[ ];   /* Control vertices. */
    short  span_size[ ];   /* Number of points desired for each span. */
{   /* begin cubic_spline_curve() */
    register float  *a, *b, *c, *d;
        /* The k-th components of the coeff. vectors. */
    float  *h0, *h1, *h2, *h3, *hi_a;
    short  i, i1, imax, k, *size;
    float  tmax, t, dt;
    Vector  *v;
    float  **space; /* Space for several arrays. */
```

```
Alloc_2d_array(float, space, 8, n);
h0 = space[0]; h1 = space[1];
h2 = space[2]; h3 = space[3];
for (k = 0; k < 3; k++) {    /* X, Y, Z */
    a = space[4]; b= space[5]; c= space[6]; d = space[7];

    /* Trigonal system. ¹*/
    for (i = 0; i < n; i++)
        d[i] = q[i][k];
    for (i = 0, imax = n − 2; i < imax; i++) {
        h3[i] = 3 * (d[i + 2] − 2 * d[i + 1] + d[i]);
        h2[i] = 1;
    } /* end for (i) */
    h2[n − 3] = 0;

    /* Dissolution of the system. */
    a[0] = 4; h1[0] = h3[0] /a[0];
    for (i = 1, i1 = 0, imax = n − 2; i < imax; i++, i1++) {
        h0[i1] = h2[i1] /a[i1];
        a[i] = 4 − h0[i1];
        h1[i] = (h3[i] − h1[i1]) /a[i];
    } /* end for (i) */
    b[n − 3] = h1[n − 3];
    for (i = n − 4; i >= 0; i−−)
        b[i] = h1[i] − h0[i] * b[i + 1];
    for (i = n − 2; i >= 1; i−−)
        b[i] = b[i − 1];
    b[0] = b[n − 1] = 0;
    hi_a = a + n − 1;
    for ( ; a < hi_a; a++, b++, c++, d++) {
        *c = *(d + 1) − *d − (2 **b + *(b + 1)) /3;
        *a = (*(b + 1) − *b) /3;
    } /* end for (a) */
    /* Store the current components of the vertices of the spline. */
    v = vertices;    size = span_size;
    a = space[4]; b= space[5]; c= space[6]; d = space[7];
    for ( ; a < hi_a; a++, b++, c++, d++) {
        dt = 1.0 / * size++;
        for (t = 0; t < (1 − EPS); t+= dt)
            (*v++)[k] = (*a *t + *b) *t + *c) *t + *d;
    } /* end for (a) */
    (*v++)[k] = *d;
}
*m = v − vertices;
Free_2d_array(space);
} /* end cubic_spline_curve() */
```

---

[1]Actually, we have to dissolve a linear system with $4n + 1$ variables. This is a very special system, however, and it would be unwise to dissolve it by means of general algorithms. (CPU time would then increase quadratically with the number of control points.)

Interpolating Surfaces

Interpolating spline curves can be used for the interpolation of surfaces that are given by a grid $Q_{i,j}$ of $(n_1 + 1)(n_2 + 1)$ vertices (Figure 3).

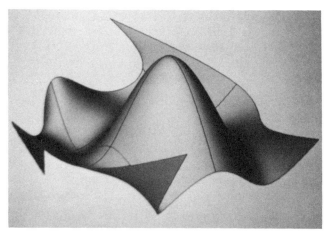

FIGURE 3. Interpolating spline surface (cubic splines).

We interpolate the n_1+1 v-lines (j constant) and the n_2+1 u-lines (i constant) by means of interpolating splines. Now the v-lines are polygons with m_2 vertices V_{ij}. Vertices V_{ij_0} with the same index j_0 ($j_0 = 0, \ldots, m_2 - 1$) determine m_2 u-lines on the surface (including the given ones). In the same way, we can determine new v-lines of the surface. The interpolated surface now consists of $m_1 m_2$ vertices. The $n_1 n_2$ patches of the surface are joined together with C^1 continuity, if we use C^1 continuous interpolating spline curves, and with C^2 continuity, if we use cubic splines.

The following C code can be used for several kinds of spline surfaces, including Akima splines, cubic splines and also the approximating B-splines, which we will discuss in the next section.

```
#define CUBIC_SPLINE 1                              (→ Macros.h)
#define B_SPLINE 2                                  (→ Macros.h)


Global Init_fptr(calc_spline_curve, cubic_spline_curve);   (→ Proto.h)
```

```
void ptr_to_calc_spline(type)                       (→ Proto.h)
    short   type;
```

```
{  /* begin ptr_to_calc_spline() */
   switch (type) {
      case AKIMA :
          calc_spline_curve = akima_spline_curve; break;
      case CUBIC_SPLINE :
          calc_spline_curve = cubic_spline_curve; break;
      case B_SPLINE :
          calc_spline_curve = b_spline_curve; break;
   }
}  /* end ptr_to_calc_spline() */
```

void *calc_spline_surface*(*m, result, ctrl_point, n, span_size, type, k*)

(→ Proto.h)

short *m*[2]; /* Size of the surface. */
Vector ***result*; /* Address of 2d-array. */
Vector ***ctrl_point*;
short *n*[2]; /* Number of control points. */
short ***span_size*;
short *type*; /* AKIMA, CUBIC_SPLINE, B_SPLINE etc. */
short *k*[2]; /* This is only for B-spline surfaces. */

```
{  /* begin calc_spline_surface() */
   register short i, j;
   register float *x1, *x2; /* Necessary for the macro Fast_copy(). */
   static Vector **surface = NULL; /* The desired surface. */
   Vector **aux_surf; /* Auxiliary surface. */
   Vector *aux_ctrl;

   ptr_to_calc_spline(type);
   /* Determine size of surface */
   m[0] = m[1] = 1;
   for (i = 0; i < n[0]; i++)
       m[0] += span_size[0][i];
   for (i = 0; i < n[1]; i++)
       m[1] += span_size[1][i];
   /* Allocate surface */
       Alloc_2d_array(Vector, surface, m[0], m[1]);
   *result = surface;
   Alloc_array(Vector, aux_ctrl, n[0], "tmp");
   Alloc_2d_array(Vector, aux_surf, n[0], m[1]);

   /* Calculate aux_surf */
   for (i = 0; i < n[0]; i++)
       calc_spline_curve(&m[1], aux_surf[i],
                       n[1], ctrl_point[i], span_size[1], k[1]);
```

```
#define Fast_copy(b, a) \                              (local macro)
    x2 = (float *) b, x1 = (float *) a,\
    *x2++ = *x1++, *x2++ = *x1++, *x2 = *x1
    for (j = 0; j < m[1]; j++) {
        for (i = 0; i < n[0]; i++)
            Fast_copy(aux_ctrl[i], aux_surf[i][j]);
        calc_spline_curve(&m[0], surface[j],
                          n[0], aux_ctrl, span_size[0], k[0]);
    }
    Free_array(aux_ctrl, "aux_ctrl");
    Free_2d_array(aux_surf);
}   /* end calc_spline_surface() */
```

9.2 Approximating Curves and Surfaces

For many applications, the use of "approximating splines" (and approximating spline surfaces) is advisable, because they do not necessarily have to contain the control points. For example, if we use control points that are not very reliable, and if we know, however, that the curve they should belong to is smooth, it is a good idea to use approximating splines. They can also be very helpful if we simply want to create objects with smooth shapes.

Approximating Splines

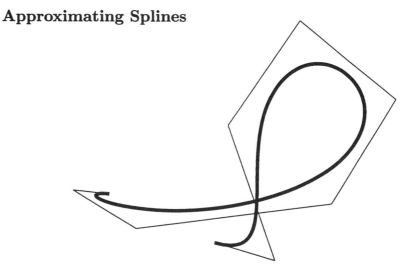

FIGURE 4. Approximating spline curves (B-splines).

Several kinds of approximating splines have been developed, among them the Bezier-splines, the B-splines [FOLE90] and the β-splines ([BARS88]). For our purposes, we only need the so-called *B-splines*. They are given by the parametric equation

$$\vec{x}(t) = \sum_{i=0}^{n} b_{i,k}(t)\, \vec{q}_i, \tag{12}$$

where $\vec{q}_0$, $\vec{q}_1$, ..., $\vec{q}_n$ are the $n+1$ control points. The index $k = 2, 3, \ldots$, determines the number of control points that have an influence on the points of the curve. The curve is then C^{k-2} continuous, i.e., we have C^2 continuity for $k \geq 4$.

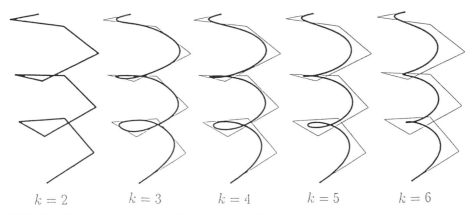

$$k = 2 \qquad k = 3 \qquad k = 4 \qquad k = 5 \qquad k = 6$$

FIGURE 5. B-splines with different continuities.

On the parameter interval $0 \leq t \leq n - k + 2$, we define the constant values

$$c_i = \begin{cases} 0 & \text{if } i < k; \\ i - k + 1 & \text{if } k \leq i \leq n; \\ n - k + 2 & \text{otherwise,} \end{cases} \tag{13}$$

which lead to the knots (breakpoints) C_i of the $n - k + 2$ spans of the curve. The coefficients $b_{i,k}(t)$ of an arbitrary curve point belonging to the parameter t are defined recursively by means of the constants c_i:

We start with

$$b_{i,1}(t) = \begin{cases} 1 & \text{if } c_i < t < c_{i+1}; \\ 0 & \text{otherwise,} \end{cases} \tag{14}$$

and then we calculate $b_{i,2}$ $b_{i,3}, \ldots$, $b_{i,k}$ as a weighted linear combination of the coefficients of lower degree:

$$b_{i,j}(t) = \frac{t - c_i}{c_{i+j-1} - c_i}\, b_{i,j-1}(t) + \frac{c_{i+j} - t}{c_{i+j} - c_{i+1}}\, b_{i+1,j-1}(t). \tag{15}$$

Only inside k intervals are these coefficients non-vanishing. Therefore, calculation time increases only linearly with the number of control points.

Figure 5 shows typical B-splines. For $k = 2$, the spline will be the polygon itself. For $k = 3$, all the line segments $Q_i Q_{i+1}$ will be tangents of the curve. For $k > 3$, this is only true for the first and the last spans of the polygon. If we want to force the B-spline to get closer to a control point Q_i, we count Q_i more than one time. (If we count Q_i k times, the curve will go through Q_i. In this case, however, the curve will have a sharp bend, which is not what we usually want.)

Points on the curve can be calculated by means of the following C code:

```
void b_spline_coeff(b, t, n, k, c, i1)                    (→ Proto.h)
    float  **b;
    float  t;
    short  n, k;
    short  *c;      /* B-spline constants. */
    short  i1;
{   /* begin b_spline_coeff() */
    register float  *b_ij;
    register short  i, j, *ci, *cj;
    float  *max_b  =  &b[n + 1][0];
    short  delta_b  =  b[1] − b[0];
    short  i0;

    ci  =  &c[i1];
    for  (b_ij  =  &b[i1][1];  b_ij  <  max_b;  b_ij +=  delta_b)
        *b_ij  =   (*ci  <  t&& t <=  * ++ci) ? 1 : 0;

    for  (j  =  1;  j  <  k;  j++) {
        i =  i1;  ci  =  &c[i1];  cj =  ci  +  j;
        for  (b_ij  =  &b[i][j + 1];  b_ij  <  max_b;  b_ij +=  delta_b) {
            if  ((*b_ij  =  b[i][j]))
                *b_ij *=  (t − *ci) /(*cj − *ci);
            i++;  ci++;  cj++;
            if  (b[i][j])
                *b_ij +=  (*cj − t) /(*cj − *ci) * b[i][j];
        }  /* end for (b_ij) */
    }  /* end for (i) */
    /*
    This is the "readable code":
    for  (i = i1;  i <= n;  i++)
        if  (c[i]  <  t&& t <  c[i + 1]) b[i][1]  = 1;
        else b[i][1]  = 0;
    for  (j  =  2;  j  <=  k;  j++) {
        for  (i = i1;  i <= n;  i++)
            b[i][j]  =  (t − c[i])    /(c[i + j − 1] − c[i])    * b[i][j − 1]+
                        (c[i + j] − t) /(c[i + j] − c[i + 1]) * b[i + 1][j − 1];
    }  /* end for (i) */
    */
}   /* end b_spline_coeff() */
```

#define $Zero\_vec(v)$ $(v)[X] = (v)[Y] = (v)[Z] = 0$ $(\rightarrow$ Macros.h$)$

```
void b_spline_curve(no_of_vertices, curve, n, q, span_size, k)
                                                        (→ Proto.h)
    short   * no_of_vertices;
    Vector  curve[ ];
    short   n;
    Vector  q[ ];
    short   * span_size;
    short   k;
{   /* begin b_spline_curve() */
    register  short  * c;
    register  short  i, j;
    float  t, dt, r;
    float  * *b;
    Vector  * curve0 = curve, *q1;
    short  i1, i2, i3;

    Alloc_array(short, c, n + k, "coeff");
    Alloc_2d_array(float, b, n + 1, k + 1);

    /* B-spline constants */
    i = 0; j = 1;
    while  (i < k)
        c[i++] = 0;
    while  (i < n)
        c[i++] = j++;
    while  (i < n + k)
        c[i++] = j;
    i = k − 1; i1 = i − (k − 1); i2 = i + (k − 1);
    for  ( ; i < n + 1; i++, i1++, i2++) {
        t = c[i] + EPS;
        dt = (c[i + 1] − t) /(*span_size) − EPS;
        i1 = Maximum(i1, 0);
        i2 = Minimum(i2, n);
        for  (j = 0; j < *span_size; j++, t+= dt, curve++) {
            if (t == EPS) {
                Copy_vec(*curve, q[0]);
            } else  {
                if  (j == 0 || dt > EPS)
                    b_spline_coeff(b, t, n − 1, k, c, i1);
                Zero_vec(*curve);
                for  (i3 = i1, q1 = q + i1; i3 < i2; i3++, q1++) {
                    if  ((r = b[i3][k]) != 0) {
                        (*curve)[X] += r * (*q1)[X];
                        (*curve)[Y] += r * (*q1)[Y];
                        (*curve)[Z] += r * (*q1)[Z];
                    } /* end if (r) */
                } /* end for (i3) */
```

```
            }  /* end if (t) */
          }  /* end for (j) */
          span_size + +;
        }  /* end for (i) */
        Copy_vec(*curve,  q[n − 1]);
        * no_of_vertices  =  + + curve  − curve0;


        Free_mem(c,  "coeff");
        Free_2d_array(b);
      }  /* end b_spline_curve() */
```

Approximating Surfaces

A very important application of approximating splines is the creation of smooth shapes. For this purpose, we extend the definition of the spline curve to the third dimension:

$$\vec{x}(u,\, v) = \sum_{i=0}^{n_1} \sum_{j=0}^{n_2} b_{i,k_1}(u)\, b_{j,k_2}(v)\, \vec{q}_{ij}. \tag{16}$$

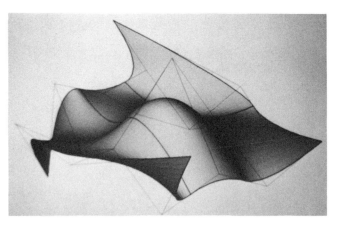

FIGURE 6. B-spline surface given by a grid of control points.

The vectors $\vec{q}_{ij}$ are the position vectors of the $(n_1 + 1)\,(n_2 + 1)$ control points Q_{ij} (Figure 6). Note that we now have two indices k_1 and k_2 in the u- and v-directions (so that we have two degrees of freedom). Lines of constant u (v-lines) are B-spline curves with the control vertices

$$\vec{q}_v(v) = \sum_{i=0}^{n_1} b_{j,k_2}(v)\,\vec{q}_{ij}. \tag{17}$$

Each of the $n_1 + 1$ given v-lines may consist of m_2 vertices V_{ij}. The $n_1 + 1$ vertices V_{ij_0} that belong to the same index j_0 are control vertices for m_2 u-lines (among them the given ones). In the same way, we can determine m_1 v-lines. The surface finally consists of $m_1\,m_2$ vertices. The given $n_1\,n_2$ patches are joined together with C^{k_1} (C^{k_2}) continuity.

The C code for the calculation of B-spline surfaces is included in the function $calc\_spline\_surface()$.

9.3 Special Curves on Polygonized Surfaces

In practice, many surfaces are given only by a limited number of points, as in the case of measured data. It is often necessary to find special curves on such surfaces. In this section, we will show that, in many cases, it is possible to get useful results without replacing the polyhedron by spline surfaces.

The Polygonization of Surfaces

We assume that we have at our disposal a certain set of points on the surface. The coordinates of these points can either be measured data (e.g., in the case of a terrain), or they can have been calculated by means of mathematical formulas. If the number of these points is comparatively small, we can also add new points by spline interpolation. If we want to have points at a particular place of the surface, such as above a grid on the base plane (e.g., to be able to use the fast hidden-surface algorithms described in Chapter 5), we have to calculate these new points by interpolation.

Then we triangulate the surface by connecting three neighbor points, each to a triangle (face). In general, each face has three neighboring faces. All the triangles taken together form a polyhedron, which approximates the surface more or less satisfactorily, depending on how detailed the dissection has been. Another kind of polygonization that can be used for implicit surfaces is described in [BLOO87].

Example 1: Contour Lines. We replace the contour of a surface by that of the approximating polyhedron, which is composed of specific edges of the polyhedron. Each face has a normal vector. We assume that the surface can be oriented and that all the normals point to the same side of the surface. With reference to a given perspective we can now distinguish between two types of faces: those, where the normal vectors are inclined towards the projection center, and the others, where this is not the case. For solid objects, they are called frontfaces and backfaces (Chapter 5). Two triangles of a different kind have one edge of the contour polygon in common.

Consequently, we check for each face, whether the angle enclosed by the projection ray and the oriented normal of the face is smaller or greater than $\frac{\pi}{2}$. Then we compare the type of each face with that of its neighboring faces. The contour line of a surface is particularly useful for plotter drawings, especially when we do not want to display too many images of parameter lines.

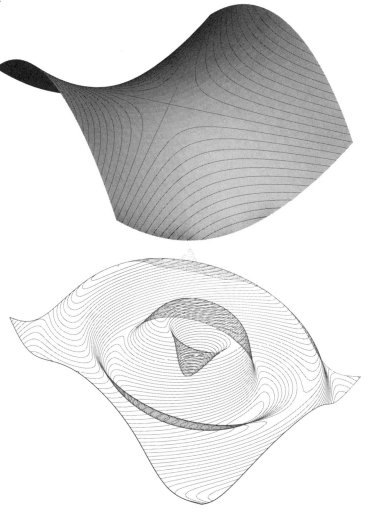

FIGURE 7. Contour lines and lines of intersection of function graphs.

If we replace the contour line of a surface by the contour polygon of an approximating polyhedron, we usually get reasonably accurate pictures with a minimum of calculation time. The reason for the good correspondence between the contour lines lies in the fact that the faces that carry the edges of the contour polygon are nearly projecting (i.e., the image of the polygon is almost a straight line). This means that the deviations of the *image* of the contour polygon of the approximating polyhedron from the *image* of the contour of the surface are reduced to a minimum, even though the respective lines may have completely different positions in space.

Example 2: Isophotes. Analogously to Example 1 we can trace the lines of equal illumination. Again we divide the faces of the approximating polyhedron into two kinds: those where the angle enclosed with the light ray is smaller than the prescribed angle of inclination, and those for which the opposite is true. The polygon though, which represents the set of edges that two faces of different type have in common, does not approximate the actual isophote very well in the projection onto the screen because, in most cases, the faces that carry the edges are not projecting at all. In order to get nice pictures, we can still apply spline interpolations to the projections of the polygons. These interpolations, however, are not always reliable enough, so that sometimes we have to resort to more precise but slower methods ([LANG84], [POTT88]).

Example 3: Lines of Intersection. The approximation of surfaces by means of polyhedra is a very good method of dealing with intersections. Instead of applying the time-consuming algorithm described in Section 8.2 (Example 3), we simply check for all the faces of the polyhedron on which side of the intersecting surface they lie. Most of the faces will not penetrate the intersecting surface. For the few faces on which a part of the vertices is on a different side of the intersecting surface than the other part, we simply consider the straight line between the two intersection points of the edges of the (always convex) face as a part of the line of intersection. If the number of faces is small, we can smooth the intersecting polygon by means of spline interpolation.

Figure 7 shows the lines of intersection of a function graph, which were mentioned in Section 8.2 when we tried to get arbitrary curves on mathematical surfaces as the solution of a function $f(u, v) = 0$.

9.4 Spatial Integral Curves

In addition to the parametrized curves $\vec{x} = \vec{x}(t)$ on surfaces and the curves that fulfill a condition $f(u, v) = 0$, there are other interesting curves on surfaces: the solution curves of vector fields. They are characterized by a differential equation in u and v, for which we have an infinite number of solution curves on the surface (e.g., the lines of steepest slope). Let us assume that in each point of the surface, the tangent vector of the corresponding curve is known so that the direction $dv : du$ of the line of solution is given. We now want the computer to calculate the integral curve of the vector field. The direction of the curve is indicated by the tangent vector in the tangent plane, which can be given as a linear combination of the tangent vectors of the parameter lines through the point (these vectors are the difference vectors $\vec{x}_u$ and $\vec{x}_v$ in Equation 25):

$$\vec{t} = \vec{x}_u.du + \vec{x}_v.dv \quad or \quad \begin{pmatrix} t_x \\ t_y \\ t_z \end{pmatrix} = \begin{pmatrix} x_u \\ y_u \\ z_u \end{pmatrix} du + \begin{pmatrix} x_v \\ y_v \\ z_v \end{pmatrix} dv. \tag{18}$$

Thus, a point that is close to the point with the position vector $\vec{x} = (u, v)$ has the position vector $\vec{x}(u + \varepsilon.du, v + \varepsilon.dv)$. The closer the points lie together, the more likely it is that the graphically integrated curve really corresponds to the actual lines of solution of the vector field. A branch of the curve ends when the parameter values belonging to the point are outside the rectangular domain of definition, or when one, while still proceeding in the same direction, comes back to the starting point (i.e., when the curve is closed in a circle).

If the vectors $\vec{t}$, $\vec{x}_u$ and $\vec{x}_v$ are given, the parameters du, dv in Equation (18) can be evaluated by

$$du = \frac{t_x y_v - t_y x_v}{D}, \quad dv = \frac{t_y x_u - t_x y_u}{D} \text{ (with } D = x_u y_v - y_u x_v), \tag{19}$$

provided that the determinant D does not vanish. (Otherwise we use another pair of coordinate equations in Equation (19)).

A pseudo-code of the relevant part of the program might look like this:

> Starting point $P_0 := \vec{x}(u, v)$
> Determine normalized tangent vector $\vec{t_0}$ in P_0
> $P := P_0$
> $\vec{t} := \vec{t_0}$
> **repeat**
> > determine tangent vectors $\vec{x}_u$, $\vec{x}_v$ of parameter lines
> > determine du, dv from $\vec{x}_u$, $\vec{x}_v$ and $\vec{t}$ (Equation (19)
> > $u := u + \varepsilon.du, v := v + \varepsilon.dv$
> > $P := \vec{x}(u, v)$
> > determine normalized tangent vector $\vec{t}$ in P
> **until** (u, v) outside domain of definition $\lor$
> > (distance(new point, P_0) $< \varepsilon \land$ angle($\vec{t}$, $\vec{t_0}$) small) $\lor$ $\vec{t}$ is not real

For accurate results, the factor ε has to be very small. On the other hand, it should not be too small, for that would increase calculation time.

After these general considerations, we will now give two examples of how we can find the tangent vector $\vec{t}$ for specific families of curves:

Example 1: Loxodromes. Loxodromes are lines that intersect a given family of curves on a surface (e.g., a family of parameter lines or the section lines) at a constant angle α.

Through each point of the surface goes one curve of the given family, the tangent of which may be interpolated by the straight connection between two neighbor points. If we normalize the corresponding direction vector and rotate it about the normal of the surface by the constant section angle α, we get the desired tangent vector $\vec{t}$ of the loxodrome. Special cases of loxodromes are the lines of steepest slope, which intersect the lines of intersection orthogonally.

Example 2: Generalized Helices. Generalized helices are those curves on a surface that have constant angles of elevation. If the normal vector of the surface has the components $\vec{n} = (n_x, n_y, n_z)$, the direction of the horizontal tangent has the components $\vec{h} = (-n_y, n_x, 0)$. The vector product

$$\vec{f} = \vec{n} \times \vec{h} = (-n_x n_z, \, -n_y n_z, \, n_x^2 + n_y^2) \tag{20}$$

determines the direction of the tangent with the greatest possible angle of elevation, the so-called tangent of steepest slope. Any other direction of a tangent is then a linear combination of the two vectors $\vec{h}$ and $\vec{f}$:

$$\vec{t} = (t_x, t_y, t_z) = \vec{h} + \lambda.\vec{f} = \begin{pmatrix} -n_y - \lambda\, n_x\, n_z \\ n_x - \lambda\, n_y\, n_z \\ \lambda\,(n_x^2 + n_y^2) \end{pmatrix}. \tag{21}$$

If $\vec{t}$ is to have the constant angle of elevation β, we have the condition

$$\tan\beta = \frac{t_z}{\sqrt{t_x^2 + t_y^2}} = \lambda.\sqrt{\frac{n_x^2 + n_y^2}{1 + \lambda^2.n_z^2}}, \tag{22}$$

which leads to a quadratic equation in λ. Every real solution

$$\lambda = \pm\frac{\tan\beta}{\sqrt{n_x^2 + n_y^2 - n_z^2 \tan^2\beta}} \tag{23}$$

determines a tangent vector $\vec{t}$.

Let us now extend the method for the determination of the integral curves of direction fields to approximating polyhedra. Of course, there is no more guarantee for perfect accuracy, but we have to consider that sometimes there is no other way to get such curves. Apart from that, the proposed algorithm is comparatively fast.

We assume that, for each face, we can determine a real or not real direction vector of the field. In the case of generalized helices, for example, this is – similar to Example 1 in this section – the tangent vector that has a constant angle of elevation with respect to the base plane. Let us start from a point A at the inside of a face (Figure 8).

The straight line that is determined by the point and by the direction vector of the face may be called the *field line* through A. (For certain applications, e.g., for trajectories, this line has to be oriented.) It intersects the border of the face in two points A_1, A_2. The edge between these two points is stored as a part of the "integral polygon." A_1 and A_2 lie on edges the face has in common with two neighbor faces. We now continue the polygon in the directions of both these neighbor faces until we reach a criterion to break off the search.

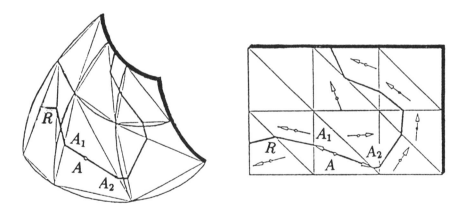

FIGURE 8. The search algorithm for "integral polygons" on approximating polyhedra.

Naturally, the vertex of our first edge also lies on an edge of the neighbor face and, together with the direction vector of this neighbor face, it determines a new *field line*. We determine the residual section point R of this line with the neighbor face. If there is another face on the polyhedron that shares the edge through R with the current face, we can apply the same procedure once more. If there is no other neighbor face on the polyhedron or if the polygon is closed, we break off the search for more points. Since all the problems that are described here can be solved by simple methods of analytic geometry, without the use of time-consuming mathematical functions like sine or tangent, we may assume that the algorithm will be done very quickly.

A pseudo-code illustrates the problem even more clearly (compare with the pseudo-code at the beginning of this section):

Choose starting point inside an arbitrary face f_0
Intersect the corresponding *field line* with the border of the face
Determine the (in general 2) neighbor faces (starting faces)
for all starting faces
    previous face := f_0
    current face := starting face
    repeat
        residual section point R of *field line* with current face
        if neighbor face through R exists
            previous face := current face
            current face := neighbor face
until no more neighbor face $\lor$ polygon closed $\lor$ field direction not real

In this way, we can again trace loxodromes, orthogonal trajectories, generalized helices and many other curves on surfaces.

9.5 Some Examples of Applications

Example 1: "Landscapes." The algorithms described in the previous sections can easily be applied to landscapes, which of course do not submit themselves to mathematical rules. A partial approximation by means of mathematical surfaces may be acceptable, but does not necessarily correspond to reality. Therefore, the simple approximation by a polyhedron is justified as well, especially if one completes the number of measured points by means of spline interpolation – preferably done by the AKIMA-interpolation ([PURG85]), which is indifferent to the multiple differentiabilty of the surface.

Provided that the terrain does not have any overhanging rocks, the surface may be interpreted as a function graph above a two-dimensional domain of definition (usually a rectangle). If the normal projections of the measured points of the surface onto the ground plane do not belong to a grid, we interpolate the spot heights of the grid points in order to be able to use specific hidden-line or hidden-surface algorithms ([GLAE88/1], [HEAR86]).

Then we triangulate the surface by splitting the skew patch above four adjoining grid points into two triangles. We can now apply all the algorithms of the previous sections to the approximating polyhedron. Of course, the lines of intersection are of great importance. The contour line is very useful for plotter drawings. The generalized helices on the surface are important for the construction of roads with constant angle of elevation.

Of particular interest to biologists and forestry engineers are the lines of steepest slope, along which rain water, and also, avalanches and landslides, will seek their way (Figure 9).

Example 2: Potential Areas. The author was motivated to write this section when dealing with the problem of how to find the equipotential lines and field lines of electrical potential areas. From the geometrist's point of view this is nothing but the tracing of lines of intersection and their orthogonal trajectories on function graphs. In the top view, these lines form an orthogonal net. Figure 9 shows such a surface, given by the equation

$$z = \left| \frac{w-1}{w+1} \right| \quad (z \ real, \ w = x + iy \ complex) \tag{24}$$

$$\left(\Rightarrow z = \sqrt{\frac{x^2 + y^2 + 1 - 2x}{x^2 + y^2 + 1 + 2x}} \right). \tag{25}$$

The normal projections of the equipotential lines and field lines on the ground plane are, as is well known, two orthogonal pencils of circles. The results of the integrations of the curves can hardly be distinguished from the accurate solutions of the differential equations.

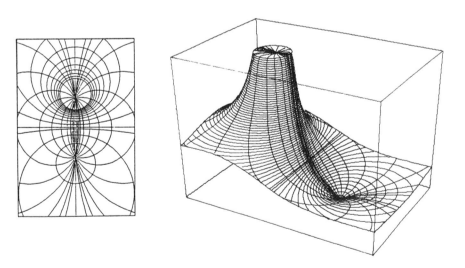

FIGURE 9. Equipotential lines and field lines on an electrical potential area. Their normal projections on the ground plane are two orthogonal pencils of circles.

10

Computer-Generated Movies

In the previous chapters, we saw how it is possible to create realistic computer-generated images and how we can manipulate a scene by way of changing the position of its eye point. In this chapter, we will develop subroutines that permit us to store the frames of a movie efficiently in a "video file."

We will introduce a new program (a "movie previewer") that reads this file and replays it as quickly as possible. Such a file is independent of the hardware that is used so that it can be replayed on any graphics computer. On graphics workstations with fast graphics hardware, this previewer may be so fast that the whole movie can be displayed on the screen in real time, so that we just have to position a film camera in front of the screen and to record the scene. (In fact, this is probably the most economical way of producing a computer-generated movie.) If we do not have such a sophisticated workstation at our disposal, we can still record the movie frame by frame.

10.1 An Economical Way of Storing a Movie

Our graphics program package produces two kinds of output: a set of lines (wire frames) and/or a set of filled polygons (shading and shadows).

Usually, we build our frames by plotting the image polygons in the correct order (with the exception of depth-buffered polygons). It turns out to be much more efficient to store the information about the polygons rather than to store the screen pixel by pixel. What is even more, the storing of polygons makes us independent of the screen resolution.

Our final goal is to be able to transfer the stored movie to any other computer (even to one that has only a minimum of graphics facilities) and to replay it there without having to change anything. In this way, the quality of the output can be improved if we switch to a more sophisticated graphics computer. (Of course, we can also store our images in other standards like the IFF-standard, but in our special case – we only store polygons – this is the most economical way.)

Let us try to store a movie in such a way as to make it fully compatible with other graphics computers. We will distinguish between 8-bit integers int_8 (**char**s), which are in the interval $\mathbf{I}_8(0 \leq int_8 < 2^8)$, and 12-bit integers int_{12}, which are in the interval $\mathbf{I}_{12}(0 \leq int_{12} < 2^{12})$. Numbers of different type will be stored in different files so that no disk space is wasted.

First we predefine some numbers:

#define	*MAX_12_BIT*	(**short**) $0xff$	$(\rightarrow$ Macros.h$)$
#define	*NEW_FRAME*	$(MAX\_8\_BIT - 1)$	$(\rightarrow$ Macros.h$)$
#define	*END_MOVIE*	*MAX_8_BIT*	$(\rightarrow$ Macros.h$)$

Numbers of the type int_8 are stored in the file `"<filename>.vd1"`, numbers of the type int_{12} in the file `"<filename>.vd2"`. While switching from one output file to another (depending on the type of the number) we store

1) the characteristic ID-number
    (int_8) *MAX_8_BIT*, (int_{12}) *MAX_8_BIT*
   at the head of each file, so that the
   computer can recognize the files as a "movie."
2) the **Boolean** expressions
    (int_8) *Smooth_shading*.
   (If *TRUE*, the polygons have to be smooth-shaded.)
3) the active palettes as follows:
    (int_8) *palette_index*,
    (int_8) lower RGB values $r1$, $g1$, $b1$ (transformed into $\mathbf{I}_8$)
    (int_8) upper RGB values $r2$, $g2$, $b2$ (transformed into $\mathbf{I}_8$).
4) one frame after the other, starting with the keyword
    (int_8) *NEW_FRAME*.
   Now we store the **Bool** variable
    (int_8) *New_image*,
   which indicates whether the current frame differs from the previous one.
   (In a movie an image may be "frozen" for a while. It would be
   a waste of disk space to store the same image several times.)

   If *New_image* is *TRUE*, we store all the polygons in the following way:
        (int_8) number n of vertices
        (int_8) *color* (palette index),
        (int_8) **if** *Smooth_shading*
            (int_8) *shade* of color (transformed into $\mathbf{I}_8$)
        else
            (int_8) n shades of color (transformed into $\mathbf{I}_8$)
        (int_{12}) n pairs of normalized device coordinates x, y
            (transformed into $\mathbf{I}_{12}$)
5) the
    (int_8) *END_MOVIE*
   constant.

Numbers of the type int_8 are efficiently stored as characters by means of the C macro *putc()* and re-read by means of the macro *getc()*.

To store 12-bit integers, we use fast bitwise operators, which pack eight such numbers into three **long** variables (with 32 bits each). Figure 1 shows how the function *pack_or_unpack_96_bits()* works.

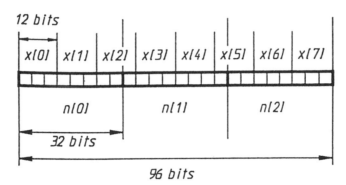

FIGURE 1. How to pack eight 12-bit integers into three **long** variables.

typedef unsigned long Ulong; $(\to$ Types.h$)$

---

void *pack_or_unpack_96_bits*$(n,\ x,\ pack)$ $(\to$ Proto.h$)$
  Ulong $n[3],\ x[8]$;
  Bool *pack*;
{ /* begin *pack_or_unpack_96_bits()* */
  if $(pack)$
      $n[0]\ =\ (x[0] \ll 20)\ |\ (x[1] \ll 8)\ |\ (x[2] \gg 4)$,
      $n[1]\ =\ ((x[2]\ \&\ 0xf) \ll 28)\ |\ (x[3] \ll 16)$
                                           $|\ (x[4] \ll 4)\ |\ (x[5] \gg 8)$,
      $n[2]\ =\ ((x[5]\ \&\ 0xff) \ll 24)\ |\ (x[6] \ll 12)\ |\ x[7]$;
  else
      $x[0]\ =\ (n[0]\ \&\ 0xfff00000) \gg 20$,
      $x[1]\ =\ (n[0]\ \&\ 0x000fff00) \gg 8$,
      $x[2]\ =\ ((n[0]\ \&\ 0x000000ff) \ll 4)\ |\ ((n[1]\&\ 0xf0000000)\ \gg 28)$,
      $x[3]\ =\ (n[1]\ \&\ 0x0fff0000) \gg 16$,
      $x[4]\ =\ (n[1]\ \&\ 0x0000fff0) \gg 4$,
      $x[5]\ =\ ((n[1]\ \&\ 0x0000000f) \ll 8)\ |\ ((n[2]\&\ 0xff000000)\ \gg 24)$,
      $x[6]\ =\ (n[2]\ \&\ 0x00fff000) \gg 12$,
      $x[7]\ =\ (n[2]\ \&\ 0x00000fff)$;
} /* end *pack_or_unpack_96_bits()* */

A 96-bit block is put into a binary file by means of the function

FILE *Video_file*[2];   ($\rightarrow$ Globals.h)
    /* Must be initialized by *Video_file*[0] = *NULL*. */

---

void *put_or_get_96_bits*(*c*, *put*)   ($\rightarrow$ Proto.h)
    register *char* * *c*;
    Bool *put*;
{   /* begin *put_or_get_96_bits*() */
    register *char* * *hi_c* = *c* + 12; /* **sizeof**(*c*[12]) = 96 bits. */

    if (*put*)
        for (; *c* < *hi_c*; *c*++)
            putc(**c*, *Video_file*[1]); /* C macro! */
    else
        for (; *c* < *hi_c*; *c*++)
            **c* = *getc*(*Video_file*[1]); /* C macro! */
}   /* end *put_or_get_96_bits*() */

An example will show how efficient this kind of storage is. A scene of medium complexity may consist of 300 polygons (quadrilaterals, for example). To store a quadrilateral, we need three 8-bit integers and eight 12-bit integers, i.e., 120 bits or 15 bytes.

Thus, a frame requires only 4.5 Kbytes! A real time movie of ten seconds and with 250 frames can be stored in a file that has a size of little more than one Mbyte. If the polygons are smooth-shaded (e.g., when we store a smooth-shaded surface of revolution), we need about 20% more space.

Let us start our graphics package. By means of an additional option, we tell the program that we want to store the images. This can be done by writing:

    progname <datafile> -v <videofile>.

in the command line (see Appendix A.3).

A flag

Bool *Init*(*Store_image*, *FALSE*);   ($\rightarrow$ Globals.h)

is then set *TRUE*. When we create the color palettes, we open the video file and store the information on the palettes that are going to be used. For this purpose, we add the following lines at the beginning of the function *create_palettes*(), which was described in Section 4.3.

```
#ifdef ANSI
#    define READ_BIN   "rb"                              (→ Macros.h)
#    define WRITE_BIN "wb"                               (→ Macros.h)
#else
#    define READ_BIN   "r"                               (→ Macros.h)
#    define WRITE_BIN "w"                                (→ Macros.h)
#endif
```

/* This may be tricky. The standard C language does not distinguish between binary files and text files. This will lead to problems, if you work in the DOS environment, where a file is closed by the character $< Ctrl > z$. (In a UNIX environment no EOF flag is set.) You should write a short test file to figure this out. */

```
#define Send_8_bit_int(n)\                              (→ Macros.h)
    putc((Ubyte) (n), Video_file[0])
#define Send_12_bit_int(n)\                             (→ Macros.h)
    send_12_bit_int((short ) (n))

    if (Store_image && !Video_file[0]) {
        Video_file[0] = safe_open("<filename>.vd1", WRITE_BIN);
        Video_file[1] = safe_open("<filename>.vd2", WRITE_BIN);
        Send_8_bit_int(MAX_8_BIT);
        Send_12_bit_int(MAX_8_BIT);
        Send_8_bit_int(Smooth_shading);
        init_video_buffer(); /* This function will be explained soon. */
    }  /* end if (Store_image) */
```

At the end of the function $make\_spectrum()$ (Section 4.3), we send the index of the palette and its characteristic RGB values to the file:

```
    if (Store_image) {
        n = pal  − Parent_palette;
        Send_8_bit_int(n);
        Scale_vec(rgb, pal−>lower_rgb, MAX_8_BIT);
        for (n = 0; n < 3; n++)
            Send_8_bit_int(rgb[n]);
        Scale_vec(rgb, pal−>upper_rgb, MAX_8_BIT);
        for (n = 0; n < 3; n++)
            Send_8_bit_int(rgb[n]);
    }  /* end if (Store_image) */
```

A function $send\_12\_bit\_int()$ receives a short between 0 and $0xfff = 2^{12} - 1 = 4095$ and integrates it into a field that is 96 bits long. As soon as eight **shorts** have been buffered, the bit field is sent to $Video\_file[1]$.

```
void send_12_bit_int(s)                                    (→ Proto.h)
   short s;

{  /* begin send_12_bit_int() */
   static Ulong buffer[8];   /* Buffered numbers. */
   static Ulong space[3];    /* Reserves 96 bits. */
   static short i = 0;       /* How many numbers in buffer. */


   if (s ≥ 0)
      buffer[i++] = s;
   else        /* Flush buffer. */
      while (i < 8)
         buffer[i++] = 0;
   if (i == 8)
      pack_or_unpack_96_bits((char *) space, buffer, TRUE),
      put_or_get_96_bits(space, TRUE),
      i = 0;
}  /* end send_12_bit_int() */
```

In the next section, we will need the reverse function $receive\_12\_bit\_int()$ to extract the compressed numbers from the file:

```
short receive_12_bit_int()                                 (→ Proto.h)

{  /* begin receive_12_bit_int() */
   static Ulong buffer[8];   /* Buffered numbers. */
   static Ulong space[3];    /* Reserves 96 bits. */
   static short i = 7;


   i = ++i % 8;
   if (i == 0)
      put_or_get_96_bits(space, FALSE),
      pack_or_unpack_96_bits((char *) space, buffer, FALSE);
   return (short ) buffer[i];
}  /* end receive_12_bit_int() */
```

Every time a polygon (or a line) is drawn, the coordinates of its vertices are sent to a buffer. For the respective code, we introduce a new type and some variables, which are global in the current module.

```
typedef struct {
    Ubyte no_of_vertices;
    Vector2 * vertices;
    Ubyte color, shade;
    Ubyte * smooth_shade;
    short xmin, xmax, ymin, ymax;
    float area;
} Poly2d;                                          (→ Types.h)
```

Poly2d * *All_polys*, **Cur_poly2d*, **Hi_poly2d*;
Vector2 * *Vbuffer* = *NULL*, **Cur_v* = *NULL*;
short *No_of_saved_frames* = 0;
Ubyte * *Shade_pool*, **Cur_s*;

#define *MAXPOLY*   3000   (*local macro*)
#define *BUFSIZE*   20000   (*local macro*)

The buffer is initialized for the first time when we open the video files. (It will be reinitialized every time a frame has been stored.)

```
void init_video_buffer()                           (→ Proto.h)
{   /* begin init_video_buffer() */
    if (!Vbuffer) {
        Alloc_array(Poly2d, All_polys, MAXPOLY, "vbuf");
        Alloc_array(Vector2, Vbuffer, BUFSIZE, "vbuf");
        if (Smooth_shading)
            Alloc_array(Ubyte, Shade_pool, 4 * MAXPOLY, "smooth");
    }
    Cur_v = Vbuffer;
    Cur_poly2d = All_polys;
    Cur_s = Shade_pool;
}   /* end init_video_buffer() */
```

When we buffer a polygon (or a line), we have to make sure that the polygon (line) has been clipped! The polygon has to be stored in an array of **Vector2**s. When the polygons are smooth-shaded, the shades have to be stored in an array

Ubyte *Shades_of_vertices*[*MAX_POLY_SIZE*];   (→ Globals.h)

When plain shading is applied, the current palette and the current shade have to be stored by means of the global variables

Ubyte *Cur_shade*, *Cur_palette*, *Cur_poly_color*;   (→ Globals.h)

```
void buffer_line(p, q)                                    (→ Proto.h)
   Vector2 p, q;
{  /* begin buffer_line() */
   register  Poly2d * cp  =  Cur_poly2d;

   cp->color  =  Cur_palette;
   cp->shade =  Cur_shade;
   cp->no_of_vertices  =  2;
   cp->vertices  =  Cur_v;
   Copy_vec2(*Cur_v, p);  Cur_v++;
   Copy_vec2(*Cur_v, q);  Cur_v++;
   Cur_poly2d++;
}  /* end buffer_line() */
```

```
void buffer_polygon(n, vertices)                          (→ Proto.h)
   short  n;
   Vector2 * vertices;
{  /* begin buffer_polygon() */
   register  Poly2d * p  =  Cur_poly2d;
   register  short  x, y;
   register  Vector2 * v, * hi_v  =  vertices + n, * v1;

   p->no_of_vertices  =  n;
   p->color  =  Cur_poly_color;
   if  (!Smooth_shading)
       p->shade =  Cur_shade;
   else  {
       p->smooth_shade =  Cur_s;
       for  (x = 0; x < n; x++)
           * Cur_s++  =  Shade_of_vertex[x];
   }  /* end if (Smooth_shading) */
   p->vertices  =  Cur_v;

   /* Store vertices in buffer. */
   for  (v = vertices; v < hi_v; v++,  Cur_v++)
       Copy_vec2(*Cur_v, *v);

   /* Bounding rectangle of polygon. */
   v = vertices;
   p->xmin  =  p->xmax  =  (*v)[X];
   p->ymin  =  p->ymax  =  (*v)[Y];
```

```
for (v = vertices + 1; v < hi_v; v++) {
    x = (*v)[X]; y = (*v)[Y];
    if (x < p->xmin) p->xmin = x;
    else if (x > p->xmax) p->xmax = x;
    if (y < p->ymin) p->ymin = y;
    else if (y > p->ymax) p->ymax = y;
} /* end for (v) */


/* Area of polygon. */
p->area = 0;
for (v = vertices + 1, v1 = v + 1; v1 < hi_v; v++, v1++)
    p->area += fabs(Area_of_2d_triangle(*vertices, *v, *v1));
if (p->area > 4) Cur_poly2d++;
} /* end buffer_polygon() */
```

When the screens are swapped, we simply flush this buffer. Some of the polygons, however, may have been completely erased during the drawing process. Thus, it is worthwhile to check whether a polygon really has to be drawn. Even though this takes some computation time, it will both save space and – what is even more – reduce the replay time.

Bool *Init*(*New_image*, *FALSE*);   (→ **Globals.h**)

```
void release_buffer()                                    (→ Proto.h)
{   /* begin release_buffer() */
    register Poly2d *p;
    register Vector2 *v, *hi_v;
    short i, total, n;
    static float scale_xy = 0, scale_shade;

    if (!scale_xy)
        scale_xy = 4096/Maximum(Window_width, Window_height),
        scale_shade = (float) MAX_8_BIT / PAL_SIZE;
    Send_8_bit_int(NEW_FRAME);
    if (!New_image && No_of_saved_frames > 0) {
        Send_8_bit_int(TRUE);
        No_of_saved_frames++;
        return ;
    } else
        Send_8_bit_int(FALSE);
    Hi_poly2d = Cur_poly2d;
    if (Hi_poly2d - All_polys) == 0)
        return ;
    for (p = All_polys; p < Hi_poly2d; p++) {
```

```
        n  =  p–>no_of_vertices;
        if  (n  >  2 &&  !necessary_to_plot(p))
            continue;
        hi_v  =  (v =  p–>vertices)  +  p–>no_of_vertices;
        Send_8_bit_int(n);
        Send_8_bit_int(p–>color);
        if  (!Smooth_shading || n == 2)
            Send_8_bit_int(scale_shade * p–>shade);
        else
            for  (i =  0;  i <  n;  i++)
                Send_8_bit_int(scale_shade * p–>smooth_shade[i]);
        for  ( ;  v <  hi_v;  v++) {
            Send_12_bit_int((*v)[X]  * scale_xy);
            Send_12_bit_int((*v)[Y]  * scale_xy);
        } /* end for (v) */
    } /* end for (p) */
    No_of_saved_frames++;
    init_video_buffer(); /* Reset the global pointers. */
} /* end release_buffer() */
```

The important optimizing function *necessary_to_plot*() will reduce the size of the file by $\approx 20\%$ ($\pm 10\%$):

```
Bool necessary_to_plot(p)                              (→ Proto.h)
    register  Poly2d *p;
{   /* begin necessary_to_plot() */
    register  2Poly2d *q, *q0;
    Vector2 *p1;
    Vector2 *which_poly;
    short  n1, n2;
    static Vector2 *clipped  = NULL;

    if (p–>color  == NO_COLOR)
        return  FALSE;
    if (!clipped)
        Alloc_array(Vector2, clipped, MAX_POLY_SIZE, "clip");
    n1  =  p–>no_of_vertices;
    p1  =  p–>vertices;

    /*  Check whether the current polygon is hidden by any of the following
        polygons or by the previous polygon when it had the same color. The
        latter case occurs especially when shadows are plotted on large faces. */
```

```
for  (q0  =  p − 1;  ;  q0−−)
    if  (q0−>color ! = p−>color) break;
for  (q  =  Hi_poly2d − 1;  q > q0;  q−−) {
    if  (q == p) continue;
    /* A very efficient way of checking whether the polygon is obscured by
       the contours of other objects. */
    if  (q−>color ! = NO_COLOR) continue;
    /* p can only be hidden by q if Area(q) > Area(p). */
    if  (p−>area > q−>area) continue;

    /* Does the bounding box of q contain the one of p? */
    if  (p−>xmin < q−>xmin || p−>xmax > q−>xmax ||
         p−>ymin < q−>ymin || p−>ymax > q−>ymax)
        continue;

    /* Final decision: intersect polygons. */
    n2  =  q−>no_of_vertices;
    if  (clip_convex(n2, q−>vertices, n1, p1,
                     clipped, &which_poly), 2)
        if  (which_poly == p1)
            return  FALSE; /* Do not save polygon! */
}  /* end for (q) */
return  TRUE;
}  /* end necessary_to_plot() */
```

We must not forget to send the *END_MOVIE* constant to the stream *Video_file*[0] at the end of the program. Because we always quit the program by calling the function *safe_exit*() (Section 3.1), we add the lines

```
if  (Video_file[0]) {
    Send_8_bit_int(END_MOVIE);
    Send_12_bit_int(−1); /* To flush the 96-bit block. */
    fclose(Video_file[0]); fclose(Video_file[1]);
}  /* end if (Video_file[0]) */
```

to this function.

10.2 A Fast Movie Previewer

The video files that have been created in the described manner can now easily be re-read by means of a new program **replay.c**. Here is the pseudo-code:

Open video files
Read (int_8) *MAX_8_BIT* (int_{12}) *MAX_8_BIT* for identification.
Open a back screen and a front screen
    with coordinates $0 \leq x < 4096$, $0 \leq y < 4096$.
Clear back screen.
Read (int_8) *Smooth_shading, palette_index*
while *palette_index* $\neq$ *NEW_FRAME*
    read RGB values (int_8) r_1, g_1, b_1, r_2, g_2, b_2
    make palette (linear color spectrum) with shades in $[0,255]$.
    read (int_8) *palette_index*
Read (int_8) *New_image, n*
while $n \neq$ *END_MOVIE*
    while $n \neq$ *NEW_FRAME*
        read n (int_{12}) pairs of normalized device coordinates
        read (int_8) *color* (palette index)
        if *Smooth_shading* read n (int_8) shades
        else read (int_8) *shade*
        display polygon (line) on back screen in given shade(s) of color
        read (int_8) *n*
    swap screens, clear back screen
    read (int_8) *New_image*
    if **not** *New_image* delay *1/30* second
    read (int_8) *n*

The source code of **replay.c** is not listed. You can find it on your disk. The module has to be linked with several other modules of the programming system. Please have a look at the **makefile**.

Appendix A

The Programming Package
on Your Disk

A.1 The Contents of the Disk

This book comes with a $3\frac{1}{2}''$-diskette, formatted under MS-DOS 5.0 with 1,44 MBytes. You will need a DOS environment to read the diskette. If you work in a UNIX environment, you have to transfer the files to your system.

The disk contains a UNIX version and a DOS version of the graphics package. If you work in a DOS environment, call the program **install** in order to copy the contents of the disk to your harddisk. Otherwise, there are a few files that you should copy first: a **read.me** text file and the C files **zp.c** and **uzp.c**.

The ASCII-file **read.me** contains information about the installation of the disk and about the author and his Email-address – in case you have any problems.

The disk also contains several directories:

Directory CODE: It contains the entire source code of the graphics package (i.e., the ***.c** files and the ***.h** files) except the system-dependent module **g_functs.c** and the macro file **G_macros.h**. The code is compressed to the file **source.zp** by means of the file **zp** and has to be uncompressed by means of the corresponding file **uzp**.

Directory SYSTDEPS: In this directory you can find the system-dependent module **g_functs.c** and the macro file **G_macros.h** plus a **makefile** for the Silicon Graphics environment, using the *Silicon Graphics Library* functions, and for the DOS environment, using a WATCOM C compiler. The package was developed on Silicon Graphics Workstations: first on the "good old" *Iris 3020*, then on the *SG-35* and finally on the *Indigo*[2]. By means of the WATCOM C compiler Version 10.0 it was possible to make the programs run in a DOS environment as well. The corresponding files are compressed to files named **sg.zp** and **pc.zp**.

A former version of the package used to run on an *Impuls* Workstation (under UNIX) and on the *Commodore Amiga* (together with the *Aztec C compiler 3.0*). Both versions used to work fine ([GLAE90]).

If you want to implement the programming package on other graphics computers, this should be possible if you change the corresponding system-dependent macros and the system-dependent functions (see Appendix B).

Directory DATA: In this directory, some dozens of sample data files are stored. The files are compressed to the single file **data.zp**.

Directory ANIM: In this directory, a few sample animation files are stored. The files are compressed to the file **anim.zp**.

A.2 How to Install the Program Package

- **You are working in a UNIX environment:**

    1. Create a working directory, e.g., **FAST3D**, and change to this directory:

       ```
       mkdir FAST3D
       cd FAST3D
       ```

    2. Create the following subdirectories

       ```
       mkdir SOURCE
       mkdir DATA
       mkdir ANIM
       mkdir VIDEO
       ```

    3. Compile the files **zp.c** and **uzp.c**:

       ```
       cc zp.c -o zp
       cc uzp.c -o uzp
       ```

    4. Copy the file **source.zp** and the system-dependent code **sg.zp** into the **SOURCE**-directory and decompress the files:

       ```
       cd SOURCE
       ../uzp source.zp
       ../uzp sg.zp
       cd ..
       ```

5. Copy the file `data.zp` into the directory `DATA` and the file `anim.zp` into the directory `ANIM`. Then decompress these files in a similar way.

6. Change to the `SOURCE`-directory and create the executable files `try`, `replay` and `speed`. To do so, just write

   `make all`

7. If you work on a Silicon Graphics Workstation, everything should be okay now. The executable files are stored in your working directory `FAST3D`. Change to this directory:

   `cd ..`

   If you do not work on such a workstation, you will have to adapt the system-dependent module `g_functs.c` and the system-dependent macros in `G_macros.h`.

- **You are working on a PC:** Switch to the disk-device and write `install`. Then follow the instructions of the installation file.

  If you have a WATCOM C compiler at your disposal, you can recompile the files: change to the `SOURCE` directory and write `make all`. This calls the batch file `make.bat` that does the job. If you do not want to recompile the code, unzip the executable files by means of the widely spread program `pkunzip.exe` (Version ≥ 2.04). If you want to use another C compiler, you have to adapt the system-dependent module `g_functs.c` and the system-dependent macros in `G_macros.h`.

  Note that the executable programs requires a mathematical coprocessor and at least 4 MB RAM (preferably 8MB and more!).

A.3 How to Use the Program

Once you have managed to compile the package – this will take a while, because it consists of dozens of modules – your compiler will create two executable file named `try` and `replay` in the UNIX environment or `try.exe` and `replay.exe` in the DOS environment.

The usage of the program `try`[1] is:

   `try <name of a data file> [ options ]`

Valid options are

   `-a <name of animation file>`

or

   `-v <name of video file>`

---

[1]The name `try` has historical reasons: it took a while until the first data files worked, thus each attempt was always a try.

To give an example: The command

```
try pencil
```

starts the program that reads the data file `pencil`[2] – a pencil is displayed interactively on the screen and can be rotated and viewed from any side by means of the keyboard:

key	function
w, h	draw mode: wire frame, hidden lines
s, c	draw mode: shading, cast shadows
j	hidden lines by means of painter's algorithm
f, F	freeze / auto rotation
a, A, <, >	change azimuth
e, E, ^	change elevation
t, T	change twist
x, X	enlarge image (decrease fovy angle)
d, D	change distance
← → ↑ ↓	change target point
1, 2, 3	top view / front view / right side view
4, 5, 6	bottom view / back view / left side view
u	undo special view (back to former perspective)

Additional options are:

key	function
g, G	geocentric / heliocentric
k, K	show color map / undo
b, B	show bounding boxes / undo
o, O	show outlines / undo
m, M	show axes / undo
l, L	show lights (can be changed interactively) / undo
z, Z	software z-buffering / undo
p	create a PostScript file
v	create a video file (default name VIDEO/tmp)
q	quit program

When we use the the -a option in the command line

```
try pencil -a ANIM/pencil
```

---

[2]The data file should either be in the current directory, or – more clearly – in the default directory DATA: the program will automatically look for the file there.

the animation is done by the animation file **ANIM/pencil**. [3]

The command

    try pencil -v VIDEO/pencil

will store your whole animation in the two files **VIDEO/pencil.vd1** and **VIDEO/pencil.vd2**[4]

When you use the the **-a** option and the **-v** option together you can create a little movie:

    try pencil -a ANIM/pencil -v VIDEO/pencil

To replay the movie, type

    replay VIDEO/pencil [5]

Provided you have a fast graphics computer, you have now created your first real time animated film.

A.4 How to Write Data Files and Animation Files

Chapter 3 dealt with the writing of data files. However, this was just an introduction. The program **try** can read quite a lot of information. Unfortunately, its HELP-options are comparatively poor. The program is not very flexible as far as the order of keywords is concerned.

The best way of learning how to write a data file is to edit the data files **Learn.1**, **Learn.2**, ..., and to vary it slightly. After a while you check out what you can or cannot do. It would fill pages to describe all the possibilities you have.

The same is true for the writing of animation files. Just edit one of the files that are on the disk and make some slight variations. For example, change the drawing mode, the number of frames, the eye point and so forth.

A.5 How Fast Is Your Computer?

The program **speed**, which you can find on the disk, allows you to test the performance of your configuration (compiler plus hardware).

When we write programs that take a lot of computation time, such as graphics programs, it is quite useful to know how fast our computer can carry out various tasks.

---

[3]In the DOS environment, the slash has to be a backslash!! This is true for the whole section. Furthermore, the directory **ANIM** is the default directory for animation files.

[4]The directory **VIDEO** is the default directory for video files.

[5]Since **VIDEO** is the default directory for video files, you can also write **replay pencil**

In this section, we give the listing of a program that is system-independent and that can be used for the testing of your machine.

The test results still depend on the compiler that is used (there are considerable differences!) and on the values chosen for the test variables. Nevertheless, the program shows which system calls or which library functions can be used without any problems and which of these calls would be "bottlenecks" in your programs. Here is the listing of the program **speed.c**:

```c
#include <stdio.h>
#include <math.h>
#include <time.h> /* prototype of clock() */
/*
   How fast is your computer?

   This program analyzes how long it takes your computer
   to carry out various tasks, e.g., to multiply two floats
   or to increment an integer or to pass a parameter to
   a function. This enables you to find out the bottlenecks
   in your programs.
*/
#define COMPILER "indigo2"
#ifndef _LANGUAGE_C_PLUS_PLUS
#   define _LANGUAGE_C_PLUS_PLUS
#endif
typedef float Real;

/* Global variables */

const long Factor = 300000L;
      /* Increase this number if your computer is very fast. */
long Repetitions, I, J;
Real Time0, TimeForLoop = 0;
FILE *f; /* The log-file. */
typedef struct { /* A typical structure (30 bytes) */
      int a, b, c;
      Real d[3];
      char *e, *f, *g;
   } A_struct;

Real time_since_prog_start(void)
   {
      return (Real) clock() / CLOCKS_PER_SEC;
   }

void prt(char *txt)
{
   printf(txt);
   fprintf(f, txt);
}
```

```
void prt2(char *format, char *txt, Real microsec)
{
    printf(format, txt, COMPILER, microsec);
    fprintf(f, format, txt, COMPILER, microsec);
}

Real t(char *str)  /* Prints time in microsecs. */
{
    Real t0 =
        1e6 * (time_since_prog_start() - Time0) / Repetitions;
    prt2("%15s%10s%6.2f␣microsec\n", str, t0 - TimeForLoop);
    return t0;
}

void g(void)  /* Prepare the test: set globals. */
{
    Time0 = time_since_prog_start();
    I = Repetitions; J = 0; while (I--) if (++J) ;
    TimeForLoop =
        1e6 * (time_since_prog_start() - Time0) / Repetitions;
    I = Repetitions; J = 0;
    Time0 = time_since_prog_start();
}

void bytes(void)  /* Operations with short ints (bytes) */
{
    register unsigned char x, y, z;
    Repetitions = 12 * Factor;  /* For more accuracy. */
    prt("\noperations␣with␣bytes:\n");
    x = 143; y = 23;
    g(); z = 0; while(I-- > 0) if (++J) z++; t("inc");
    g(); while (I-- > 0) if (++J) z = x & y; t("log.␣and");
    g(); while (I-- > 0) if (++J) z = x | y; t("log.␣or␣");
    g(); while (I-- > 0) if (++J) z = x ^ y; t("log.␣xor");
    g(); while (I-- > 0) if (++J) z = x >> 1; t("shift␣1");
    g(); while (I-- > 0) if (++J) z = y / 2; t("div␣2");
    g(); while (I-- > 0) if (++J) z = x + y; t("+");
    g(); while (I-- > 0) if (++J) z = x - y; t("-");
    g(); while (I-- > 0) if (++J) z = x * y; t("*");
    g(); while (I-- > 0) if (++J) z = x / y; t("div");
    g(); while (I-- > 0) if (++J) z = x % y; t("mod");
    if (z) ;  /* In order to suppress a warning. */
}

void shorts(void)  /* Tests operations with shorts (2 bytes) */
{
    register int x, y, z;
    Repetitions = 12 * Factor;  /* For more accuracy. */
    prt("\noperations␣with␣integers:\n");
    x = 23; y = 103;
    g(); z = 0; while(I-- > 0) if (++J) z++; t("inc");
    g(); while (I-- > 0) if (++J) z = x & y; t("log.␣and");
```

```
        g(); while (I-- > 0) if (++J) z =  x | y; t("log.⎵or");
        g(); while (I-- > 0) if (++J) z =  x ^ y; t("log.⎵xor");
        g(); while (I-- > 0) if (++J) z =  x >> 1; t("shift⎵1");
        g(); while (I-- > 0) if (++J) z =  y / 2; t("div⎵2");
        g(); while (I-- > 0) if (++J) z =  x + y; t("+");
        g(); while (I-- > 0) if (++J) z =  x - y; t("-");
        g(); while (I-- > 0) if (++J) z =  x * y; t("*");
        g(); while (I-- > 0) if (++J) z =  x / y; t("div⎵");
        g(); while (I-- > 0) if (++J) z =  x % y; t("mod⎵");
        if (z) ; /* In order to suppress a warning. */
}

void longs(void) /* Tests operations with long ints (4 bytes) */
{
        register long x, y, z;
        Repetitions = 6 * Factor; /* For more accuracy. */
        prt("\noperations⎵with⎵longint:\n");
        x = -543210; y = 123456;
        g(); z = 0; while(I-- > 0) if (++J) z++; t("inc");
        g(); while (I-- > 0) if (++J) z =  x & y; t("log.⎵and");
        g(); while (I-- > 0) if (++J) z =  x | y; t("log.⎵or");
        g(); while (I-- > 0) if (++J) z =  x ^ y; t("log.⎵xor");
        g(); while (I-- > 0) if (++J) z =  x >> 1; t("shift⎵1");
        Repetitions /= 10; /* Divisions take a lot of time! */
        g(); while (I-- > 0) if (++J) z =  y / 2; t("div⎵2");
        Repetitions *= 10;
        g(); while (I-- > 0) if (++J) z =  x + y; t("+");
        g(); while (I-- > 0) if (++J) z =  x - y; t("-");
        g(); while (I-- > 0) if (++J) z =  x * y; t("*");
        Repetitions /= 10; /* Divisions take a lot of time! */
        g(); while (I-- > 0) if (++J) z =  x / y; t("div");
        g(); while (I-- > 0) if (++J) z =  x % y; t("mod");
        if (z) ; /* In order to suppress a warning. */
}

void floats(void)  /* Tests operations with floats (4 bytes) */
{
        register Real x, y, z;
        Repetitions = 3 * Factor; /* For more accuracy. */
        prt("\noperations⎵with⎵floats:\n");
        x = 1.2432434; y = -562.15; z = 0.1413;
        g(); while (I-- > 0) if (++J) z =  x + y; t("+");
        g(); while (I-- > 0) if (++J) z =  x - y; t("-");
        g(); while (I-- > 0) if (++J) z =  x * y; t("*");
        g(); while (I-- > 0) if (++J) z =  x / y; t("/");
        Repetitions = 1 * Factor;
        g(); while (I-- > 0) if (++J) z =  fabs(z); t("fabs");
        g(); while (I-- > 0) if (++J) z =  sqrt(x); t("sqrt");
        g(); while (I-- > 0) if (++J) z =  sin(x); t("sin");
        g(); while (I-- > 0) if (++J) z =  cos(x); t("cos");
        g(); while (I-- > 0) if (++J) z =  sin(x)/cos(x); t("tan");
        g(); while (I-- > 0) if (++J) z =  atan(x); t("atan");
```

```
    }
      g( ); while (I-- > 0) if (++J) z = exp(x); t("exp");

void f1f(Real x) { };
void f2f(Real x, Real y) { };;
void f3f(Real x, Real y, Real z) { };;
void f1i(int i) { };;
void f2i(int i, int j) { };;
void f3i(int i, int j, int k) { };;
void f1stp(A_struct *s) { };;
void f1str(A_struct s) { };;

void function_calls(void)
   {
      register Real x = 1.2345;
      register int y = 1234;
      static A_struct z = { 0 };
      Repetitions = 10 * Factor;
      prt("\nfunction␣calls:\n");
      g( ); while (I-- > 0) if (++J) f1f(x); t("1␣Real");
      g( ); while (I-- > 0) if (++J) f2f(x, x); t("2␣Real");
      g( ); while (I-- > 0) if (++J) f3f(x, x, x); t("3␣Real");
      g( ); while (I-- > 0) if (++J) f1i(y); t("1␣short");
      g( ); while (I-- > 0) if (++J) f2i(y, y); t("2␣short");
      g( ); while (I-- > 0) if (++J) f3i(y, y, y); t("3␣short");
      g( ); while (I-- > 0) if (++J) f1stp(&z); t("1␣address");
      g( ); while (I-- > 0) if (++J) f1str(z); t("1␣struct");
   }
/* Just for C++:
   Macros are fastest (sometimes together with inline-functions).
   Ordinary function calls take a lot of time. The same is true
   for operators. Even if some people call it "macromania":
   fast C programs still depend heavily on the use of macros!
*/
#ifdef _LANGUAGE_C_PLUS_PLUS
struct V2d { /* A 2d-vector */
  Real x, y;
  V2d() { };
  V2d(Real x0, Real y0) { x = x0; y = y0; }
  friend V2d operator + (V2d &u, V2d &v)
     {
       return V2d(u.x + v.x, u.y + v.y);
     }
};
#else
typedef struct {
  Real x, y;
} V2d;
#endif
void sum(V2d *w, V2d *u, V2d *v)
   {
      w->x = u->x + v->x;
```

```
        w->y = u->y + v->y;
    }
#ifdef _LANGUAGE_C_PLUS_PLUS
inline void in_sum (V2d &w, V2d &u, V2d &v)
    {
        w.x = u.x + v.x;
        w.y = u.y + v.y;
    }
#endif
#define SUM(w, u, v) ((w).x = (u).x + (v).x, (w).y = (u).x + (v).y)
void compare_macros_and_functions(void)
{
    V2d a, b, c;
    Real the_time[5], min_time;
    a.x = 1.5; a.y = -3.5; b.x = -5.4; b.y = 7.5;
    Repetitions = 5 * Factor;
    prt("\nmacros␣as␣opposed␣to␣function␣calls:\n");
#ifdef _LANGUAGE_C_PLUS_PLUS
    g(); while (I-- > 0) c = a + b, a.x += 0;
    the_time[1] = t("operator");
    g(); while (I-- > 0) in_sum(c, a, b), a.x += 0;
    the_time[2] = t("inl.function");
#endif
    g(); while (I-- > 0) sum(&c, &a, &b), a.x += 0;
    the_time[3] = t("ord.function");
    g(); while (I-- > 0) SUM(c, a, b), a.x += 0;
    the_time[4] = t("macro");
    prt("relative␣result:\n");
    min_time = 1e10;
#ifdef _LANGUAGE_C_PLUS_PLUS
    I = 1;
#else
    I = 3;
#endif
    for (; I < 5; I++)
        if (min_time > the_time[I])
            min_time = the_time[I];
#define PERCENT(i) 100 * the_time[i] / min_time
#ifdef _LANGUAGE_C_PLUS_PLUS
    prt2("%15s%10s%5.0f\%\n", "operator", PERCENT(1));
    prt2("%15s%10s%5.0f\%\n", "inl.function", PERCENT(2));
#endif
    prt2("%15s%10s%5.0f\%\n", "ord.function", PERCENT(3));
    prt2("%15s%10s%5.0f\%\n", "macro", PERCENT(4));
}

FILE *open_logfile(void)
{
    f = fopen("speed.log", "w");
    if (!f) printf("Cannot␣open␣log␣file!\n");
    return f;
}
```

```
int main()
{
  if (!open_logfile()) return 1;
  prt("\nPERFORMANCE␣TEST\n");
  prt("(The␣values␣depend␣on␣the␣test␣numbers!)\n");
  bytes();
  shorts();
  longs();
  floats();
  function_calls();
  compare_macros_and_functions();
  printf("The␣result␣has␣been␣written␣into␣<speed.log>\n");
  return 0;
}
```

Finally, we give a table of the results of the program with the following configurations:

- A 486/50MHz PC in connection with a Borland C++ compiler, Version 3.1 (compiler option "fastest code").

- A Personal Iris SG35 with a UNIX C compiler (options **-float -O2**).

- An Indigo2 with a UNIX C compiler (options **-float -O2**).

This is the result:

```
                    PERFORMANCE TEST
        (The values depend on the test numbers!)
              Numbers in microseconds

                         BC-3.1  SG-35 INDIGO2
        operations with bytes:
                    inc      0.08   0.11   0.03
              log. and      0.05   0.09   0.02
              log. or       0.03   0.08   0.02
              log. xor      0.06   0.08   0.02
              shift 1       0.05   0.08   0.02
              div 2         0.23   0.09   0.02
                    +        0.03   0.09   0.02
                    -        0.08   0.08   0.02
                    *        0.05   0.08   0.02
                    div      0.06   0.08   0.02
                    mod      0.05   0.08   0.02
```

```
operations with integers:
          inc       0.08    0.08    0.02
     log. and       0.05    0.08    0.02
      log. or       0.02    0.08    0.02
     log. xor       0.06    0.08    0.02
      shift 1       0.03    0.08    0.02
        div 2       0.21    0.08    0.02
            +       0.08    0.08    0.02
            -       0.05    0.08    0.02
            *       0.03    0.08    0.02
          div       0.05    0.08    0.02
          mod       0.03    0.08    0.02
operations with longint:
          inc       0.09    0.08    0.02
     log. and       0.12    0.08    0.02
      log. or       0.09    0.08    0.02
     log. xor       0.09    0.08    0.02
      shift 1       0.12    0.08    0.02
        div 2       0.92    0.06    0.02
            +       0.09    0.08    0.02
            -       0.09    0.08    0.02
            *       0.09    0.47    0.16
          div       0.92    0.11    0.02
          mod       1.22    0.11    0.02
operations with floats:
            +       0.37    0.08    0.03
            -       0.31    0.08    0.03
            *       0.31    0.08    0.03
            /       0.37    0.22    0.17
         fabs       0.37    0.53    0.20
         sqrt       2.93    4.10    2.48
          sin       7.69    2.50    1.85
          cos       7.51    3.47    1.79
          tan      16.67    5.83    3.62
         atan      11.17    4.63    2.86
          exp      15.02    3.43    1.79
function calls:
       1 Real       0.75    0.41    0.15
       2 Real       0.97    0.46    0.17
       3 Real       1.34    0.52    0.20
      1 short       0.35    0.40    0.15
      2 short       0.33    0.46    0.17
      3 short       0.35    0.52    0.20
    1 address       0.27    0.40    0.16
     1 struct       2.71    1.37    0.68
macros as opposed to function calls:
     operator       4.69    0.62    0.22
 inl.function       2.31    0.33    0.13
 ord.function       2.20    0.80    0.45
        macro       1.39    0.31    0.13
relative result:
     operator       296%    172%    146%
 inl.function       152%    106%    100%
 ord.function       148%    214%    264%
        macro       100%    100%    100%
```

Appendix B

System Dependencies and Other Programming Languages

B.1 How to Change the System-Dependent Commands

In Chapter 4, we talked about writing programs that are independent of the hardware and the compiler that is used. We said that we collect all the system-dependent functions in one file named **g_functs.c**. Additionally, all the system-dependent macros are written into one include file named **G_macros.h**.

In order to get an idea how such files look like, let us have a look at the two files that were developed for an IBM-PC in connection with the WATCOM C compiler (Version 10.0) and pick out some examples.

Example 1: The system-dependent macros
$G\_opengraphics(\,)$, $G\_close\_graphics(\,)$, $G\_clear\_screen(\,)$ and
$G\_swap\_screens(\,)$ in **G_macros.h** call functions
$PC\_open\_graphics(\,)$, $PC\_close\_graphics(\,)$, $PC\_clearscreen(\,)$ and
$PC\_swapbuffers(\,)$ in **g_functs.c**:

#define $G\_open\_graphics(\,)$ $PC\_open\_graphics(\,)$
#define $G\_close\_graphics(\,)$ $PC\_close\_graphics(\,)$
#define $G\_clear\_screen(\,)$ $PC\_clearscreen(\,)$
#define $G\_swap\_screens(\,)$ $PC\_swapbuffers(\,)$

For the time being these functions may have the following (simplified) system-dependent code:

```
void PC_open_graphics()
{
    _setvideomode(_VRES256COLOR);
            /* Standard VGA resolution with 256 colors at the same time.
               May be set to _XRES256COLOR (1024 × 768) if your video
               card supports that resolution. */
}
void PC_close_graphics()
{
    _setvideomode(_DEFAULTMODE);
}
void PC_clearscreen()
{
    _rectangle(_GFILLINTERIOR, 0, 0, 640, 480);
            /* 640 × 480 is the standard VGA resolution.
               Has to be changed for other resolutions. */
}
void PC_swapbuffers()
{
    _setvisualpage(1 - _getvisualpage());
    _setactivepage(1 - _getactivepage());
}
```

Example 2: The macros *G_move*() and *G_draw*() may directly insert the system-dependent functions _moveto() and _drawto():

```
#define G_move(v)  _moveto((short) (v)[X], (short) (v)[Y])
#define G_draw(v)  _drawto((short) (v)[X], (short) (v)[Y])
```

The macros *G_area_move*(), *G_area_draw*() and *G_area_close*() should insert the functions *poly_move*(), *poly_draw*() and *poly_close*() of Section 4.6.

Example 3: The macros

```
#define G_set_color(a) PC_setcolor((short) a)
#define G_get_color() PC_getcolor()
#define G_set_pixel(x, y) PC_setpixel((short) x, (short) y)
#define G_get_pixel_color(x, y) PC_getpixel((short) x, (short) y)
```

insert calls of the system-dependent functions

```
void PC_setcolor(col) /* For the time being. */
    short col;
{
    _setcolor(col);
}
int PC_getcolor() /* For the time being. */
{
    return _getcolor();
}
void PC_setpixel(x, y) /* For the time being. */
    short x, y;
{
    _setpixel(x, y);
}
short PC_getpixel(x, y) /* For the time being. */
    short x, y;
{
    return _getpixel(x, y);
}
```

If it was just the function calls, one should definitely insert the system-dependent function calls directly into the macro so as not to waste time (see Appendix B.2)!

———— • ————

One problem with the writing graphics software for PCs, however, is that there are so many different video cards on the market. Thus, the above mentioned functions will only cover a certain number of video cards.

The WATCOM C compiler supports standard VGA modes and most of the VESA 256 color modes on Super VGA's (SVGA). The VESA specifications only standardize the video mode numbers and the "bits per pixel memory organization" (8 bits per pixel = 1 byte per pixel for 256 colors). So far, however, there is no standard for screen pages. Thus, in order to support doublebuffering on standardized video cards, we have to write our own graphics primitives.

The actually implemented code for *PC_open_graphics*() first tests whether there are two screen pages available or not and will use two pages if supported (the boolean variable *TwoScreens* is then set *TRUE*).

When we can only use one screen page (this is true for most of the video cards), we buffer the whole drawing into a "pseudo screen" in ordinary RAM and not into video RAM. When is comes to page flipping, we put the image back on the screen. This is a slow solution, but ist works fine for most video cards. (On some video cards you have to load a VESA driver before using the program!)

The pseudo screen is built up line per line with no additional bytes at the end of a line (n pixels per line). Since we need one byte for each pixel, a pixel with the coordinates (x, y) has the linear position number $(n\,y + x)$ in our pseudo screen.

There are very fiew basic functions (macros) that actually change the pseudo screen: The function $PC\_setpixel(\,)$ ($PC\_set\_xor\_pixel(\,)$), the function $PC\_clearscreen(\,)$ and the macro $PC\_HORLINE(x1,\ x2,\ y)$ that "draws" a horizontal line from (x_1, y) to (x_2, y).

char *CurCol*; /* Number of color in color lookup table: $0 \leq CurCol < 256$. */
Bool *DrawInBack*;
 /* *TRUE* when *TwoScreens* = *FALSE* and not XOR-mode. */
typedef struct {
 short *xsize, ysize, BitsPerPixel*;
 char *Data*[ ];
  /* Huge array that is able to store a screen of the dimensions *xsize* ×
   ysize. Must have the size *xsize* ∗ *ysize*. */
} **PC_image**;
PC_image **Pseudo_screen*;
 /* Has to be allocated in *PC_open_graphics*( ):
  Pseudo_screen = (**PC_image** ∗) *malloc*(6 + *xsize* ∗ *ysize*);
 */
char **Pseudo_line*[768];
 /* *Pseudo_line*[k] points to the beginning of the k-th line on the pseudo
  screen:
  for ($k = 0$; $k < ysize$; $k{+}{+}$)
   Pseudo_line[k] = &*Pseudo_screen* –> *Data*[*xsize* ∗ k];
 */

void *PC_setcolor*(*col*) /* new version */
 short col;
{
 if (*DrawInBack*)
  Curcol = col;
 else
  _setcolor(*col*);
}

void *PC_setpixel*(*x, y*) /* new version */
 short x, y;
{
 short reg;
 if (*DrawInBack*) {
  Region(*reg, x, y*);
  if (!*reg*) *Pseudo_line*[x][y] = *CurCol*;
 } **else**
  _setpixel(*x, y*);
}

Drawing general lines, filling (convex) polygons, etc., is done by means of the routines in Chapter 4.

Now we redefine the macros *G_move*( ) and *G_draw*( ):

```
#define G_move (v)   PC_moveto ((short) (v)[X], (short) (v)[Y])
#define G_draw (v)   PC_drawto ((short) (v)[X], (short) (v)[Y])
```

They call the functions

```
void PC_moveto (x, y )
     short x, y;
{
    if (DrawInBack) {
        CurX = x;
        CurY = y;
    } else {
        _moveto (x, y );
    }
}
void PC_drawto (x, y )
     short x, y;
{
    if (DrawInBack)
        _lineto (x, y );
    else
        plot_line (CurX, CurY, x, y);
    CurX = x; CurY = y;
}
```

The code of the function PC_swapbuffers ( ) finally looks like this:

```
void PC_swapbuffers ( )
{
    if (TwoScreens) {
        _setvisualpage (1 − _getvisualpage ( ));
        _setactivepage (1 − _getactivepage ( ));
    } else if (DrawInBack)
        _putimage (0, 0, (char *) Pseudo_screen, _GPSET);
}
```

B.2 'Macromania': C, ANSI C or C++ ?

In this book, the standard C language [KERN86] has been used. It can easily be adapted to the ANSI Standard for the C language [DARN88].

One major advantage of the ANSI Standard is that the parameters of the function calls are checked during the compilation. This makes programming much safer. Also, the call of functions will be a little bit faster (the type **float**, e.g., does not have to be converted to the type **double**).

The most elegant development of the C language is the C++ language[AT&T90]. Actually C++ is a "pseudo language," since it is based on the C language:

as a first step a preprocessor creates a C program that is then compiled by the standard C compiler. There is no question that C++ is one of the most convenient languages for the writing of readable code. Furthermore, C++ allows the protection of variables and the so-called "multiple inheritance."

However, C++ has one disadvantage: It will slow down C code like the one you can find throughout this book. Here is a typical example:

Let us redefine the type **Vector** as a **class**:

class Vector {
    float x, y, z;
    public:
    friend float operator $*$ (**Vector** v, **Vector** w) {
        return $v.x * w.x + v.y * w.y + v.z * w.z$;
    };
    $\vdots$
};

If now a and b are two **Vectors** and c is a **float** variable, we can write very comfortably

    $c = a + b$;

The C++ preprocessor translates such a line into something like

    $c = some\_function(\&a, \&b)$;

Since no macro can be used, the C++ version of the dot product of two **Vectors** runs more slowly than the macro version. If you have a C++ compiler at your disposal, use the program listed in Appendix A.5 to check how much the loss of speed is for your own configuration. It will most probably be more than 50%.

Thus, if you write a program in C++ and your program runs too slowly, look out for segments that are visited frequently and replace the operator by a macro or at least by a so-called **inline** function! (Some people may call this "macromania.")

B.3   Pointer Arithmetic in PASCAL

Many high-level programming languages like PASCAL do not support pointer
arithmetic, because it is tricky and because it can create hard-to-find errors since
it allows the user to write over non-allocated memory.

The reason why we make intensive use of pointer arithmetic throughout this
book is that it speeds up the programs and enables us to write compressed code.
(Some people call the C language a "veiled assembler.")

If you prefer to write PASCAL programs while still using code listed in this book
you can do this by using a unit *pointers*. The unit contains the functions *pp*
and *mm*() corresponding to ++, += and −−, −= and a function *smalle*
which compares two addresses.

Here is the listing of such a unit for an IBM-PC and with "Turbo-PASC
Since the functions are not optimized, they will not run as fast as an o
PASCAL code. If they are implemented as assembler routines, they wi
up the code.

```
unit pointers;

interface

    type
        ptr = record
            offs, segm : word;
        end;
    procedure pp(var p; s : integer);
    procedure mm(var p; s : integer);
    function smaller(var p1, p2) : boolean;

implementation

    procedure pp(var p; s : integer);
        begin inc(ptr(p).offs, s) end;

    procedure mm(var p; s : integer);
        begin dec(ptr(p).offs, s) end;

    function smaller(var p1, p2) : boolean;
    var s1, s2 : word;
    begin
        s1 := seg(p1); s2 := seg(p2);
        if s1 = s2 then smaller := (ofs(p1) < ofs(p2))
        else smaller := (s1 < s2);
    end;

end. (* unit pointers *)
```

To give you an idea of how this unit can be used, we list a sample program.
First the listing of the C file:

```
#define X 0
#define Y 1
#define Z 2
#define N1 30
#define N2 20
typedef float Vec3 [3];
typedef float Vec2 [2];

Vec3 v3[N1][N2], *p3;
Vec2 v2[N1][N2], *p2, *p_array[N1], * * pptr;
float * r, *hi_r;
int i, j, k;

void main()
{
    /* Example 1: Initialize array with zeros. */
    /* First the ordinary C code. */
    for (i = 0; i < N1; i++)
        for (j = 0; j < N2; j++)
            v3[i][j][X] = v3[i][j][Y] = v3[i][j][Z] = 0;
    /* Now the same with pointer arithmetic. */
    r = (float *) v3;
    hi_r = r + 3 * N1 * N2;
    while (r < hi_r)
        * r++ = 0;

    /* Example 2: Copy arrays of different types. */
    /* First the 'readable' code. */
    for (i = 0; i < N1; i++)
        for (j = 0; j < N2; j++) {
            v2[i][j][X] = v3[i][j][X];
            v2[i][j][Y] = v3[i][j][Y];
        }
    /* Now the same with pointer arithmetic. */
    p2 = (Vec2 *) v2;
    p3 = (Vec3 *) v3;
    for (i = 0; i < (N1 * N2); i++) {
        (*p2)[X] = (*p3)[X]; (*p2)[Y] = (*p3)[Y];
        p2++; p3++;
    }

    /* Example 3: How to use pointers to pointers. */
    pptr = p_array;
    for (i = 0; i < N1; i++)
        * pptr++ = v2[i];
    pptr = &p_array[N1 - 1];
```

```
for  (i = 0; i < N1; i++) {
    p2 = *pptr - -;
    for  (j = 0; j < N2; j++) {
        (*p2)[X] = 0;
        (*p2)[Y] = 0;
        p2++;
    }
}
}
```

This is the one-to-one translation into PASCAL:

```
program pointer_test;
    (* This sample program shows how to use the unit
        pointers. *)
uses pointers;
const
    X = 0; Y = 1; Z = 2;
    N1 = 30; N2 = 20;
type
    Vec3 = array[X..Z] of real;
    Vec_ptr3 = ^Vec3;
    Vec2 = array[X..Y] of real;
    Vec_ptr2 = ^Vec2;
    Real_ptr = ^real;
    ppt = ^pointer;
var
    v3 : array[0..N1 - 1, 0..N2 - 1] of Vec3;
    v2 : array[0..N1 - 1, 0..N2 - 1] of Vec2;
    p3 : Vec_ptr3;
    p2 : Vec_ptr2;
    r, hi_r : Real_ptr;
    pptr : ppt;
    p_array : array[0..N1 - 1] of Vec_ptr2;
    i, j, k : integer;
    zero3 : Vec3;
(* * * * M A I N * * * *)
begin
    (* Example 1: Initialize array with zeros. *)
    (* First the ordinary Pascal code. *)
    zero3[X] := 0; zero3[Y] := 0; zero3[Z] := 0;
    for  i := 0 to N1 - 1 do
        for  j := 0 to N2 - 1 do
```

$$v3[i,j] := zero3;^1$$

(* Now the same with pointer arithmetic. *)
$r := @v3;$
$hi\_r := r;\ pp(hi\_r,\ 3\ *N1\ *N2\ *\textbf{sizeof}(r\hat{}\,));$
while $smaller(r\hat{},\ hi\_r\hat{}\,)$ **do begin**
    $r\hat{} := 0;\ pp(r,\ \textbf{sizeof}(r\hat{}\,));$
end;

(* Example 2: Copy arrays of different type. *)
(* First the 'readable' code. *)

for $i := 0$ **to** $N1 - 1$ **do**
    for $j := 0$ **to** $N2 - 1$ **do begin**
        $v2[i,j,X] := v3[i,j,X];$
        $v2[i,j,Y] := v3[i,j,Y];$
    end;

(* Now the same with pointer arithmetic: *)
$p2 := @v2;$
$p3 := @v3;$
for $i := 0$ **to** $N1\ *N2\ -1$ **do begin**
    $p2\hat{}[X] := p3\hat{}[X];\ p2\hat{}[Y] := p3\hat{}[Y];$
    $pp(p2,\ \textbf{sizeof}(p2\hat{}\,));\ pp(p3,\ \textbf{sizeof}(p3\hat{}\,));$
end;

(* Example 3: How to use pointers to pointers. *)
$pptr := @p\_array[0];$
for $i := 0$ **to** $N1 - 1$ **do begin**
    $pptr\hat{} := @v2[i];$
    $pp(pptr,\ \textbf{sizeof}(pptr));$
end;
$pptr := @p\_array[N1 - 1];$
for $i := 0$ **to** $N1 - 1$ **do begin**
    $p2 := pptr\hat{};\ mm(pptr,\ \textbf{sizeof}(pptr\hat{}\,));$
    for $j := 0$ **to** $N2 - 1$ **do begin**
        $p2\hat{}[X] := 0;\ p2\hat{}[Y] := 0;$
        $pp(p2,\ \textbf{sizeof}(p2\hat{}\,));$
    end;
end;
end.

---

[1] *zero3* is an array of **real**. This would not work in C!

References

[AMME92] Ammeraal, L.: *Programming Priciples in Computer Graphics*. John Wiley & Sons, Chichester.

[ANGE90] Angel, E.: *Computer Graphics*. Addison-Wesley.

[ANGE87] Angell, I. O. and Griffith, G.H.: *High-resolution Computer Graphics Using FORTRAN 77*. Macmillan Education Ltd.

[ATHE77] Atherton, P.R., Weiler, P., et al.: *Polygon Shadow Generation*. Computer Graphics **12**(3).

[BARS88] Barsky, B. A.: *Beta-Splines*. Springer, Tokyo.

[BISH86] Bishop G. and Weimer, D.M.: *Fast Phong Shading*. Proc. SIGGRAPH 86, Computer Graphics **20**(4): pp 103-106.

[BOEH85] Böhm, W., Gose G. and Kahmann J.: *Methoden der numerischen Mathematik*. Vieweg.

[BROT84] Brotman, L.S. and Badler, N.I.: *Generating Soft Shadows with a Depth Buffer Algorithm*. IEEE Computer Graphics and Applications 4(10):5-12.

[BUIT75] Bui-Tuong, Phong, and Crow, F.C.: *Improved rendition of polygonal models of curved surfaces*. Proc. 2nd USA-Japan Computer Conf.

[BURG89] Burger, P. and Gillies, D.: *Interactive Computer Graphics*. Addison-Wesley.

[BYKA78] Bykat, A.: *Convex Hull of a Finite Set of Points in Two Dimensions.* Inform. Proc. Lett. **7**, 296-298.

[CHIN89] Chin, N. and Feiner, St.: *Near real-time shadow generation using BSP trees.* Computer Graphics **23**(3):99-106.

[CROW77] Crow, F.C.: *Shadow algorithms for computer graphics.* Proc. SIGGRAPH'77, Computer Graphics **13**(2):242-248.

[DARN88] Darnell, P.A. and Margolis, P.E.: *Software Engineering in C.* Springer/New York.

[EARNSHAW] Earnshaw, R.A. and Wyvill, B. (Eds.): *New advances in computer graphics.* Proceedings of CG International 89. Springer Tokyo.

[ENCA83] Encarnção J. and Schlechtendahl E.G.: *Computer Aided Design. Fundamentals and System Architectures.* Springer Berlin.

[FELL92] Fellner, W.D.: *Computergrafik.* B.I. Reihe Informatik Band 58

[FOLE90] Foley J., van Damm, A., et al.: *Computer Graphics: Principles and Practice.* Addison-Wesley.

[FUCH80] Fuchs, H., Kedem, Z.M. and Naylor, B.F.: *On visible surface generation by a priori tree structures.* Computer Graphics **14**(3), pp.124-133.

[GARC86] Garcia, A.: *Efficient Rendering of Synthetic Images.* PhD Thesis, Massachusetts Institute of Technology.

[GLAE81] Glaeser, G.: *Über die Rotoidenwendelflächen.* Sitz.ber. Öst. Akad. Wiss. 190, pp.285-302, Vienna.

[GLAE86] Glaeser, G.: *3D-Graphik mit Basic.* B.G.Teubner, Stuttgart.

[GLAE88/1] Glaeser, G.: *Ein schnelles Verfahren zur Herstellung realistischer Bilder.* Informatik Fachberichte, Springer/Heidelberg.

[GLAE88/2] Glaeser, G.: *Visualization of minimal surfaces.* Proc. of the 3rd Int. Conf. on Eng. Graphics and Descriptive Geometry, Vol. I, pp.180-184, Vienna.

[GLAE90] Glaeser, G.: *Amiga 3D-Sprinter. Interaktive Echtzeit-Animation.* Markt&Technik, Munich.

[GLAS90] Glassner, A.S., et al. *An Introduction to Ray Tracing.* Academic Press, San Diego.

[GORA84] Goral, C., et al.: *Modeling the interaction of light between diffuse surfaces.* Comput. Graph. **18**, pp. 213-222 (SIGGRAPH 84).

[GOUR71] Gouraud, H.: *Continuous shading on curved surfaces.* IEEE Transactions on Computers C-20(6):623-629.

[HEAR86] Hearn, D. and Baker., M.P.: *Computer Graphics.* Prentice Hall International.

[HECH74] Hech, E. and Zajac A.: *Optics*. Addison-Wesley, p.159.

[HECK84] Heckberth, P. and Hanrahan, P.: *Beam tracing polygonal objects*. Computer Graphics **18**(3), pp.119-127.

[HOSC89] Hoschek, J. and Lasser, D.: *Grundlagen der geometrischen Datenverarbeitung*. B.G.Teubner.

[JANK84] Jankel, A. and Morton, R.: *Creative Computer Graphics*. Cambridge University Press.

[KERN86] Kernighan, B.W. and Ritchie, D.M.: *The C Programming Language*. Prentice Hall.

[LANG84] Lang., J.: *Zum Konstruieren von Umrissen im Computer Aided Design*. CAD 33, Vienna.

[NEWE72] Newell, M.E. and Sancha, T.L.: *A new approach to the shaded picture problem*. ACM National Conf., 443-450.

[NEWM84] Newman, W.M. and Sproull, R.F.: *Principles of Interactive Computer Graphics*. McGraw-Hill.

[NISH74] Nishita T. and Nakamahe, E.: *An algorithm for half-tone representation of three-dimensional objects*. Proc. Information Processing Society of Japan 14:93-99.

[PARK85] Park, Chan S.: *Interactive Microcomputer Graphics*. Addison-Wesley.

[PAUK86] Paukowitsch, P.: *Konstruieren spezieller Flächenkurven*. CAD 39, pp.2-13, Vienna.

[PLAS86] Plastok, R.A. and Kalley G.: *Computer Graphics*, McGraw-Hill.

[POTT88] Pottmann, H.: *Eine Verfeinerung der Isophotenmethode zur Qualitätsanalyse von Freiformflächen*. CAD und Computergraphik 39/4, Vienna.

[PURG85] Purgathofer, W.: *Graphische Datenverarbeitung*. Springer, Vienna.

[PURG89] Purgathofer, W. and Schönhut, J. (Eds.): *Advances in Computer Graphics V*. Springer, Heidelberg.

[ROGE85] Rogers, D.F.: *Procedural Elements for Computer Graphics*. McGraw-Hill.

[ROGE87] Rogers, D.F. and Earnshaw, R.A.: *Techniques for Computer Graphics*. Springer New York.

[ROGE90] Rogers, D.F. and Earnshaw, R.A.: *Computer Graphics Techniques. Theory and Practice*. Springer New York.

[SEYB77] Seybold, H.: *Beitrag zur konstruktiven Computergeometrie*. Computing 17, pp.281-287, Springer Verlag.

[THAL87] Thalmann, D. and Magnenat-Thalman, N.: *Image Synthesis*, Springer Tokyo.

[THAL90] Magnenat-Thalmann, N. and Thalmann D.: *Computer Animation. Theory and Practice*. Springer Tokyo.

[THAL91] Magnenat-Thalmann, N. and Thalmann D. (Eds.): *Computer Animation 91*. Springer Tokyo.

[TANA91] Tanaka, T. and Takahashi, T. *Shading with Area Light Sources*. Eurographics 91 (Post, F.H. and Barth, W. Eds.), North Holland, pp. 235-246.

[TOSI85] Tosiyasu, L.K. (Ed.): *Computer Graphics. Visual Technology and Art*. Springer Tokyo.

[SEDG92] Sedgewick, R.: *Algorithms in C++*. Addison-Wesley.

[SHIR87] Shirai, Y.: *Three-Dimensional Computer Vision*. Springer Tokyo.

[SUTH74/1] Sutherland, I.E. and Hodgman, G.W.: *Reentrant Polygon Clipping*. Comm. ACM **17**:43.

[SUTH74/2] Sutherland, I.E., et al.: *A Characterization of Ten Hidden Surface Algorithms*. ACM Computing Surveys, 6(1), 1-55.

[VINC92] Vince, J.: *3-D Computer Animation*. Addison-Wesley, Don Mills.

[WATK92] Watkins, C. D. and Sharp, L.: *Programming in 3 Dimensions*. M&T Publishing, San Mateo.

[WATT92] Watt, A.: *Fundamentals of Three-Dimensinal Computer Graphics*. Addison-Wesley.

[WEIL77] Weiler, K. and Atherton, P.: *Hidden surface removal using polygon area sorting*. Proc. SIGGRAPH'77, Computer Graphics **11**(2): 214-222

[WILL78] Williams, L.: *Casting curved shadows on curved surfaces*. Comput.Graph., Vol. 12, pp. 270-274 (SIGGRAPH78).

[WHIT80] Whitted, T.: *An Improved Illumination Model for Shaded Display*. Commun. ACM **23**(6).

[WUND54] Wunderlich, W.: *Beitrag zur Kenntnis der Minimalspiralflächen*. Rend. Mat. 13, pp.1-15, Rome.

[WUND66] Wunderlich, W.: *Darstellende Geometrie I, II*. B.I. Hochschultaschenbücher, Mannheim.

Index